PETER CLAVER

El V. P. P.º Clauer Catalan de la Compª. de Jesus Professo de quatro votos Yllustre
en Santidad Profecias y milagros Varon Apº. 40 años Exercitò El ministº. de
los Negros delos quales conuirtio 350 gentiles y muchos moros: reduso a nraSª. Fee muchos hereses. Siruio muchos años a los leprosos de S. Lazaro fue penitentiss.mo muy humilde
y ardiente caridad Murio Virgen en el Coleg.º de Cartax.na delas Indias de hedad de 71
años à 8 de Sept.e de 1654 Conserba nro. S.r cassi todo su cuerpo Incorrupto y con
buen olor.   Marcus Orozco Sculpsit M.ti

The first published portrait of St Peter Claver

PETER CLAVER

Saint of the Slaves

by

ANGEL VALTIERRA, S.J.

With a Preface by

JAMES BRODRICK, S.J.

THE NEWMAN PRESS
WESTMINSTER · MARYLAND

This translation of *El santo que liberto una raza:*
San Pedro Claver S. J. (Imprinta nacional, Bogotá, 1954)
was made by
JANET H. PERRY and L. J. WOODWARD

NIHIL OBSTAT: ADRIANUS VAN VLIET, S.T.D.
CENSOR DEPUTATUS
IMPRIMATUR: E. MORROGH BERNARD
VICARIUS GENERALIS
WESTMONASTERII: DIE XXV SEPTEMBRIS MCMLIX

The Nihil obstat *and* Imprimatur *are a declaration that a book or pamphlet is
considered to be free from doctrinal or moral error. It is not implied that those who
have granted the* Nihil obstat *and* Imprimatur *agree with the contents, opinions or
statements expressed.*

English translation © Burns & Oates Ltd 1960

PRINTED IN GREAT BRITAIN

PREFACE

THIS book, which comes from Colombia, Latin America, the land of St Peter Claver's appalling labours and sufferings, is bound to make on any reader bold enough to go through with it the impact of a sledgehammer. He will dwindle in his own esteem to the size of a pinhead, which is mighty good for him. There are several other accounts of the Slave of the Slaves in English, including Maud Petre's pioneering work, *Aethiopum Servus*, Father Martindale's brief and brilliant sketch based on it in *Captains of Christ* and Sir Arnold Lunn's most stimulating and instructive book, *A Saint in the Slave Trade*. Father Valtierra's book goes far beyond any of those earlier attempts to probe the psychology of one of the most heroic and baffling of God's saints. He sets out the evidence of those who watched St Peter at work more completely and critically than has been done before, and adds to it much new evidence hitherto unpublished. He is impatient of legends, even charming ones, and mentions them only to discard them. St Peter's cloak did not remain miraculously clean and sweet-smelling after he had countless times wrapped it about plague victims and lepers. It stank to high heaven and had to be washed seven times a day. Padre Valtierra spares his readers nothing. He challenges their twentieth-century squeamishness on almost every page. Peter Claver, a well-bred and sensitive Spaniard, was as squeamish as any of us, and shrank from dirt and stench every bit as much as we do. But he learned in his never broken communion with Christ crucified so to master his natural nausea that it became habitual with him to kiss the dreadful sores on the negroes' bodies, caused by the brutality and greed of white men calling themselves Christians, even to suck the killing poison out of them with his own lips. A few saints are recorded to have done that kind of thing once in a burst of pity and love. Peter Claver did it almost every day of his life for close on forty years. It was not for him, a quiet, gentle person, sad of face because he lived so intensely on his chosen Golgotha, to argue the rights and wrongs of slavery or to encourage some Spartacus among the negroes who adored him to rise against their oppressors. It would have been futile anyway. No; the suffering and the degradation were there before his eyes, so let others, the priests and the levites, argue to their hearts' content while he trudged off daily to the ghastly hospitals and lepers' huts to pour into gaping wounds his oil and his wine. It may comfort the reader to know that by constant assaults on the charity of the rich whites, Peter accumulated vast stores of clothing, mosquito nets, tobacco, brandy and wine, honey, dates, oranges and lemons, even eau de Cologne, for the solacing of his beloved negroes and lepers. He seems to have been a fusion in one man of the Curé d'Ars, St Francis Xavier and Father Damian. He would hear his negroes' confessions for eight or twelve hours on end, he would spend a whole day without bite or sup in loving attendance on a dying man or woman, he would be first on the scaffold if any man, white or black, was condemned to the rope, and he performed, not once but a score of times, the sublime act of charity which brings tears to the eyes when read in the life of St Catherine of Siena. Let the reader test his nerve on the chapter of this book entitled, 'Facing the World of Pain' and see whether he too is not feeling for his handkerchief. It is horrifying and—heavenly. Pope Leo XIII said once: 'No life, except the life of Christ, has so moved me as that of St Peter Claver.'

JAMES BRODRICK, S.J.

CONTENTS

PART I

SEEKING THE WAY
(1580–1622)

PART II

THE DYNAMIC SOCIAL WORKER
(1622–1650)

PART III

THE INTIMATE SAINT

PART IV

FROM PAINFUL ECLIPSE TO SUPREME GLORY
(1650–1654)

ILLUSTRATIONS

PART I

SEEKING THE WAY
(1580—1622)

CHAPTER I

A CHILD IS BORN IN VERDÚ

THE Catalan village of Verdú lies at one end of the Urgel valley in the province of Lérida, about two and a half miles from Tárrega and fifty-four from Barcelona. Now a municipality of 1,600 inhabitants, in Claver's time it had 2,000.

Verdú's High Street—narrow, cobbled, between low houses with wide balconies—has not changed much in three centuries. Along it still walk sturdy Catalan peasants, the local style of cap on their heads and in their cheeks a tinge as sallow as the olives on the surrounding plains. A mule bought at the celebrated local fair may be crossing the street, or a country girl carrying on her head one of the pitchers that are the pride of Verdú's domestic industry. Half-way down the street, no higher than the other houses, the porch of a late-nineteenth-century church displays no particular attraction. The visitor would pass it by if he did not know that there, three centuries ago, in the former spacious farmhouse, Peter Claver was born. His actual birthplace is now in the choir of the church built on the site. The room, converted into a chapel, could not be simpler. About ten feet wide by thirteen feet high, it has a vaulted arch resting on five blackened beams. At one side of the altar a marble tablet reads: 'Here St Peter Claver, the Apostle of the Negroes, was born. He was baptized in the parish church of this town on 26 July 1580. He died in Cartagena de Indias on 8 September 1654. He was solemnly canonized by Leo XIII on 15 January 1888.'

In the South American town of Cartagena in another simple chapel with a plain altar, blackened beams and a bright red tiled floor like the one in Verdú, a tablet reads: 'Here in this room Peter Claver died on 8 September 1654.' . . . A relic, sent from Cartagena and taken from the body of the Saint which lies beneath the high altar there, lies today on the altar at Verdú.

A child was born in Verdú in the early summer of 1580. Youngest of the family, his elder brothers and sister were called Juan, Jaime and Isabel. Their father could barely sign his own name, yet rose to be mayor and chief alderman.[1]

Incredible though it may seem, Peter Claver's biographers had given wrong dates for his birth until 19 December 1854, when Father Isidoro Duarri sent a copy of the entry in the baptismal register in the parish archives of Verdú to Father Bruguero, translator of Father Fleurieau's life of the Saint. The parchment cover of the baptismal register bears the title in Catalan: *Llibre dels Batejats en esta Iglesia di Verdú de* 1570 *fins a* 1595—'Book of those baptized in the Church of Verdú from 1570 until 1595'; the literal text of the document taken from the register is as follows: 'On 26 June of the above year 1580 in the aforesaid Church of Verdú, Juan Pedro, son of Pedro Claver of the *Calle Mayor* and of his wife Ana, was baptized. The godfather was Juan Borrell, dealer in earthenware, and the godmother Magdalena, wife of Flavian Colom, hosier, both of Verdú. God make him a good Christian.'[2]

In the beatification process drawn up in Cartagena he is stated to have been 'born in 1585', a wrong date accepted by Father Andrade in his *Lives of Famous Members of the Society of Jesus*, by Father José Fernández, the Saint's second biographer, and among modern biographers by the Frenchman Gabriel Ledos, who admits that he can give no reason for or against either 1580 or 1585 as a hypothetical date. Father Cassani explains the uncertainty by stating inaccurately that the parish archives of Verdú had disappeared. In the official papal documents, in the Bull of beatification issued by Pope Pius IX, the date 1585 is implicitly accepted, for the Saint is said to have entered the Jesuit Order at the age of seventeen in 1602. On the other hand, Leo XIII in the Bull of canonization formally established the correct date, 26 June 1580. The latest historian of the Society of Jesus in Spain makes the

---

[1] Luis Fiter, S. J., *Apéndice documental a la vida de S. Pedro Claver de Fernández Sola*, Barcelona, 1888. This is the most complete study of the critical period of his childhood, and little can be added to his researches. See Appendix 12.

[2] Fiter, *op. cit.*, Appendix 3.

same statement. Corroborated by the baptismal certificate, this date would seem incontrovertible.

Most of the difficulties over the date of baptism arose from the common custom in Spain of using the second name without the first, and also from the presence in Verdú of baptismal entries of other Clavers, a common surname in Catalonia. Naturally we have given the date of baptism, not of birth, but the traditional custom in Verdú is to baptize infants on the day after birth, unless the infant's life is in danger. We may therefore accept the date of 25 June as virtually certain to be that of his birth.

Another error in the recorded life of St Peter Claver concerns his parents' surnames. Most biographers, and here we must include the beatification process, follow the opinion of his first biographer, Father Alonso de Andrade (who assumed the name of *Licenciado* Suárez de Somoza), that Peter Claver's parents were called Pedro Claver and Ana de Sobocano. In fact the correct names of his parents were Pedro Claver y Mingüella and Ana Corberó y Claver. An examination of the parish archives of Verdú shows how common the surname of Claver was in the town, and to make matters worse a number of Clavers were called Pedro. Most of them give no second surname, using instead the name of the street where they live. So we find: Pedro Claver of Church Street, Pedro Claver of New Furnace Street, Pedro Claver of the High Street. In spite of this vagueness, we can identify the parents of St Peter Claver with certainty.

In 1886 three wills of Pedro Claver were found in the parish archives bequeathing a legacy to his son, 'Pedro Claver, a member of the Society of Jesus'. The testator is Pedro Claver of the *Calle Mayor* of Verdú, that High Street where the house in which the Saint was born is preserved to this day as the church of St Peter Claver.

In the first will legally drawn up on 9 April 1608 we read: 'Furthermore I leave to my son, Pedro Claver, now a religious of the Order of the Fathers of the Society, who is at present residing in Majorca, as his legitimate inheritance and supplement to it and all other rights pertaining to him in my properties twenty pounds of Barcelona minting to be freely disposed of by him.' In the second will, drawn up on 17 August 1615, and in the third, dated 2 March 1621, there is the same clause relating to the legacy of twenty pounds, but no longer stating that the son is resident in Majorca; for in April 1610 he sailed for America. In his latest will the father of Peter Claver said: 'He is suffering from a bodily ailment from which he fears to die', and he adds 'this last will is made of the house my habitual residence which I have and possess in the *Calle Mayor* of this town of Verdú'. This puts it beyond doubt that the Saint's father was the Pedro Claver who lived in the High Street of Verdú.

The third incorrect assertion made by the Saint's biographers refers to his noble birth. The nobility and wealth of St Peter Claver which so beguiled the early biographers has no existence in reality. The truth is simple. From the amounts assigned by Pedro Claver y Mingüella to his sons as their inheritance it may be deduced that he was no millionaire, although neither was he poor. According to the latest documents discovered in Verdú in the book of inventories, we find that the family owned eighteen properties;[1] and the endowment of the Nativity of Our Lady founded by the Clavers comprised eleven properties; once this is ascertained we may consider the Clavers were rich. Neither the father nor the mother of Peter Claver was of noble origin, and their friends, as we see from the wills and baptismal documents, were simple people—hosiers, farmers and the like. Pedro Claver himself was a farmer. The surname Claver or *Clahuer* in Catalan means keeper of the keys, one who has charge of the economy of the house; and it might give rise to confusion that in the orders of chivalry of Calatrava and Alcántara Clavero was a title of honour and dignity as relating to the custody of the keys of the castle.

In Castile the officials appointed by the kings or by the overlords of the towns administer their houses, and, exempted from taxation, were known as *claveres*, key-bearers or stewards. This variety of office and employment associated with the word *claver* caused much confusion. The Clavers of Verdú were all of humble rank, and though well-to-do had no claim to nobility or to relationship

[1] Fiter, *op. cit.*, Appendix 2.

with the Clavers of Tarragona, who were really noble. They belong to two quite different branches. Again the assertion that the surname Claver is one of the most illustrious of Catalonia is unfounded, for it does not figure in the general history of Catalonia or in the royal documents of the period or even in particular accounts of the county of Urgel and Poblet. In corroboration a modest farmhouse which bore no signs of noble origin could be seen up to the year 1886. It was the spacious home of a wealthy country farmer, but nothing more. The true nobility of Peter Claver was conferred on him by his sanctity.

CHAPTER II

AN UNEVENTFUL CHILDHOOD

WITNESSES in the beatification process, especially Brother González and several of his fellow novices such as Father Sobrino, refer to Peter Claver's childhood and show the deep impression left on him by the piety of his family.

We have concrete evidence of the parents' piety. In the third will the testator leaves a legacy to provide oil for a lamp before the Blessed Sacrament on the altar of St Stephen and makes a further disposition for the perpetual celebration of a monthly low Mass at the altar of Our Lady of the Rosary. A religious family. In the will of his mother's brother, Antonio Corberó, provision is also made for the celebration of six Masses at the altar of Our Lady of the Rosary, in order that she 'may be the more honoured with her only Son'. Devotion to the Blessed Sacrament and the rosary were the two devotions of the family; and the famous crucifix of Verdú, which is venerated in the parish church and the feast of which is observed every January with magnificent ceremony, left in Peter Claver such a deep devotion to the Cross that later on in Cartagena it was to be one of the favourite themes of his preaching. We know very little about this period of his life in Verdú. The child must simply have spent his time like any other farmer's son helping with the farm work.

Two distressing events must have had a great influence on his future outlook—the death of his beloved mother which took place on 17 January 1593 and, a few days later, the death of his brother, Jaime, aged twenty years and seven months. Then thirteen years old, at the crossroads of life, Peter dedicated himself to a priestly career. Furthermore the family ties must at that time have been weakened to some extent, as his father soon after got married for the second time, to Angela Escarrer, and when she died a third marriage followed to Juana Grenyó, both marriages without issue. His sister Isabel married Jaime Cabestany in Rocafort de Vallbona. Peter Claver was not a cold man for whom family ties were of little importance. The only letter of his that has been preserved, an incomplete one written later in Majorca, reflects this love:

I have wished for a long time to write this to you in order to fulfil my obligation to some extent . . . The Lord will reward you for it, and also that you might know the joy that a good Christian must have in governing himself and his family well. Furthermore I entreat you, my father, and you, my brother, that you earnestly and truly endeavour to . . . the house will work in harmony and I trust that if you go forward in this way . . . and follow this road, all will imitate you. If you wish to give good news, write me how things are going with you . . . in this respect. All other news with this will give me great pleasure and everything else without it bitterness. Many remembrances and respectful greetings in token of gratitude to my sister-in-law to whom I owe so much, to my sister and to my uncle, Jaime Corberó, and my other relatives. Warmest regards to Magín, Sebastián, Catalina and other friends. Our Lord Jesus keep you all from sin and give you grace to carry out what I have written to you. From Majorca . . .[1]

An event of supreme importance in his life took place on 8 December 1594. The Bishop of Vich, Don Pedro Jaime, who ruled that diocese from 1587 to 1597 and figures in the annals of the Society of Jesus for having been one of the principal witnesses in the preparation of the Process of St Ignatius, conferred on him the first tonsure in the church of Verdú. Peter Claver must have learnt his first lessons with the community of beneficed clergy who served the parish church of Santa María. At six years old, in 1586, he was greatly impressed when the Archbishop of Tarragona and Viceroy of Catalonia, Juan Terés, a native of Verdú, solemnly consecrated with great splendour the parish church which had just been completed. This eminent prelate, a pupil of

[1] Archives of the Society of Jesus, Barcelona. This letter is now published in a biography of St Peter Claver for the first time.

the Jesuits in Valencia, later became Bishop of Tortosa, won the confidence of Philip II and subsequently Philip III. The Jesuits of the province of Aragon owe a great debt to his memory, for he laid the foundation stone of the novitiate of Tarragona where Peter Claver was to enter in 1602.

The document, authentic record of the tonsure, produced in the process of beatification at Cartagena by the witness, Tomás de Victoria, reads as follows:

> Be it known to all that we, Padre Jacobo, by the grace of God and the favour of the Apostolic See, Bishop of Vich, and royal counsellor, on Friday 8 December 1595 in the parish church of the town of Verdú in our bishopric of Vich, with all the due and requisite solemnities, do consider that the first clerical tonsure should be conferred on our beloved in Christ Pedro Claver, son of Pedro Claver, farmer, of the aforesaid town of Verdú, and of Ana, his wife, confirmed and found to be suitable in age and skilled in letters; and so we rightly, duly and canonically promote him. In testimony of which we sign with our hand and seal these presents. Given at Verdú the above day, month and year. Pedro, Bishop of Vich.

A note written above this text runs: 'Juan Vinyes, notary and substitute for him, Jacobo Frabegat; process of beatification, sheet 368.'

Now that he had received the tonsure and decided on an ecclesiastical career, Claver's parents considered it time for him to go and study in the capital. The recent creation of the bishopric of Solsona made it improbable that an adequate course of ecclesiastical studies should have already been established there. So we find Claver in Barcelona during the years 1596–7 pursuing his studies at the university, usually called then *studium generale*. He went as an external student and probably took up his residence at the house of relatives of his father's third wife, Juana Grenyó, previously widow of Juan Managuerra, a citizen of Barcelona.

At that time it was possible to take the full ecclesiastical course in the schools of the *studium generale*. At this university Peter Claver Corberó studied three years of grammar and one of rhetoric, for at that time the Jesuit Fathers had only chairs of philosophy and theology at their College at Belén.

The *studium* or university was situated at the western end of the *Rambla* close to the San Severo gate in the so-called *Pez de Palla*, now the *Rambla de Canaletas*. This was near the Jesuit college of Belén, founded by St Francis Borgia on the very spot indicated by St Ignatius. He must have passed by the college and the church of the Society on his way to the university.

When he came to Barcelona, the church had been completed, a magnificent feat of architecture and already then enjoying a flourishing attendance. On the other hand, contact with the Jesuits might have been brought about by a regulation laid down from 1559 that a priest of the college of Belén should go every day to the *studium* of Barcelona to bring the children who were learning to read in the college to the church, where they were taught the catechism from two to three in the afternoon and were then escorted back to the university by the same priest. This catechetical work might have impressed the young Claver.

Moreover, St Ignatius and the Society of Jesus had left an indelible mark on Barcelona. Precisely at this time all the prelates of the ecclesiastical province of Tarragona were petitioning Rome for the beatification of the founder of the Jesuits. Peter Claver was present at the solemn feast celebrated by the Lord Bishop of Barcelona in the church of Belén for the placing of a great reredos of the holy Trinity. About the year 1601, having completed his course of rhetoric, he probably entered the college of Belén under the direction of the Jesuits. The lists of pupils for that period have been lost, so there is no absolute certainty on this point, but his continued residence in Barcelona from August 1602, dealings with the priests of the college and the possibility of his attending the philosophy classes as an external student allow us to affirm so.[1]

Another point which has worried the biographers and cannot be cleared up completely is the question of Peter Claver's membership of the sodality of our Lady which the fathers had in the college of Belén in Barcelona. The early biographers, Fathers Andrade and Fernández, say nothing about this. Centuries later,

[1] Fiter, *op. cit.*, Appendix 4.

historians of the sodalities, like Fathers Delplace and Grasset and still later Father Carayón, are inclined to the affirmative without giving any definite proof. We may draw the following conclusion: while Peter Claver was studying grammar and rhetoric at the university he could not be a member of the sodality. Later he must have studied philosophy for a year at the college of Belén. So if we remember that the pupils most distinguished for knowledge and virtue belonged to such sodalities, and if we add Peter's singular love for the blessed Virgin, we may certainly affirm that Peter Claver belonged to the Barcelona sodality. The problem would solve itself if the register of the sodality of the students of the former college of Belén, which already numbered 357 folios in 1611, had not disappeared.

Peter Claver did not know it, but a young saint had fifteen years earlier passed through these cloisters thronged with young people. The Empress, Doña María, sister of Philip II, had visited Barcelona, accompanied through the town as lady-in-waiting by Doña María Manrique de Lara, foundress of the college of the Society of Jesus in Barcelona. In the Empress's train was a young Italian called Aloysius Gonzaga, then fourteen years old and acting as page to the heir apparent. Did they visit the college? Very probably they did, given the devotion of Doña María and young Aloysius Gonzaga to the Jesuits.

Peter Claver was now treading the path of a great saint. The first stage in his career was nearing its end. At twenty-two his heart was not satisfied by the gay noisy town of Barcelona with its *sardanas* and pilgrimages, with the bustle of its port and the magic of the Mediterranean. His soul was ever more ardently drawn to the priesthood. He was about to take a new step, mount a fresh rung of the ladder. Among his fellow students he was outstanding in ability and diligence. He applied for minor orders to the Bishop of Barcelona, Don Alonso Coloma, son of the Count and Countess of Elda. The Bishop made enquiries and gladly granted Peter Claver's wish, for he had discovered—as he testified later—that 'he surpassed the rest not only in learning, but also in piety and religious observance'.

This was the final step towards his vocation. He spent long hours in the college church, and there, surrounded by the chosen young members of the sodality, he listened to the sermons and every Sunday used to go with half a dozen companions to the hospital of Santa Cruz to care for the poorest of the sick. It could even have been this contact with reality which moved him to dedicate his life to the poor and suffering.

One day—we do not know exactly when—he approached the spiritual director of the college and told him that he wished to become a Jesuit. He was referred to Father Antonio Clar, a Majorcan, who in turn put him in touch with the Father Provincial, at that time Father Melchor de Valpedrosa, the same who on 7 August 1602 gave Claver permission to enter the novitiate at Tarragona.

What opinion did Peter Claver form of the Society of Jesus when he entered it in Barcelona?[1] Not many years before, on 31 July 1556, Ignatius of Loyola had died in Rome, leaving one hundred Jesuit houses with more than 1,000 members scattered over twelve districts or provinces. In the year of Claver's birth, 1580, the fourth General of the Jesuits died, and a little later, in 1581, a Neapolitan, Claudio Aquaviva, was elected to this office, in which he ruled the Society of Jesus until 1615. It was he who admitted Peter Claver to the Society.

In 1599 a Jesuit, Robert Bellarmine, was created a Cardinal. Doubtless too Peter Claver had heard a great deal about Francis Borgia, Viceroy of Catalonia, who became a Jesuit and died a saint. On 27 July 1609 the Church confirmed the sanctity of St Ignatius by beatifying him. In the time of Father Aquaviva a great missionary movement spread abroad, and the names of Ricci in China, Valignani in India, Aquaviva in Mongolia, were as well known throughout Europe as were the letters of the great Francis Xavier at an earlier date.

Over in distant America, where conversions were filling the gap left by heresy in Europe, there were flourishing missions. In 1574 there were already twenty-three Jesuits in Mexico and

[1] Antonio Astrain, S. J., *Historia de la Compañía de Jesús en la Asistencia de España*, 7 vols., Madrid.

in 1568 they were in Lima. Residences were established in Quito in 1586, in New Granada (now Colombia) in 1589, in Bogotá and Cartagena, and Father Sandoval began catechizing the negroes. In distant Africa, Barreira in Guinea, Fathers Bogado and Verez in the Congo and Angola, exercised a great apostolate among the negroes and in 1599 alone had converted 15,000 of them. At that time perhaps the greatest success of the Jesuits lay in their missionary work, apart from the education given in their popular missions at home. Peter Claver communicated the news of his decision to his father, who soon had a room ready for him in the *Calle de Xucla* in a house for residents behind the college of Belén. The memory of his stay there is still preserved. The nuns of the Order of Retreat, who later occupied the house, converted the room into a chapel which is maintained with great veneration.

The road from Barcelona to Tarragona is not long. Claver firmly made his way there, and on 7 August 1602 entered the house as a novice. By some caprice of history Claver seemed always destined to live in walled towns—first Verdú, then Tarragona and later Cartagena.

When Claver arrived at Tarragona the novitiate was prosperous and flourishing. It had been first at Valencia, then in Gandía, later in Saragossa, until finally it settled down in Tarragona. Peter Claver may almost be called one of its founders. The house was already six years old. We can really say very little about his life as a novice, although early biographers discourse long and piously upon the utterances of the Saint on arriving at his cell, on seeing the chapel and on various other occasions during his novitiate. These same expressions of piety, placed between inverted commas as though taken down word for word, unfortunately have no historical foundation. Apart from some maxims duly proved to be the original work of the Saint and reported under oath in the Process at Cartagena by one or other of his fellow novices who knew these writings, we know in fact very little. In a small notebook—now lost—which he kept by him all his life, Peter Claver wrote down these four precepts which he himself says a novice of the Society of Jesus should observe:

First, to seek God and endeavour to find him in all things. Second, to use all his strength to obtain in himself perfect interior and exterior obedience, subjecting his judgment and his will to his superiors as if to the very person of Christ our Lord. Third, to direct all his actions to the greater glory of God. Fourth, and last, to seek nothing in this world but that which Christ our Lord sought so that as he came into the world to save souls and to die for them on the Cross, he (the novice) should try to win them for Christ and expose himself gladly to any labour or death itself for them, accepting any indignity offered to him for our Lord's sake with pleasure and delight, and desiring to receive many such, provided he himself should give no cause for it nor occasion for offence to God.

An analysis of these four precepts gives the key from now on to the whole of Peter Claver's spirituality: to seek God in all things; total submission to his superiors and an indefatigable zeal for the saving of souls, in spite of humiliation, death and any personal labour that might be necessary for this purpose. This disposition is confirmed by the judgment given under oath in the Process by Father Gaspar Sobrino, former Provincial of the Society of Jesus in New Granada and a fellow novice of Claver in Tarragona, who when he saw him later on his visit to the college in Cartagena said with extraordinary admiration: 'Father Claver is still as much a novice in his attitude as he was when I knew him during his novitiate.'

Regular observance is the key to his sanctity at the time of his novitiate and in later life. God's providence caused the name of Peter Claver to be associated centuries later at his canonization with that of the young man who had been considered the perfect observer of the rules of the Society of Jesus, St John Berchmans. These two, together with their great master, St Alphonsus Rodrí- guez, were canonized on the same day.

St Peter Claver led this life during the two years of his novitiate at Tarragona. On 8 August 1604 he took the vows which joined him to the Society of Jesus. In the notebook already mentioned, known to Father Andrade and Brother González, these brief meditations were preserved.

'I shall consider,' he says, 'the great obligation assumed by one who has made the consecration of himself to God . . . I must dedicate myself to the service of God until death, on the understanding that *I am like a slave*, wholly occupied in the service of his master and in the endeavour to please and content him in all and in every way with his whole soul, body and mind.'

The logicial continuity of his religious psychology is remarkable. The idea of slavery had already at the time of his novitiate penetrated deeply into his humble mind, and the phrase 'I am like a slave of God', undefined and general in this his first profession, is to become concrete, defined and heroic in the second, when far away in Cartagena he makes his solemn profession. Then this slavery will extend its sphere of action, and he will find God in the most unhappy of his fellow-beings; he will become the slave of the negro slaves. This nascent idea, rested in his deep humility, was to constitute the distinctive character of his life. Some keen-sighted historians have perceived in certain phrases and decisions of the Saint a kind of fear which arises from this very humility. His fear of the priesthood will manifest itself in different ways, not only while he is a student, but especially as the great day approaches. God's providence will bring across his path, as we shall see, two men to light his way and leave him no doubt of his mission. St Alphonsus Rodríguez will urge him to cultivate an apostolic interior life, full of zeal for souls. Father Sandoval will be the counsellor of genius who defines this vocation still further and indicates the apostolate of the slaves as the finest fulfilment of his life.

When Peter Claver ended his novitiate he was twenty-four years old, and one of the witnesses describes him to us at that epoch as: 'vigorous, energetic and robust, with a perfect and regular countenance, lit by large black eyes through which the fire of his youthful soul shines, a body of great physical perfection not yet worn and emaciated by that melancholy which is to be typical of his last years.'

When his novitiate came to an end, his superiors sent him to another Catalan town, which made his round of the province complete. This time it was to Gerona in the north of Spain near the French frontier. The college of Gerona had not long been founded.

This town also was walled and full of historic ruins, Greek, Iberian and Roman. The climate was colder and damper than that of Barcelona or of Tarragona. In Gerona Claver was to complete his study of humane letters. He arrived in October and remained there, perfecting his knowledge of Latin, learning Greek and studying rhetoric. Later on a witness will say that Peter Claver was a specialist in the Greek language and a great orator. He could not have exercised this gift much in the years that followed, for his apostolate took him rather into the field of simple religious instruction and personal intercourse.

Nevertheless we gather from the Gerona report that he spoke and wrote perfect Latin and Greek with ease, and so far as Castilian is concerned he possessed a great virile eloquence, matter of fact and without elaboration, but always full of the fire which distinguished him all his life. Father Fernández notes that these qualities were due rather to appreciation than to natural talent. Later we shall see that contradictory judgments were frequently pronounced on the whole of his personality.

Peter Claver had now reached the moment to leave for the college in Majorca to study philosophy. There he was to find more than the human learning of Aristotle, the divine wisdom of a saint. Majorca represents for Peter Claver the crucial moment of his life. Without Alphonsus Rodríguez we should not know how St Peter Claver came to exist.

CHAPTER III

THE GOLDEN ISLE

THIS is a decisive chapter in the life-story of St Peter Claver. A great poet has called Majorca the Isle of Calm. Serenity enfolds this Mediterranean island where bright blue skies lend a soft colouring to the perpetually spring-like landscape.

Quietly on this island two Jesuit saints of the seventeenth century lived for three years, far from the turmoil of the world, in the college of Montesión at Palma—an old man of eighty and a young man of twenty-five. The world outside was not aware of their inspired colloquies, but its religious history was to present some years later an amazing picture of the heroism of the man who became a slave and chose to endure terrible martyrdom of body and mind in order to free 300,000 oppressed brethren. The apostolate of Cartagena de Indias has its roots in Majorca. St Peter Claver is the truest spiritual son of St Alphonsus Rodríguez. This is what makes it so moving to approach this abundant source of God's favour.

A marvellous island, Majorca. A college with the symbolical name of *Montesión* (Mount Zion). Two saints encouraging each other in spiritual friendship: St Alphonsus and St Peter Claver.

The modern traveller who disembarks today in the bay of Palma is amazed at the sight of the gigantic mass of the cathedral. If he goes straight on towards the old part of the town in an easterly direction, he will pass through the street of San Pedro Nolasco, and when he reaches Morey Street he may go on towards the churches of Santa Eulalia or San Francisco or make his way through a series of narrow shaded streets, *Calle de la Pureza, Calle San Alonso, Calle Montesión*. Here he will find the magnificent porch of a church and the entrance to a cloister where a statue of St

Alphonsus greets him. At the base of the statue may be read the words: *Ya voy, Señor*—'I go, Lord.'[1]

We are in the Jesuit College of Montesión, where the patron saint of Majorca, St Alphonsus Rodríguez, and St Peter Claver lived.

On the feast of St Bartholomew, 24 August 1561, five Jesuits entered the city of Palma. They were the founders of Montesión: Fathers Francisco Boldó, Bernardo Verdolay, Gerónimo Mar and the brothers coadjutors, Juan Navarro and Francisco Fortuni.

At the beginning of the seventeenth century twenty-seven religious of the Society of Jesus were resident in the college.

On 11 September 1603 Father Blas Vaylo began the course in philosophy. The number of pupils was sixty. Another memorable date in the history of the college was 11 November 1605, when a mere student from Barcelona called Peter Claver arrived to follow the full philosophy course under the famous teacher.

Father Vaylo's success continued and the number of pupils grew. By 2 September 1606 he could reckon about one hundred secular students and seven Jesuits. School tasks alternated with religious festivities. It was a time of fervour and devotion to Ignatius of Loyola whose beatification was imminent. Peter Claver was present in the church of Montesión on the solemn occasion of the erection of a great reredos begun in 1607.

In December 1604 Father Arcaina arrived to teach grammar, philosophy and theology; he was Peter Claver's teacher. In 1605 thirty-six Jesuits were resident in this house, of whom fifteen were priests, five young teachers, twenty-one students and ten lay brothers. Nothing special seemed to happen during this time, yet one person filled the whole scene. August 10, 1571 had been a date of supreme importance for Montesión. On that day the brother coadjutor, Alphonsus Rodríguez, had arrived at the college, sent there from Valencia by the Father Provincial, Antonio Cordeses.

[1] The principal documentation for this section is found in the manuscript history of the college of Montesión published in part by Father Pedro Blanco Trías, S.J., *El colegio de Ntra Sra de Montesión en Palma de Mallorca*, Palma, 1948. Also Jaime Nonell, S. J., *Vida y Obras del beato Alonso Rodríguez*, Barcelona, 1885.

The presence of a saint always exercises a powerful influence. In the register of those received into the college of Valencia—now in the archives of that town—we read: 'Brother Alonso Rodríguez, aged somewhere between thirty-five and forty, was received into this college as a lay brother on 31 January 1571.' In the manuscript history of Montesión we read this entry nearly fifty years later, for 31 October 1617: 'On account of the mild climate of this land there has been no serious illness this year among the residents, who enjoyed perfect health, except for the illness of our blessed brother, Alonzo Rodríguez, who passed away at the end of this year, or more exactly on October 31.' Thus simply was recorded the death of a saint.

St Alphonsus Rodríguez was St Peter Claver's great teacher in the life of the spirit. Father Colín, a contemporary and his first biographer, described him thus: 'of medium height, although in his old age he was so bent that he seemed small. Lean, rather sunburned and very bald, he had big eyes with tear-ducts inflamed and bloodshot from continual weeping, a small mouth slightly twisted in old age, but not ugly. During his three-day ecstasy and in death his face appeared whiter and more beautiful than before.'

The outward aspect of this eminently spiritual saint's life may be reduced to a few lines; the framework of his hidden life suggested by a few dates.

Born in Segovia on 25 July 1531, he entered the Society of Jesus on 31 January 1571, took his final vows on 5 April 1573, died in Palma in Majorca on 31 October 1617—eighty-six years of life, during which he exercised the function of doorkeeper for forty-seven years at the college of Montesión. He is the doorkeeper saint, beatified on 31 July 1824 and canonized at the same time as Peter Claver on 15 January 1888.

These dates say little, but their laconic statement conceals a life of which Leo XIII said in his Bull of Canonization:

St Alphonsus by his admirable virtue and the splendour of his divine gifts may stand comparison with the greatest saints. But he is not only remarkable for his own glory but for others to whom he showed the way of salvation, among whom St

Peter Claver may be considered to occupy the first place; for while he was still young St Alphonsus inspired him to embark on a career of the most sublime sanctity with utter joy. So it came to pass—not without God's manifest will—that the great apostle of the negroes and the humble doorkeeper of the college of Palma, illumined by the same celestial light, received the halo of sanctity on the same day.

To give a full account of his teaching would become too prolix. He left twenty-two memorials of his life which constitute an ascetic and mystical way, and his writings are collected in seven volumes full of solid practical doctrine: he lived what he taught.

One central thought in his ascetic doctrine is revealed in the following fundamental passage:

There is another exercise which is also very precious and divine for the imitation of Christ our Lord, taking the sweet for bitter and the bitter for sweet for love of him; and that is to put oneself in spirit before our crucified Lord, looking at him so full of sorrow and shedding his blood from every part of his body imbued with the many great hardships he endured for me; for love is paid for in love. What then I must do is to imitate him, sharing in spirit all his sufferings, considering how much I owe him and what he has done for me; to put these sufferings between the two, God and the soul, speaking of them in these words: 'What matters it, my God, that I should endure for thy love these small hardships, for thou, Lord, didst endure so many great hardships for me?' In this way I stimulate the heart to this exercise in the hardship and trial itself, encouraging it to endure with love, for love of the Lord who is in front of me, till I make what is bitter sweet; and in this way learning from Christ our Lord take and convert the sweet into bitter, despising oneself and all earthly and carnal pleasures, delights and honours of this life, so that the whole heart is centred solely on God . . .

The great philosophy of suffering with Christ, of the renunciation of self, is the basis of all the teachings of Alphonsus. A full biography cannot be provided here, but only the outlines needed to understand the decisive influence he exercised on Peter Claver as his spiritual instructor.

Alphonsus Rodríguez was a Segovian, born in that austere Spanish land of Old Castile.[1] Castilian austerity leads to God, to detachment; in those solitudes sounds a call to the life beyond this earth. And St Teresa, the indefatigable traveller along this world's dusty roads towards luminous mystic horizons, also belonged to that land; like Cervantes and the Cid, and like Alphonsus Rodríguez, she possessed that realism which keeps close to the earth.

St Alphonsus Rodríguez could not lose this stamp of austerity even after fifty years of smiling Mediterranean life in the lovely town of Palma in Majorca. The spirit of concentration on the cross of Christ is characteristic. St Alphonsus was divinely gifted as few are. Yet even in exalted mood he writes: 'Holiness does not consist in having visions or consoling joys nor in the gift of prophecy, nor in revelations, for all these things cost the soul little; God gives it all. Holiness costs great trials of mortification and the conquest of the soul by God's grace . . . holiness consists in the love of God and our neighbour and in deep humility of heart and obedience and resignation, and in the imitation of Christ our Lord; and in this there is no danger as in those other things. Holiness does not lie in extraordinary things, and so avoids them.' [2]

This Castilian asceticism fell on the fruitful ground of Peter Claver's soul and yielded a hundredfold. On opening the great door Alphonsus never failed to exclaim: 'I go, Lord.' He saw Christ in all the brothers who came in, as Claver would see the wounded Christ in the poor chained negroes or the lepers of San Lazaro. Without this divine transfiguration, heroic charity is impossible.

St Alphonsus writes:

The exercise he practised in his work as doorkeeper was the following: first of all, when anyone rang the bell, he used to say, raising his heart to God: 'Lord, I shall open the door to you for love of you.'

The second exercise was, when someone rang, to perform

[1] Manuel Siurot, *España: Las Castillas*, Barcelona, 1933, pp. 6, 10.
[2] *Memorial*, 7.

mental acts of rejoicing on the way to the door, as if he were going to open to God, as if he were ringing the bell; on the way thither he kept repeating: 'I go, Lord.'

The third exercise was of interior mortification, for if anyone rang loud and quickly, his heart was naturally perturbed within him; and he repressed it firmly . . . So he went toward the door calmly and opened it, as if the visitor had not rung more than once and that gently . . .

The fourth exercise was that, having grown so accustomed to the idea of going to open to Christ, he found suddenly he was there and that he was opening to him, with great joy and happiness; it seemed to this person when he went to open the door . . . that he saw him come with innumerable angels and the most holy Virgin also with him.

Devotion to Christ was the central point of his life, but again we find another mark of the realism of his spirituality. Like the Castilian Teresa, he did not exalt himself so high to the divinity of Christ as to lose touch with his humanity.

Presently we shall see the love and esteem St Peter Claver felt for images. A wooden crucifix hung upon his breast all his life and crudely painted pictures of Christ were the first things the 300,000 slaves baptized by him saw when they arrived at the port of Cartagena. It is easy to see where he learned his esteem for and practical use of images. Here is a paragraph from the memorial written by St Alphonsus in 1609 when the Saint was still in residence at the college of Montesión.

It is an amazing thing that this person passes before an image of Christ crucified and sees in it what Christ suffered for him and for the whole world, and he raises his eyes to heaven and perceives that the Lord of such glory and majesty who enjoys such bliss in heaven is he who endured all that for him and much more that he sees in his image; and that his heart awakes, saying to him: 'Lord, who would not die for love of such a master who has done such a thing for love of him and all men? And who would not serve such a master?' From this it is plain to him how valuable images are, in that they enable a man to see what he owes to God and what he has done for him and still does, God being (as he is) of such majesty, so that he may burn with love for him and with desire to serve him and please him; more particularly the images of Christ and his Mother . . .[1]

Rodríguez died as he had lived: 'And when we had finished reciting for him the recommendation of the departing soul, embracing a devout image of Christ crucified which he held in his hands, he opened his eyes which he usually kept closed, and then he opened them wide and looked at us with a clearer, livelier and happier expression than he had ever had in his life, and bending to kiss it and pronouncing the sweetest name of Jesus in a loud and sustained voice, he died. It was 31 October 1617. He was eighty-six years old.'

This was the spiritual master of St Peter Claver, whose influence was not ephemeral. Alphonsus disappeared from Claver's sight but not from his heart when he said good-bye in Palma. And a day came when God united them in the supreme honour of canonization.

From the unpublished manuscript history of the Jesuit college of Montesión, very laconic throughout, come the following lines: 'On 11 November 1605 Brothers Antonio Palao, Gabriel Alegre, Juan Humanes and Pedro Claver arrived from Barcelona. The three brothers Alegre, Humanes and Claver came to follow a three year course in philosophy, which they completed under Father Vaylo . . . ' And three years later the history adds: 'In this same month of November 1608, Brothers Humanes and Claver, who had completed the course with Father Vaylo, embarked for Catalonia in a Breton ship and arrived in good weather at the port of Salou going on from there to Tarragona.' This is all the information given about St Peter Claver. He was a mere student, and the historical account says nothing about those daily talks with the doorkeeper of the house, old Brother Alphonsus.[2]

Claver was twenty-five years of age when he was sent to

[1] *Memorial*, 125.

[2] Sources: Jaime Nonell, *op. cit.*; P. Colín, *Vida de San Alonso Rodríguez*; Ignacio Casanovas, *Alonso Rodríguez*, Barcelona, 1947; *Process of beatification and canonization of St Peter Claver*, summary, Nos. 4 *et seq.*

Majorca to study philosophy. He himself says somewhere to Brother González that he was overjoyed to hear this news, as he longed to see and talk to Alphonsus, whose holiness he had heard so highly praised . . .

One psychological trait in Peter Claver's make-up is really obscure. It is difficult to be sure exactly how conscious he was of his priestly vocation. Although he entered the Society of Jesus, various remarks suggest that he sometimes doubted his definite vocation. He felt a strong inclination for a life apart from active work and was attracted to a more monastic way. Like St Francis Xavier he came upon the right man at the right time. It was not the formidable spiritual genius of St Ignatius, but an old door-keeper, Alphonsus Rodríguez, also a good judge of character, with an ardent Castilian temperament, who understood from the very first the young student's secret struggle. Above all, he took on the task of his spiritual director, steeping him in his own solid spirituality based on self-renunciation and humility, though at the same time urging him on to conquest. Alphonsus Rodríguez countered Claver's fears of ordination as a priest by showing him the apostolic way—the saving of souls perishing in the Indies. Young Claver must have felt this struggle deeply. For three years the old man's lessons became part of his life, and perhaps the complex fear of active life left his mind, though not finally. It comes up again shortly afterwards in Barcelona, when he refuses to be ordained before leaving for the Indies. And in Santa Fe de Bogotá this indecision appears again when he tries to become a lay brother. Only his meeting with another man of genius, Father Sandoval, was to set him definitely on his way.

So the two men who most influenced the life of Peter Claver are St Alphonsus and Father Sandoval. Without them, humanly speaking, Peter Claver might perhaps have lost his bearings.

This period of three years in Montesión was the most fruitful and decisive for Peter Claver, not on account of his studies but through his providential meeting with such an extraordinary man as Alphonsus Rodríguez. It was the meeting of two saints. Alphonsus had reached the prime of his spiritual life. At this time he enjoyed a reputation for holiness known not only in the community of Montesión but in the whole Society of Jesus. For the young Jesuit student filled with desire for spiritual guidance, arrival in Majorca presented something new in his life. His reserved temperament could not hide his emotion. Scarcely had he reached the college and exchanged a glance with the doorkeeper than he went to the superior to ask for permission to communicate his spiritual problems to Alphonsus Rodríguez. They understood one another at first sight. Every day they had a quarter of an hour's private talk, as Father Claver himself tells Brother Nicolás González—so we read in the Process: 'he had permission to talk every evening for a quarter of an hour alone with Alonso about the means of attaining to evangelical and religious perfection'.

The old man was a practised director of souls of whom, in the words of Father Colín, 'it can be truly said that in all the years that he was doorkeeper, no one entered the Society of Jesus in the college in Majorca who did not confide in him his aspirations or was not stirred to live up to them by his conversations.' It seems that his particular spiritual task was the formation of missionaries for America . . . From the outset Alphonsus prayed for this choice soul of whose great mission he had a foreshadowing. One day, praying for his friend in a moment of crisis, of indecision about the future, Alphonsus was rapt to heaven accompanied by his guardian angel. There he saw innumerable thrones occupied by the souls of the blessed, and among them, the most splendid of all, an empty one. Desiring to know the meaning of that mystery, he was told: 'That is the place prepared for your disciple, Peter Claver, as a reward for his many virtues and the innumerable souls he will convert by his toil and sweat in the Indies.' The old man was greatly moved. He had before him a predestined man. He disclosed his vision to his spiritual director, who revealed it later on. To Peter Claver he said nothing about it, but in their daily talks he saw the mysterious light that shone from the predestined throne. Everything became clear so that now he could guide his friend with absolute certainty.

One day, seated beside a tree in the courtyard of the college, not far from the bay of Palma, he said to Claver: 'How many there are idle in Europe who might be apostles in America!' and exclaimed: 'A great mission, a great mission . . . Oh, why does not God's love plough these seas through which human avarice has cleft a way? Are those souls not worth the price of God's life? Did he not die for them too? Ah, Pedro, my beloved son, why do you not go, you also, to gather the blood of Christ? He cannot love who has not learnt to suffer. And there it is waiting for you—and oh, if you only knew the great pleasure he has prepared for you!'

Of the notes in Claver's diary, that precious notebook which Brother Nicolás González had in his possession, but which is now unfortunately lost, we have only scraps contributed by the same brother to the Process and recorded in private letters after Claver's death.

Another day, we read in these notes, the old man made these reflections: 'What blindness there is for lack of men to enlighten so many millions of unbelievers with the light of Christ. How many of them die without having known or loved their Creator and Redeemer! On the other hand a crowd of adventurers cross the ocean for temporal business and earthly interests. Can it be endured any longer that the worldly should be more eager to pile up merchandise and perishable goods than the servants of Christ to ransom souls which cost the Son of God so dear?'

This argument of emulation was used with special point in that century of great conquests. We find it repeatedly in the ascetic writers and with particular emphasis in the so-called *Letter of Perfection* addressed by St Ignatius to the Jesuit students of Coimbra. The same argument is frequently found in the letters of St Francis Xavier. We shall see this theme very clearly set out in one of the most brilliant chapters of Father Sandoval's famous book.

The sixteenth and seventeenth centuries were filled with heroism, courage and enterprise. The accounts coming from America, dry and brusque as they were, recorded, as well as the marvels of its wealth and topography, the mighty struggle of the men who strove even to death against untamed nature and the mysteries of the unknown: rough men from Estremadura, grave Catalans, Majorcan navigators, nobles in reduced circumstances from that Old Castile exhausted now from over-cultivation. Beside Hernán

Cortés, Pizarro, Magellan, Elcano, heroes of this world, there should be a parallel legion composed of Luis Beltrán, Claver, Rose of Lima, Toribio de Mongrovejo, the numberless missionary conquerors for Christ.

In the colloquies of Alphonsus and Claver which the early biographers give as textually correct but which really only reflect their spirit without being strictly literal, the far-off world of the West Indies appears not as an earthly Eldorado, but as a field ready for the harvest of souls.

This aspect has not been sufficiently stressed; the value of America as a spiritual ideal in the aspirations of Europe in the sixteenth and seventeenth centuries. America first as a stimulus to holy ambitions and then as an actual field for the apostolate. Exhortations did not fall on deaf ears. Peter Claver and his companion Juan Humanes wrote to their superiors asking to be allowed to work in the New World.

One interesting scene presents four persons. Alphonsus was at the door of the sacristy in company with Father Vicente Arcaina. The brother asked Father Vicente who those two were coming through the courtyard and about fifty paces away. The Father answered that they were young students, Peter Claver and Juan Humanes, fellow pupils in the philosophy course. On hearing this the old man exclaimed with great emphasis: 'those brothers will go to the Indies and will gather in a great harvest of souls.' In fact Brother Humanes would go to Paraguay where he died after enduring many hardships; the kingdom of New Granada (Colombia) was reserved for Peter Claver.

Another day Peter Claver was going out to the country, this time with Brother Miguel Serra, another disciple of Alphonsus, who died in 1665, renowned for his sanctity. The master saw them go by: a smile lit up his wrinkled face and, greeting them both, he said: 'Are you going for a walk? Remember that Jesus is on one side of you and Mary on the other.' At these words, Peter Claver wrote later in his notebook: 'I felt my heart wounded, as if I had been hit by an arrow.'

Another day he was going out to recreation with a fellow student. The doorkeeper at his post saw the two young men going out, and spoke mysteriously, first indicating Claver: 'Here the Father,' then to Claver's companion: 'Here the Son,' and then putting his hands between the two of them, 'Here the Holy Spirit.' Scarcely had he pronounced the last word when he was seized by a rapture and lost the use of his senses. There seemed to sweep over all three of them the full force of the Holy Spirit. It left Brother Alphonsus motionless, rapt in a state of ecstasy; and Peter Claver was so overcome that he could not walk a step and almost fainted. He asked his companion if he had felt anything, and the latter replied: 'A sweet feeling of love no words could describe.' Claver wished to return home, for the experience had deprived him of the strength to walk; but recollecting that recreation was of obedience, he prayed to God to enable him to fulfil it by moderating this ecstasy. Some relief he felt, but every step still cost him a violent effort. At last, with incredible difficulty he went on to join the others. All day he went about as if in a trance. This event had a lasting effect, for Claver himself recounted it to several of his friends—as is recorded in the Process.[1] It is not strange that Peter Claver should consider these three years in Majorca 'the most beautiful in his life', and that as an old man he remembered these moments with ineffable delight. That daily quarter of an hour moulded him in the spirituality of Alphonsus. There is perhaps no more remarkable case in the history of the saints: a layman saint who by formal instruction in systematic ascetical theology guides a priest saint who, in his turn, leaves no writing or theoretical instruction of any kind, but only a wonderful life of action, fruit of the ideas instilled in his mind by a humble teacher. Everything leads us to conclude that Peter Claver was the favourite pupil of Alphonsus Rodríguez. November 1610 arrived, the time for saying farewell to Brother Alphonsus. The afternoon before he had brought Claver a treasure, written out in his own hand, the Little Office of the Immaculate Conception, which Claver was to keep all his life and recite three times a week; and with this some notebooks of spiritual precepts. Alphonsus had to ask special permission of the superiors to hand over these books to his friend Claver, as the latter was going to the Indies where there

[1] Process, No. 4.

was a greater shortage of spiritual reading matter than in Spain. This permission was necessary as there had been cases of fathers being obliged to undo their bundles at the porter's lodge of the college of Montesión and ordered to give up the notes which they had received from Brother Alphonsus. Peter Claver was departing well provided. After the daily conversation he used to make his own résumé of it in a notebook. To this were added those written out by Alphonsus Rodríguez himself.

Claver left Montesión, and never in all his life did his love cool for the one whom he called 'my saintly master'. He boasted of being his pupil, spoke of him with the greatest enthusiasm, and all the witnesses in the Process dwell on the enormous influence exerted on him by the writings of Alphonsus. 'He had', they said, 'two notebooks containing spiritual matter drawn from the writings of his master, and another three, containing but a few sheets, of other precepts which he had taken down orally, noting the day, month and year when they were given to him. Apart from these notes written by himself, Claver had the original texts of Alphonsus, the little book given as a farewell gift, which Claver carried with him all his life—together with the Office of the Immaculate Conception.'[1]

These notes he always prized so highly that in his last illness he kept the books on his person with great reverence, and arranged, with the permission of his superiors, that they should be sent to the novitiate of Tunja with a letter produced by Brother González which reads:

By permission of our Father Provincial and our Father General as stated in their letter, I deposit—being about to quit this world—I say, I deposit a great treasure which I received from holy Brother Alonso Rodríguez, a book written by his own hand in which he left imprinted his soul and his virtues. And so I send it to the novitiate in order that the holy novices and their Father Master may make good use of it, as I have been unable to do. Let them take care of this treasure. I beg and entreat the man who carries it there to pray to God for this

[1] Process, No. 8. A book in the form of a novel has lately been published by Mabel Farnum, *The Wool Merchant of Segovia*.

sinner who, having so great a treasure in his possession, instead of extracting from it the gold of holiness only extracted dross; for which reason I ask no reward or payment, but pardon and mercy. Cartagena, 28 October 1651. Pedro Claver.'

What would we not give to possess those notes which were lost on the expulsion of the Jesuits, as well as the others which remained in the hands of Brother González in Cartagena?

A final illustration of the great love of Claver for Alphonsus Rodríguez was given during his last illness when Brother Nicolás entered the sick man's room and told him the great news. 'Here, your Reverence,' he said, 'is the life of the holy Brother Alonso Rodríguez of which a printed copy has just arrived, to give you this consolation before you die.' It was the biography written by Father Francisco Colín, a Catalan, entitled: *Life, deeds and doctrines of the Venerable Brother Alonso Rodríguez*, published in Madrid by Domingo García y Morera in 1652. The saintly old man displayed great joy. Taking the book he touched his forehead with it, saying: 'Blessed be God who has allowed me to see in print something I longed for so much.' Brother Nicolás opened the book to show him the portrait of Brother Alphonsus well reproduced from the original. Father Claver's eyes shone, and he seemed so eager to talk that Brother González thought the moment opportune to put some questions to him on matters about which he had always been very reserved. The brother asked him if holy Brother Alphonsus had told him he would go to the Indies, to New Granada (Colombia) and more particularly to Cartagena. The sick man answered that he had told him so very often. Brother González pressed him for more details of his friendship with Alphonsus Rodríguez and it was then that he revealed the incident we have already related of the Holy Spirit.

Brother Nicolás, when the Saint's first joy had faded, took away the biography of Brother Alphonsus; but the arrival of this book had made such an impression on Peter Claver, and he was so anxious to read it, that he got dressed and eagerly, half dragging himself along, went down to the sacristy in search of Brother Nicolás once more to console himself with the sight of the life of his dear master. There he found some old college friends, among them Don Antonio Betancur, governor of Jamaica, who were all amazed at his action, but he began immediately to talk to them of his old friend. Claver's poverty did not permit him to have objects of value in his room, but his devotion induced him to affix a print of Brother Alphonsus on a wooden tablet which hung at the head of his bed. This picture he used to hold up to the sick he visited and also when he went on missions. It was the only picture with him until death, when his devotees ransacked his cell in search of relics. A member of the order saved the picture and kept it at the head of Peter Claver's bed until he breathed his last; for he knew the sight of it was one of the most precious things he could have at the hour of his death. Among his heavenly patrons there was one he invoked every day, saying: 'And thou also, my dear Alonso.'

Certainly in religious history there are few saints for whom friendship and supernatural influence have been so combined as in the case of St Alphonsus Rodríguez and St Peter Claver. Both were canonized on the same day in the year 1888.

It is difficult to distinguish among the documents attributed to Peter Claver the authentic originals from the spiritual commentaries. Fundamentally, although the original text of the spiritual precepts given him by St Alphonsus may have been lost, we have historical assurance of their authentic if indirect derivation from that source. In the Process Brother Nicolás González said: 'These notebooks of St Alonso were lent to Brother González when he was a novice by Father Claver in order to stimulate his fervour.' And elsewhere: 'These notes were left by the Saint before his death to be sent to the novitiate at Tunja.' Brother González sent a complete account of Peter Claver's life to the Spanish Provinces, and Father Andrade in Madrid assures us that he saw a copy of these notes. We can therefore be certain of the genuineness of writings which, apart from this evidence, are in complete harmony with the letter and spirit of St Alphonsus Rodríguez.

THE PRINCIPAL PRECEPTS PRESENTED BY ST ALPHONSUS TO PETER CLAVER

The health and perfection of a man's soul is in the performance of the will of God our Lord, which he should regard at all moments of his life and in all his actions in order to perform them with great zeal; and the more closely he follows it, the higher perfection he will attain.

To do God's will it is necessary for a man to despise the doing of his own will in all things; for the more he dies in this, the more he will live to God; and the more he purges himself of self-love and pride, the more he will abound in the love of God. And in order to fulfil the will of God, a man must love him, for the measure of his love will be the fulfilment of God's will.

In order to love God a man must first set aside his own will and free it from all worldly and carnal love and affection; he must love God alone, or if he love any other thing, he should do so for God's sake and in no other way.

The highest perfection consists in this, that all a man's thoughts, words and actions be directed solely to the honour and glory of God. A man ought to work with the supreme desire of making his will conform in every way to the will of God, and of bringing it into such close union with him that he not only rejects evil but even the good which God may not desire. In every adversity that may befall him in temporal or spiritual matters he must endeavour not to let his soul's peace be disturbed, desiring what God wishes, gives and sends him from his own hand.

In order to desire what God wishes, he must deny his own will with great constancy; for one who denies his own and performs God's will, does what best pleases Him, and has the Creator with him.

The perfection of a religious does not consist in keeping the body enclosed within walls but in having his soul accompanied by virtues.

To win a real victory he must be silent when men insult, reproach and ill-treat him, whether he is to blame or not, and not defend himself: and however much they persist he ought to give way in silence without replying.

If he wishes to gain a real victory, let him keep watch on his tongue; let him not lose by speaking what he has won by silence, for the latter keeps great blessings in the soul. Let him see to it then that there be quietness and peace, truth and edification in all his words; and brevity, few words and of much substance and matter that is of God.

If he wishes to gain much and speak well, let him talk always of God and with God, living humbly with him alone.

Let him never prefer anything or anyone, save only a superior, to the least obligation of obedience, subjecting himself to every creature for God's sake, and saying 'yes' to all things, accepting everything, doing what he can with great peace of mind. And if he does not do it, when asked he should answer, 'I have not been able to'; for nothing else will do; and let him observe great silence, answering nothing, nothing, nothing at all to whatever may be said to him; let him be completely silent, silent, silent, not answering a single word; for in this silence great perfection, holiness and profit lie concealed; for in this way a man conquers himself, not defending himself, but for the love of God accepting everything that is not contrary to God's will and his obedience.

Go deep in self-knowledge, for this is knowledge firmly based; a man who knows himself despises himself; one who does not know himself becomes vain.

The good religious must be like Melchisedech without father or mother, without family or relatives; for he must have as little to do with them as if he did not possess them.

There must be no more than God and you in the world, for he alone must be all things to you.

Look for God in all men and serve them as images of him.

Let him pray to God for those who offended him and do them greater benefits than they did him wrongs.

Let him give the first fruits of the day to our Lord, offering to him his heart and all the actions of that day.

Let him offer his works to God at the beginning, the middle and the end; at the beginning directing his attention to his greater glory and service; in the middle uniting them all with those of Jesus Christ that they may be precious and acceptable to his Majesty; and at the end offering them for his soul and those of his fellow men.

Let him keep God present in his heart and not do or say anything without asking his permission and communicating it to him.

Let him retire at all times to the privacy of his own heart to revere God and ask him for grace to serve him and not offend him.

Let him never leave his room without cause, nor without asking our Lord for permission and for grace not to offend him; and on his return let him examine himself to see if he is returning as he left it.

Before leaving the house let him visit our Lord in the church and ask him to accompany him and always go with him.

Let him not use his senses except for necessary things and the service of God. Let him not look at curious things or listen to useless tittle-tattle which dries up the heart.

Let him never speak of food or clothing, nor ask for it, even for his room. Let him act in all things as one who is dead to the world and lives for God alone.

Let him eat no sweet or dainty food, or anything beyond what is needed to sustain life. One who admits the gratification of the body loses that of the spirit, and one who takes delight in men loses the delights of God.

Let him consider praise as blame, remembering what he is in God's sight; men look at the outside, but God our Lord looks at the heart.

Let him rejoice in abuse and insults on account of those which Christ suffered for him. Let him humble himself in affronts, for he deserves more for his sins.

Let him meditate continually on the four last things, especially on death to which he must soon come; and let him be eager to work and suffer, for his time for acquiring merit will soon come to an end.

Let him meditate often on the passion of our Lord; let him remember every hour what he suffered for him and give him great praise, and ask for his cross and carry it with pleasure for his love.

Let him meditate on the virtues, especially the religious ones which are proper to his state; let him consider that arduous and great tasks are presented to him in each one, such as difficult acts of obedience and great hardships; and let him not cease till he surrender his heart to bear them with joy for love of God.

Let him speak well of all and ill of himself.

Let him reproach and punish himself for any faults he incurs, asking God to pardon him and to give him his hand to keep him from falling.

Let him avoid occasions into which he has once fallen or is in danger of falling, for they are snares of the devil whom he must resist until he conquers.

Let him serve Mass whenever he can, remembering that the angels assist and serve the Lord who is offered therein. Let him look at him on the altar as on Calvary and with the priest offer him as a sacrifice to his eternal Father.

Let him detach his heart from all created beings and fix it on God alone. Let him do many loving acts daily, stirring the fire in in the sanctuary of his heart.

Let him cultivate great devotion to the blessed Virgin, loving her and serving her with his whole heart; let him visit her many times each day; let him offer her all his works; let him say her rosary and, if he can, the Little Office and let him waste no opportunity of doing her some service; let him contemplate her virtues and take courage to imitate them by the grace of God.

Let him show devotion to his holy guardian angel and to our father St Ignatius, love him as a son and revere him as a father, and take both of them as intercessors to obtain whatever he asks of God.

Let him venerate the images of the saints, as if they were actually present; let him remember their virtues, how they served God, and how quickly their sufferings were over and the reward they earned through them; the brevity of this life and the eternity of the next; and all will become light and easy to endure for the love of God.

Wake much and sleep little; whatever is saved from sleep is added to life and to merit.

Study with care the necessary and not the superfluous; suitable knowledge profits and the superfluous puffs up.

Let him look for God in all things and he will find him and will have him always at his side.

The sanctity of Peter Claver was nourished faithfully on these ideas. In the history of religion he is one of the most faithful followers of a concrete religious philosophy. Alphonsus Rodríguez excercised with his writings the most direct intellectual influence ever exerted by one man over another. For this reason it has been necessary to insist on this fruitful friendship. To understand the ascetic mentality of St Alphonsus is to penetrate the depth of Peter Claver's religious psychology.

CHAPTER IV

FROM SEVILLE TO CARTAGENA

AFTER three decisive years at Montesión Claver was twenty-eight and had brilliantly completed his course in philosophy under Father Vaylo. On the return journey from Majorca to Barcelona old Alphonsus figured constantly in conversation with Juan Ballester, Antonio Gual and Pedro Juan Pons, the three novices who accompanied Claver, and especially with his friend, Brother Juan Humanes. Moreover, he shared with this last a secret ambition, to go to the Indies. The old man had seen them both in a supernatural vision. Unconsciously they followed the route he had marked out. They had made their decision; their ideal was there in the far-off Indies, as the Saint had again repeated to them when he bade them farewell at the door of Montesión.

After a good journey Peter Claver saw at last the coast of Tarragona. In a new light he saw his native land, which now seemed foreign. In imagination he was already in the Indies. He was only anxiously awaiting an affirmative reply from his Provincial. Two years he waited for permission to go to the New Kingdom of *Tierra Firme*, as it was called. In the meantime he continued to fulfil his duty.

In the college at Barcelona, which held so many memories for him, Claver began to study theology. Since the year 1597 this faculty had existed in the college of Belén. At this time Father Lorenzo de San Juan was rector, having been appointed on 12 June 1607, and he continued in this office until June 1610. Father José de Villegas was still Provincial of Aragón. Peter Claver studied theology at Barcelona from November 1608 until the end of January 1610. The rest of the course he completed in Santa Fe de Bogotá. Of this life during his stay in Barcelona we have a first-hand account from his fellow student, Father Gaspar de Garrigas, who wrote to Father Alonso de Andrade from the residence at Valencia on 15 August 1656 the following illuminating note:

I should like to have been his confessor during the time when I was a fellow student of Father Pedro Claver, for then I should doubtless have much to relate about his life which was as admirable and perfect as I understand it has always been. While he was studying theology—when I knew and conversed with him—I can only say that I never observed anything in him unbecoming to a perfect and holy religious. Modest, gentle and friendly, he edified us all, trying to please and help everyone. I never heard him complain. Always he spoke of God and of things bearing on spiritual progress, and as far as possible, he increased and advanced his own. He was very humble and no less exact in obedience, showing remarkable submission to his superiors in everything. I can give no very personal details, as he was very silent and reserved. What is certain is that I never saw him break, or fail in the observance of any rule, even in the smallest particular. In all things he tried to imitate our holy Brother Alonso Rodríguez. In his possession were some notebooks that Brother Alonso Rodríguez had given him, written in his own hand and containing some precepts on prayer and mortification which the said Brother himself practised, and Claver did the same. So I am not surprised that God should work miracles through him, for he led such a holy life.

This letter is a sure synthesis of the psychology and behaviour of the Saint at this period. It throws much light on certain aspects of his personality. Kindness and friendliness are noted as fundamental traits of his character; humility and submission as his pivotal virtues: silence and reserve as typical of his temperament; faithful observance of the rules of his institute as the general pattern of his life; and the example of the master he had left at Majorca, Alphonsus Rodríguez, as the motive force which stimulated his endeavours.

During this period of theological studies two out-of-the-way incidents reveal the remarkable mystical side of Peter Claver. One day passing through the narrow streets of old Barcelona his companion happened to suggest that they continue their walk outside the city walls. They went on past the Convent of Our

Lady of the Angels by the road which leads from Barcelona to
Mataró as far as a place called Llacuna. On the stretch between
the above-mentioned old convent and a porch called *Portal de
San Daniel*, seventy-seven years earlier, some young men had
beaten and injured St Ignatius and his companion, Mosén Pujol,
because the Saint had found fault with their conduct. Some millers
who were passing carried Ignatius to the house of his great
benefactress, Inés Pascual. The place was a lonely spot near the
convent. Now after all those years as Peter Claver was passing this
spot he was mentally reconstructing the whole scene, when his
companion, a religious who was a good servant of God, spoke.
'It was here, brother,' he said, 'that they gave such a beating to
our father, St Ignatius; this is the very spot.' Scarcely had Claver
heard this when he stood still, gazing up at the sky, and remained
in a state of ecstasy for a little while. Such was the effect of this
supernatural communication that afterwards in America, relating
the incident to a confidant who later bore witness to it in the
process of beatification, he again became tongue-tied, and then
burst into tears.

Peter Claver's devotion to St Ignatius was remarkable and without doubt contributed powerfully to his vocation. In the Processes
of Barcelona Ignatius of Loyola had just been called 'one of the
chief glories of Catalonia'. During the festival of his beatification
celebrated with magnificence, Claver was in Barcelona. A contemporary account describes the event thus:

This year (1609) was one of the happiest by reason of the
welcome news of the beatification of our Father which delighted the whole town, and indeed the whole principality.
The vicar general gave orders that the feast should be announced
in every parish church, and apart from this it was also proclaimed
throughout the city to the sound of drums and trumpets.
When the bell was rung in one church all the churches of the
city replied, and everywhere at night there were very great
and wonderful illuminations. Don Juan de Moncada, brother
of the Marquis of Aytona and shortly after Bishop of this city,
undertook the decoration of a church, which with the wealth
of tapestries, the multitude of lights, the variety of precious

objects and their advantageous display seemed a very heaven.
An enormous crowd attended the service there, and a Dominican father preached to the admiration of all. Afterwards a
banquet was held which was honoured by the presence at table
of the viceroy, Don Juan de Moncada, a great many canons, all
the superiors of the various orders, and fourteen Dominican
friars who spent a great deal of time looking at the many and
varied poems which were publicly displayed for the glorification
of the Saint.

An altar was also erected in the house where the Saint had
resided when he was studying grammar here; and on it they
placed the crucifix before which the Saint had often said his
prayers. This house, which was that of Inés Pascual, gave its
name to the street, still called *Calle de San Ignacio.*

The demonstrations of rejoicing shown by Barcelona doubtless
found an echo in Peter Claver's heart. All his life he was to preserve
a deep love for his founder.

Still his petition was not granted. An event hastened the decision.
Some seven years earlier the Jesuit province of New Granada, the
present Colombia, had been founded and was urgently in need
of active members. In 1609 all the Spanish provinces received
from their common superior, Father Claudio Aquaviva, an order
for every Jesuit province in the peninsula to provide each year a
missionary for the young province of New Granada. Those
chosen should possess suitable qualities for such a difficult and
distant mission. God's hour had come. The Father Provincial,
José de Villegas, decided to send one of the most promising young
men. Years after the Father Provincial, Manuel de Arcos, was to
say publicly in the college of Tunja that 'six of the most dilligent
and fervent young men did not do as much work as Father Peter
Claver'. In conformity with the wishes of the Father General and
his own earnestly repeated requests, Brother Claver received the
following letter from his Provincial:

We must no longer oppose the will of our Lord, which I
have always seen inspires your desire to employ yourself in his
holy service among the Indians who by God's grace will be
greatly aided by you. And although I have kept you back as

long as possible, it seems to me now that I can no longer stand
in the way of your holy and efficacious desires and purposes.
Therefore as soon as the Father Rector gives his consent—
which will be soon, for Father Alonso de Mejía is urging the
matter from Seville where he awaits you—you should set out
for Tarragona to go with the others as far as Valencia, and from
there you are to start for Seville in the company they will
provide for you in accordance with my orders. You must send
me word of your journey and arrival when you reach Seville
to relieve my mind. Nothing more, but may the Lord grant
you his full blessing and order your affairs and works to his
greater glory as I pray him to do. Tarragona, 23 January 1610.
José de Villegas.

Peter Claver's desires had been fulfilled. The ideal visualized by
Alphonsus Rodríguez shortly before had become a reality.

The Father Provincial had given him an order—to make haste.
Peter Claver took the order literally. He set out immediately
without sending word to his family or saying good-bye to them.
In Barcelona he had got to know a young man called Domingo
del Prado, who afterwards joined the Jesuits and went to New
Granada. So great was his friendship for Claver—and we must
recall here the affection that Claver inspired in those around him—
that shortly after Claver's departure without taking leave of his
family, Domingo del Prado went to Verdú to make their acquaintance; and the father, brother and sister with other members of his
family complained bitterly of his departure without even sending
them a letter. They made the same complaint to Father José de
Alitrán, who passed through Verdú about that time and was later
appointed rector of the college of Mompox in New Granada.
This he disclosed in the Process. Saints are like that. St Francis
Xavier also refrained from bidding his family farewell, though he
passed only three miles away from their castle at Xavier.

Claver's self-surrender was complete. One of his characteristic
traits as recorded by the witnesses in Cartagena was his deliberate
detachment from ties with the homeland. Only three things
interested him: the virtues he saw in some perfect members of
religious orders, to reproach himself for not profiting by their

example; the sermons of apostolic preachers in Advent; and thirdly the festivals celebrated throughout Europe for the beatification of Ignatius. Little beyond these.

The road from Barcelona through Tarragona and Valencia to Seville was marked out for him. A few days' journey by those ways and inns about which St Teresa speaks so graphically, along the Mediterranean coast of so many memories. Brother Peter Claver arrived at last in Seville. It was the last town in Spain in which he was to stay. It was his good-bye to Europe.

Francisco Rodríguez Marín in his introduction to Cervantes' 'exemplary' novel, *Rinconete y Cortadillo*—the most vivid picture of the Sevillian thieves' community ever penned—gives a perfect reconstruction of Seville in the seventeenth century. The following is a short extract from it:

On 22 March 1595 the silver ships from the Indies arrived at the quays of the river at Seville where they started unloading and placing in the *Casa de Contratación* 332 wagon-loads of silver, gold and pearls of great value. On 8 May 1595 they took from the *Capitana*[1] 103 wagon-loads of silver and gold, and on 23 May they brought by land from Portugal 583 loads of silver, gold and pearls taken from the *Almiranta*[2] which docked at Lisbon, and from there they brought the cargo overland on account of the storms. It was a wonderful sight, for loads from that ship never ceased passing over the Triana bridge for six days. In that year there was greater treasure than men have ever seen in the *Casa de Contratación* because they collected silver there from three fleets. This treasure was held there on the King's behalf for more than four months, and it overflowed from the store-rooms, and outside in the courtyard were many bars and chests. This was written by an eyewitness.[3]

Beside all this wealth there was also destitution. Before embarking Peter Claver could have walked along the banks of the

[1] The ship in which the leader of the fleet sailed.
[2] The ship in which the second in command sailed.
[3] Edición principe of Cervantes' *Rinconete y Cortadillo*, edited by Rodríguez Marín, Revista de Archivos, Madrid, 1926; Antonio Domínguez Ortiz, *Orto y Ocaso de Sevilla*, Siglos XVI y XVII, Seville, 1946.

Guadalquivir and seen with his own eyes for the first time negro slaves, of whom there were great numbers in Seville in those days. Their sturdy arms, their sad stare, the strange expression in their eyes must have made a deep impression on him. The sight of these negroes in Seville, in Europe itself, was a significant foreshadowing of his far-away apostolate.

The slaves were at the bottom of the social scale. At the beginning of the modern age the plague of slavery was becoming widespread for two reasons: factually as a result of the discoveries which created the slave-trade; ideologically through the rising importance of Roman Law which gave it a legal basis. A small book by Sr Gestoso provides us with interesting data about slavery in Seville. At first it dealt almost exclusively in Moorish prisoners of war.

In 1847, as a result of the surrender of Malaga, 2,300 Moslems arrived from that town to be sold, or ransomed for thirty doubloons apiece. In 1504 several *Moriscos* from Hornachos who tried to escape to Portugal were seized on their way there and declared slaves of the Crown. Thirty-five of these *Moriscos* were sold on the *Gradas*[1] (the steps of Seville Cathedral) by public auction which lasted five days and produced 671,502 *maravedis*.

Thanks to the magnanimous intervention of the Spanish sovereigns and the Sevillian Dominican, Las Casas, the Indies were not converted into an immense slave-market. Only during the first half of the sixteenth century do we find any mention of some Indian slaves in Seville.

The negroes, unfortunately, did not find such determined protectors. The Portuguese had for some time past practised this infamous traffic, and habit had hardened consciences. It is true that some writers protested against the trade in negroes. Mercado censures the cruelty of the Portuguese and criticizes severely the merchants of the *Gradas* who dealt in negro slaves from Cape Verde, but other more tolerant moralists thought that the slave-trade practised by the Portuguese should not be condemned, 'because we must believe there is some justification as we see that very learned and pious bishops of that kingdom tolerate it and

---

[1] Cervantes, *Comedias y Entremeses*, Vol. II, Ed. Schevill and Bonilla, p. 29. Explanatory note in *El Rufián Dichoso*.

forbear to condemn it. The same is true of the learned men of that kingdom.'

There were in Seville in the year 1565 more than 6,000 slaves, mostly negroes, and doubtless this number increased greatly in the following years. For this reason Gracián said of this town that its inhabitants 'were neither all white nor all black', and another author that they were 'like pieces in chess, as many black as white, for the large number of slaves there are in the town'. There were also a fair number of Turkish and Berber slaves, less docile and in worse condition than the negroes.

In 1655 a Fleming, Antoine de Brunel, made a journey through Spain, of which he has left an interesting account:

'Trade with the Indies has in this country restored the legality of slavery, so that in Andalusia one hardly ever sees servants who are not slaves. The majority of these are Moors or converts. According to Christian law those who embrace the Faith should be free, but this law is not observed in Spain.' This second-hand report (for Brunel did not go to Andalusia) is not correct. Domestic slavery preceded the Discovery, although it is true that the latter gave it a great stimulus. As for the emancipation of the slaves on conversion, this never existed as a legal obligation but it was a common practice to grant it, at least as a testamentary disposition.

Considering the extent of this trade, it is not astonishing that there should be people who specialized in it. In 1548 a certain Martín Sánchez, who lived in the *Plaza de San Francisco*, figures as a 'slave-dealer'. Another such dealer is mentioned in 1564, and an agent (in slaves) in the 1691 census list. As a property mark and to make escape difficult, slaves were branded on the face, either with an 'S' and a nail, or with the owner's name.

The famous archbishop Don Pedro Vaca de Castro y Quiñones said that as soon as he entered Seville (coming from the diocese of Granada) he noticed that there were a great many negroes, men and women, in the town. He wished to know where they had been baptized, who had performed the marriage ceremony for the married couples and where it had been celebrated; because for many years a great number of these negroes had been brought into Spain so ignorant and untaught that, when they were em-

barked, they were baptized without instruction in the Faith and
without any knowledge of what they were accepting. To remedy
these evils the prelate assembled a committee of learned men, in
agreement with whom he determined to re-baptize all and make
their marriages valid.

In 1639 a cruel provision ordered all the slaves in Seville to be
sent to the galleys on account of the great shortage of rowers.
Their owners resisted this order as far as possible, keeping them
hidden for a long time, and they succeeded in freeing from the
galleys those who were Christians by paying one hundred *ducats*
per head for substitutes.

Although slavery is repugnant to modern sensibility we must
admit that the treatment of slaves in Seville was comparatively
humane. Some slaves were employed in rough work—for instance
in the soap factories—but the majority were destined for domestic
service and there is no reason to believe that they were harshly
treated. When they had been in service for some time it was
usual to set them free. At the beginning of the seventeenth
century a healthy adult male slave was worth a hundred *ducats*
or more, while a woman slave fetched hardly half that sum. After
the separation of Portugal from Spain the prices paid for slaves
rose greatly; for this reason and through the custom of freeing
them their numbers decreased in the eighteenth century until they
were reduced to a few individual slaves kept by some great houses
for curiosity or show.

The day came for the mission to embark. Father Alonso Mejía,
the leader of the expedition, arranged that all those under his charge
who had taken minor orders should be ordained as subdeacons.
Brother Claver excused himself humbly and simply. Perhaps the
fear complex which had troubled him previously returned again.

When Claver was due to embark for America, there existed a
special house in Seville where the Jesuits who were to leave for the
New World stayed.[1] According to the deed of royal patronage the
kings of Spain had promised faithfully to protect and promote the

[1] Antonio Astrain, *op. cit.*, Vol VI., Bk. 3, p. 372, El Patronato Real; Padre
Constantino Bayle, *España en Indias*, Ed. Nacional, 1944.

propagation of the faith as part of the engagement formulated by Pope Alexander VI when he conceded to the kings of Spain the dominion of the West Indies recently discovered by Christopher Columbus. The state gave economic aid to the missionaries who went out to America. Above all, the king, so to speak, took under his care the Spanish missionary in whatever college or house in Spain he might be, provided him with a complete outfit appropriate to his order and gave him a mattress, a blanket and a pillow for sleeping on board, thus making the journey as comfortable as possible in those days. The king also paid the expenses of the journey from the traveller's college to Seville, furnishing him with a certain amount of money calculated on the basis of an average of twenty-four miles a day. When the missionary arrived at the Andalusian capital, he was maintained at the king's expense for the whole time he had to wait for the departure of the fleet. The sea-journey was also, of course, paid for by the state. When the missionaries landed, the king ordered due payment to be made to the carriers who transported their books and garments. Not content with this generosity, the king provided the missionaries with a chalice and vestments to celebrate Mass. He paid for the wine to be used in the Holy Sacrifice and the oil for the lamp before the Blessed Sacrament. Moreover, he assigned to the missionaries an allowance on which each could keep himself without needing payment from his poor converts.

Every parish or *doctrina*, as the community of recent converts was called, had a definite income assigned to it; for instance, in Marañón in the middle of the seventeenth century every missionary received 300 *escudos* for each *doctrina*. In 1687 the Jesuit Father Diego Francisco de Altamirano compiled a book entitled: *Summary of the money which the Catholic Kings of Spain assign to transport the religious of the Society of Jesus to the Indies and to maintain them there.* In it the following statistics for a year in different provinces are given. For New Granada (Colombia) 57,100 *escudos;* Philippines 42,500; New Mexico 80,400; Peru 6,000; Paraguay 28,925; Chile 4,325. Ten thousand more for special expenses made the total amount 229,250 *escudos*. Of course, everything human has defects and this royal patronage had very serious ones, chief of them the

minute and exaggerated intervention in certain ecclesiastical
affairs sometimes practised by unscrupulous ministers; but it cannot be denied, as the great historian Father Astrain asserts, that in
our days, accustomed as we are to the hostility of modern states
towards the Church, we find it difficult to realize the genuine
protection and encouragement given by the former kings of Spain
to the propagation of the Faith.

By good fortune in the Archives of the Indies[1] we find among
the lists of passengers, legajo 5318, the list and description of the
sailing which included Peter Claver. Here is the transcription of
this remarkable document published for the first time.

List of passengers No. 35. *Casa de Contratación*. Legajo 5318.

List and memorandum of passengers attested by the aforesaid
Don Diego Canales de la Cerda, general purveyor to His
Majesty for the Royal Armada and convoy fleets for the voyage to the Indies who are travelling this year 1610 in the Royal
Galleon Fleet in charge of Don Gerónimo de Portugal y
Córdoba, captain-general of the said fleet, according to the
visits of inspection made the by above-mentioned purveyor in
a fortnight of the month of April of this year 1610, who are
the following:

Galleon San Felipe, Capitana

Fray Pedro Leonardo, of the Augustinian order.
Fray Pedro de Fuentes, his companion of the same order.

Galleon San Pablo, Almiranta

Fray Diego Ramírez, of the Dominican order.

Galleon San Pedro

Don Diego Mexía.
Father Alonso Mexía, Theatine.[2]
Father Juan Gregorio, of the same order.
Father Juan de Cabrera.
Father CLAVEL, etc.

On 15 April 1610 in the spring sailing, three galleons left port
bound for America; in the galleon *San Pedro* there was a person
called Father Clavel, a mistake for Claver, with Father Alonso

[1] Archivo de Indias, Sección Pasajes, legajo 5318.
[2] Jesuits were also known in early years as Theatines, an order now extinct.

Mexía (Mejía), Jesuit, Father Juan Gregorio, Jesuit, Father Juan de Cabrera, Jesuit.

The document records his farewell to the continent of Europe, which he was never to see again.

On that April day in the year 1610, the farewell scene then familiar in the port of Seville was enacted near the *Torre del Oro*. The Jesuit fathers of the Andalusian city came to see off the missionaries. Father Mejía was going as Visitor of Peru. The young student Peter Claver, who walked by his side, probably attracted little attention. People were not to hear of him until years later when his fame had spread throughout Europe.

A great authority on America, Father Constantino Bayle, has left us an almost unrivalled description of the moment when the fleets sailed from the port of Seville. This is what he says in his book *Santa María en Indias*.[1]

> The wharves swarm with people; there are heaped-up casks of water, barrels, some filled with jerked beef, others with chick-peas and beans which travel better in barrels to preserve them from the sea-water which might pour in whenever a nail worked loose or a frame gave way; endless strings of garlic, the main condiment for sailors and cabin-boys; jars of honey, cases of figs, rose-coloured sugar paste, orange-flower water by the gallon and other strange cooling drinks used rather as medicine than for enjoyment; rigging, sail-cloth, spare anchors; and among all these obstacles a motley crown of men singing, weeping and saying good-bye perhaps forever to their friends, if these are going to the Indies attracted by the dream of gold which began to dance before their eyes in the ploughed fields of Andalusia or the hot pasture-lands of Extramadura; or if they are members of the crew they bestir themselves to get on board the masses of ship's stores, cargo and other impedimenta.
>
> At the street corners of the city and among the huts of the strand and the port of Las Muelas, the regulations to be observed for the voyage are read out to the sound of fifes and drums; first that no one should embark without going to confession

[1] Constantino Bayle, S.J., *Santa María en Indias*, A. Prensa, Madrid, 1928, p. 369, and Chap. II, 'A las Indias van los hombres', pp. 40 *et seq.*

and receiving the sacraments; dice and card games are forbidden, severe penalties are prescribed for blasphemy, women
of doubtful antecedents are excluded; and other requirements—
not always observed—for the good government of sailors,
soldiers and passengers.

The day before the embarkation was a day of pilgrimage:
the images of the hundred-odd invocations of the blessed
Virgin venerated in Seville were never left a moment without
worshippers; some would go to the Virgin of the Pomegranate
in her former chapel, the canons' burial place, where now the
Sagrario[1] of the cathedral stands; some to the *Norabuena lo
pariste* which is situated behind the cathedral sanctuary and
dedicated to the Holy Child alluded to in the title; some to
Our Lady of Rocamadour, a Byzantine mural painting in San
Lorenzo; others to Our Lady of 'la Antigua', a much venerated
image that seems to date from the fourteenth century, although
tradition or legend makes it much older, going back to the time
of St Hermenegild, in whose chapel, built by the great cardinal
of Spain who is buried there, are also many fetters and chains
of captives, many models of ships and galleons, all sent there
on account of the many and continuous miracles to which the
invocation of this image has given and still gives rise in different
parts of the world; others were drawn by their devotion to
Our Lady of Victory, well-tried patroness for the dangers of
the sea since she went round the world in Elcano's famous
ship; some went to Our Lady of Favourable Winds, patroness
of the boatmen of the Guadalquivir, venerated in the Chapel
of the Holy Christ of Zalamea near the gate of St John of Acre;
the Sevillians especially did not forget the Virgin of the Kings,
the chief treasure of their city, a heritage from St Ferdinand.
The last visit was paid to Our Lady of Good Weather, for her
chapel was near the river in front of the *Torre del Oro*; there
she was and still is, though the public cult and devotion to her
has diminished owing to the demolition of her sanctuary and
the erection of the college of St Elmo, in the chapel of which
she occupies the high altar.

Peter Claver was thirty years of age when he left his native
land. He was going with an ideal of conquest in his mind. It was

---

[1] See the plan of Seville Cathedral in a guide-book.

not the gold and silver of the New World that attracted him, but the treasure of souls that drew him across the ocean.

'They set sail and arrived successfully in Cartagena.' In these words Father Cassani, the historian, sums up the journey of the missionaries in Father Alonso Mejía's party. Nevertheless, the so-called 'Indies' route was somewhat awe-inspiring in the vast distance it covered. The journey of Peter Claver from smiling Seville to the tableland of the Andes at Santa Fe de Bogotá took about five months. The intinerary of the fleets across the Atlantic at the beginning of the sixteenth century was already laid down.[1]

'The fleet commander sails in the ship called the *Capitana* . . . this is the first to leave and enter the ports and always goes at the head to guide the fleet; in order to be recognized it carries the flag on the mainmast by day and by night a lantern in the stern; twice a day, once in the morning and again in the evening, all the ships fire a salvo and salute it. The admiral sails in another ship with his flag on the foremast and he is charged with keeping the fleet together so that no ship remains behind, all keeping close to one another but without colliding.' On his voyage Peter Claver sailed in the galleon *San Pedro*, which was neither the *Capitana* nor the *Almiranta*.

At the end of the sixteenth century, according to Haring,[2] from sixty to seventy ships sailed annually from the port of Seville *en route* for the West Indies. This is more or less the itinerary which they followed: from Spain they sailed through the Gulf of Yeguas[3] as far as the Canary Islands; this stage lasted from eight to ten days. They usually called at these islands to revictual the fleet and especially to take on water. From there they sent despatches to the king, and sometimes a tender (*patache*) was sent on ahead to Cartagena and Portobello. In the first, reports were sent to the capital, and in the second, the approaching arrival of the fleet was announced. In the main the route followed was the same as that taken by

[1] Gonzalo Menéndez Pidal, *Imagen del mundo hacia* 1570, Madrid, 1944.
[2] C. H. Haring, *Le commerce et la navigation entre l'Espagne et les Indes*, Paris, 1939.
[3] *Golfo de las Yeguas* is the open sea between Europe and America.

Columbus on his second voyage. The captain-general who directed
the fleet had orders not to call at any port not included in his
instructions, and in case they were forced to do so by storms only
to remain in such a port twenty-four hours.

Every year two fleets were organized to undertake the voyage
to America, one destined for the southern continent (*Tierra
Firme*) going to Cartagena and Portobello, and the other to Vera
Cruz and New Spain (Mexico). The first, known as the galleon
fleet, was under the command of a captain-general and left Spain
between February and April. It usually wintered in Havana,
returning with what was more properly called the Fleet—the
Mexican one—in the spring of the following year. The galleon
fleet consisted generally of from five to eight ships. Our convoy had
only three. On its departure the commander received three sealed
packets: the first, to be opened at the Canary Islands, gave the
name of the West Indian island where they were due to arrive
first; the second, to be opened at Cartagena, contained instructions
for the return of the fleet in the same year or for wintering in
America; the third, not to be opened until after leaving the
Bahama Channel on the return voyage, contained the route they
were to follow. The international organization was rigid.

From the Canaries the ships had to take a south-westerly route
to avoid the calms and cyclones of the north Atlantic. The voyage
from the Canaries to the first American island lasted from twenty-
five to thirty days; sometimes the wind shortened the time. The
point of arrival in the Indies was most frequently the island of Dom-
inica, Guadaloupe or some other of the Lesser or Outer Antilles.
Here the routes diverged; those going to New Spain (Mexico) and
those going by the southern continent or Cartagena route separated. The latter went west in search of the Cape La Vela and then
coasted cautiously to avoid the powerful current of the Rio Grande
and arrived at Cartagena. From Cape La Vela to Cartagena the
voyage lasted a few days. Cape La Vela is at the northern end of
the Peninsula of La Guajira in Colombia.

From Cartagena the ships continued as far as Nombre de Dios,
steering west and cutting across the Gulf of Darien. Nombre de
Dios was the end of the voyage. The following year the fleets

would collect once more at Cartagena for the return to Spain. Such was the general plan of the voyage.

Life on board these ships, generally of not more than 300 tons, threatened by pirates and still more by calms, by cyclones and by sickness, was truly stirring.

During the sixteenth and seventeenth centuries the ordinary rations of the sailors and soldiers consisted of ships' biscuits, a little wine, pork, salt fish, beans, peas, oil, vinegar, rice, cheese and sometimes beef. Usually, an eye-witness tells us, the passengers were not treated with great consideration. Although there was a regulation that the ships should be of more than 800 tons, this rule was not observed; sometimes even eighty tonners were allowed. In the larger ships provided with forecastles, the passengers were housed there and in cabins erected on the lower deck.

The beds and upkeep were the private concern of the passengers. The chief problem was the drinking water, which was kept in barrels and open jars. Life on board had its picturesque touches in the midst of its hardships, and life at sea offered opportunities for missionary zeal. A modern historian, a notable observer of the American scene, has written this attractive passage:

A curious and amusing chapter and even a book might be written about the life which they led for months at a time on board these ramshackle vessels in which even the water in the casks went sea-sick, where the cockroaches and bugs invaded even the boiled beans, in which there was no room to move or even sleep, and this only when by good luck no storm was tossing them or when the sails drooped in the dead calm which held them as if fastened by hooks to the sea; and in this last case were the added difficulties of cutting down rations while the passengers were roasted alive in the tropical sun. In jocular or serious style not a few Castilian writers have used their pens and wit in depicting such scenes, from the famous bishop of Mondoñedo, Fray Antonio de Guevara, to Mateo Alemán.

To kill time the sailors used to relate their adventures, the passengers their troubles and the hopes which drew them to the Indies; dice and cards were furtively produced; at times the Captain turned his eyes away so as not to see the card party, sometimes he upheld the rigour of the law which forbade such pastimes. Cortés, fond himself of gambling in the milder sense of the word, was lenient. His dictum runs: 'As the chief occasion for blasphemy is found in card-games and dicing, you will forbid, by public proclamation or other means, anyone to indulge in these games on pain of rigorous punishment. But because in armies, and more so in those that put to sea, there is need for some kind of recreation or pastime, you will allow betting for moderate sums as you think advisable, on condition that it is done in your presence when you are there or, if you are absent, in the presence of the captain acting in your place; for in this way you will aviod blasphemy and the men will have some relaxation.'[1]

We cannot give an authentic description of the life on board of Peter Claver and his companions. Early biographers let their imagination run riot and pictured the young student as preaching assiduously to the sailors and succeeding by his holiness and pleasant manners in winning the heart of the captain, who invited him to eat at his table. We find no confirmation for these assumptions. We believe that the spirit which reigned in this group was more or less like that in which Father Manuel Uriarte evoked in his *Diary of a missionary to Mainas*. The portion of the text which refers directly to life on board is, in the opinion of one critic, worthy to be included in any anthology of sea voyages. It runs as follows:

From the very first day when I set sail, while everyone else was suffering agony from the usual sickness of those who travel by sea for the first time, I was the only one out of fifty-five Jesuits to maintain my health perfect until this day. That same night toward twelve o'clock we encountered five or six ships thought to have been English, and without knowing how, we passed through their midst without any one of them attacking us or making the slightest sign of doing so; a circumstance we all took for a miracle. After three or four days we had a fair number of calms which detained us considerably; but after a sung Mass and a sermon in honour of our apostle Xavier, and a novena started by a fervent Father, who preached every

[1] C. Bayle, S. J., *Santa María en Indias*, cap. II

Verdú: The room
where St Peter Claver
was born

Verdú: Altar of the Church of St Peter Claver's home town

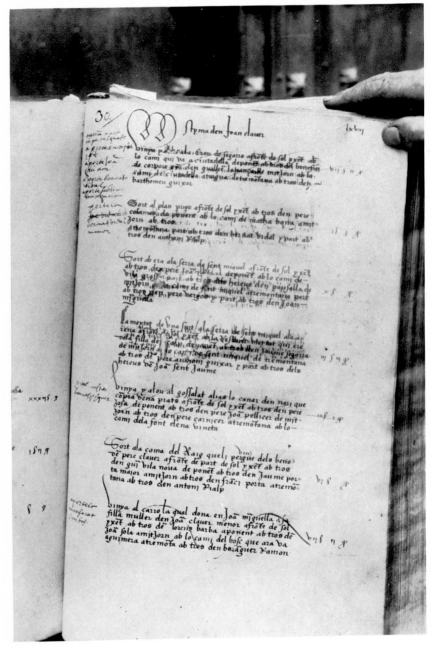

A page from the Register of Property, showing an entry for a farm belonging to St
Peter Claver's grandfather

day, to the Sacred Heart of Jesus, a favourable breeze blew
once again and lasted until the eighth day of the novena, the
feast day of St Mark the Evangelist, when with God's permission
about two in the afternoon there arose a furious south-easter,
which beat against the prow and reduced us to the laste xtremity.
The ship tottered, tossed like a straw, all of us expecting our
end with each descent into the trough of the waves. The
sailors could not control the helm, so without any great hope
they tied it up; then they hauled down the sails and all at their
wits' end thought only of confessing and preparing to die, and
I officiated with another Father now dead, as I shall presently
relate. When all were so abashed that they did not dare to call
publicly on the name of God, he gave me strength, holding up
my rosary before the picture of the blessed Virgin, to recite
it two or three times, and many litanies of our Lady and the
saints, all responding aloud; then I performed acts of faith, hope
and charity and we endeavoured to prepare ourselves as far as
possible to make a good death. While we were thus engaged,
there came a great wave so strong that it threw us all on the
ground and upset all our belongings and much of the cargo on
the right side. Our distress was increased on seeing that the *Santa
Barbara* was letting in water which the pumps were unable to
deal with; and the waves came pouring in as if the whole ship
were a sea. What worse might be coming? The fore-part sank
and was threatening to drag with it the rest of the ship; but
when a small top-sail was hoisted it came up after being almost
submerged. Many vows and promises were made to St Francis
Xavier, St Anthony and other saints, some to visit their sanctuaries barefoot, others to make various fasts and others again to
describe the miracle and to dedicate their lives to honouring
them. Finally on my advice a fast with confession and
Communion was offered to St Aloysius Gonzaga, and I attribute
mainly to this saint our deliverance from such manifest danger.
But in this moment of peril I realized the truth of the saying:
'Whoever wishes to learn to pray let him go to sea.'

On the eve of Ascension Day we sighted the American mainland, to the great relief of those who longed so much to see it.
On that great feast-day when the novena of our Lady was
completed with the same success as the preceding ones, we
began an octave to my holy patriarch and a novena to St

Anthony, both with discourses from various missionary fathers. And that you may learn briefly in what a holy way people behaved on this voyage, every morning was spent in hearing Masses, singing litanies and in other pious exercises, and the afternoons in sermons, novenas and rosaries; in the evening one of our students, a Catalan, catechized those who spoke his tongue, while I did the same in my poor way for the other Spaniards, and explained Christian doctrine, giving some prizes, such as medals, rosaries and holy pictures, which encouraged an eager and devout attendance. I assure you that among the one hundred and twenty or so passengers I found some persons of great Christian perfection, who made me feel very humble.[1]

Peter Claver's voyage must have passed in such or similar circumstances.

The day arrived when a great bay appeared before his eyes. It was Cartagena. A full account of the town deserves attention later, for here Claver was to spend practically all the rest of his life. His first reception was not very cordial; he could remain only a few days and then had to undertake a long journey up the great river Magdalena till he reached the heart of New Granada. Cassani writes the following: 'He arrived safely at Cartagena, landed and kissed the shore, not so much because he was treading solid ground again as at finding himself in his promised land. He entered the so-called college and found it a structure which looked nothing like a college or a residence. The church was one hundred feet long and the earth floor was so damp that it turned to mud. The few Jesuits there gave him a fraternal welcome.'[2]

After a few days' rest he said good-bye to Father Mejía, who was going on to Peru, and continued on his way to Bogotá. This was his second itinerary—this time by river, the great river Magdalena. He must have traversed it on other occasions and in time this journey became a familiar one. In 1615 he was to go down it to begin his life work in Cartagena—his ministry with the negroes.

[1] P. Manuel de Uriarte, *Diario de un misionero de Mainas*, revised by P. Constantino Bayle, Consejo superior de investigacaciones científicas, Madrid, 1952.
[2] José Cassani, S.J., *Historia de la Provincia de la Compañia de Jesus en el Nuevo Reino de Granada*.

CHAPTER V

IN NEW GRANADA

SHORTLY before his death, Father Claver told his companion, Brother González, that Alphonsus Rodríguez had clearly stated three things: first, that Claver's work would be among negroes; secondly, that it would be in New Granada; and thirdly, that it would be in Cartagena de Indias. These names must have sounded strange and mysterious to a Spaniard of those days. The name, New Granada, might have been familiar to him, and perhaps he may have consulted some rudimentary map of the period in the college of Montesión in order to locate the position of this unknown country. He would locate it vaguely on that narrow strip of land where two oceans met on either side of a small isthmus. New Granada owed its name to the founder of Bogotá, Jiménez de Quesada, a native of Cordova, but a lover of Granada. All the *conquistadores* saw these new lands as he did with eyes turned towards the land they had left, and so there appeared New Spain, New Andalusia, New Toledo and New Granada.

The New Kingdom of Granada formed a juridical district consisting not only of the territory occupied by present-day Colombia, but also of regions belonging to present-day Panama, Venezuela and Ecuador. At that time the presiding governor was Don Juan de Borja (1605–28), grandson of St Francis Borgia. The inhabitants were satisfied under his rule; he had unusual gifts and was known later as the father of his country. The ecclesiastical see of Bogotá was vacant in 1610, as the year before an illustrious archbishop, Bartolomé Lobo Guerrero, had died.

From 1604 the governors were at the same time presidents of the juridical district and, with few exceptions, military officers of eight years' service. New Granada had special geographical features and its culture had been influenced by them. It was one of the most fertile, vast and rich lands of the New World. Its nature was wild, and the great river Magdalena which divided it in two was its civilizing artery. One chronicler says:

> Its territory is almost completely filled with mountains, gorges and ravines, and in most of them there are many deposits of gold and other metals. There were 170,000 Indian inhabitants paying tax, not counting a larger number known to exist. A few years after the conquest in the middle of the sixteenth century there were thirty Spanish towns—with 1,800 to 2,000 householders. The wealth was extraordinary, including many mines of fine gold from which a great quantity has been and is still being extracted, also mines of rich and remarkable emeralds. The greater part of the gold brought to Spain comes from this place.

Among the oldest towns were Santa Fe de Bogotá, Cartagena, Tunja, Tocaima, Pamplona, Mérida, Vélez, Mariquita, Ibagué, Popayán and Santa Marta. New Granada was distinguished from the outset by its special addiction to learning. One curious characteristic of this new region of the world was the rapid assimilation of the indigenous element, both in language and customs, so that even at the time when Claver arrived there were very few centres of purely indigenous life; the mixing of races was the rule, not imposed by authority but arising naturally.

Peter Claver lived in three cities of New Granada representing as many cultural aspects of American civilization. Santa Fe de Bogotá, as we shall see, was the cultured Spanish city of wide interests and aristocratic atmosphere. Jiménez de Quesada, its founder, had stamped it with the seal of distinction which it was to preserve throughout its history.

Cartagena, on the other hand, was a city into which the negro element had introduced a very characteristic touch of racial mixture. Like other South American cities—Santos, for instance, in Brazil—it was to preserve throughout its history a warm gay element of coloured culture. Tunja, in its turn, was a city in which the indigenous element predominated, assimilated, it is true, but with a noticeable underlying sadness.

Between June or July 1610, when Peter Claver came from Spain to Cartagena de Indias, and 19 March 1616, the date of his

ordination in that town, was a period of interior life unmarked
by external events. It was the life of any Jesuit student preparing
himself by theological study for the day of his ordination as a
priest, the crowning point of his career. In reality this period was
too long for Claver. He had already studied a year and a half of
theology at Barcelona and in normal circumstances two years
more would have been enough for him to complete the course.
What interrupted his study? His stay at Cartagena after landing
there was very brief. The *Annual Letters* of the Society of Jesus in
1608, documents which record the Jesuit activities for each period,
now in the Archives at Rome, say of this period 1605:

> This city of Cartagena has probably more than 300 house-
> holds and among them more than 2,000 Spaniards who have
> in their service 3,000 to 4,000 negroes. There is a garrison of
> more than 200 soldiers, three forts furnished with men and two
> galleys which, apart from the pressed men, have sufficient
> soldiers for the defence and patrolling of the coast. The teaching
> of Latin to sixty or seventy boys, all well brought up, has begun.
> Sodalities exist such as the fathers of the Society are accustomed
> to found everywhere, and above all a sodality of negroes has
> been successfully started which meets every Sunday and holds
> a procession. The negroes are being accustomed to the reception
> of Holy Communion, and the chaste conduct of these negro
> members attracts the attention of the citizens. In the newly
> established college a public chapel has been built, one hundred
> feet in length, and as it cannot hold the crowd which attends,
> awnings are set in the courtyard in front of the door, and so in
> the dim light the people can hear Mass and the sermon which is
> preached in the door of the chapel itself. There are still only
> four priests in the college, so they have not been able to go out
> to hold missions, except for one priest who preached for a few
> days in two villages after Lent in 1605.[1]

When Peter Claver arrived from Spain in 1610, the college
which the Jesuits had started in Cartagena was in temporary

---

[1] *Cartas Annuas*, 3 series: 1616, 1638–43. Sebastián Hazañero, S. J., *Letras
Annuas de la Compañía de Jesus dela Provincia del Nuevo Reino de Granada desde
el año 1638 hasta el año 1643.*

quarters. The government of Spain had authorized its opening on 25 December 1603. The bishop of Cartagena, the Dominican Juan de Ladrada, a great friend of the Jesuits, gave them efficacious help. He himself went from door to door begging alms for this object, and Don Jerónimo Zueso Casasola, governor of the city, gave similar aid. A Portuguese merchant, a former pupil of the Jesuits, gave them a house which he owned near the *Plaza de La Hierba*, beside the main gate of the city, coming from the port. This building had no courtyard, and when other taller houses were built nearby it was overshadowed and left without adequate light so that other accommodation became necessary. Some land was bought in a place near the landing pier where the college now stands, with access to the sea and close to the ramparts. At first there was not even one brother. Father Cassani remarks on the restricted space of the new college, saying: 'The room that served as a church was thirty feet long, damp and muddy. The fathers had to live two in a room.'

A fresh reinforcement came from Lima with Father Alonso de Sandoval, the great practical initiator of the work among the negroes. There came also to the college a lay brother, Bobadilla by name, born in Granada in 1583, a man of great spirit, who had acquired, when he died, the reputation of a saint. Peter Claver on his arrival at Cartagena seems more likely to have gone directly to the house belonging to the Portuguese benefactor, rather than to this newly established college.[1]

In any case, while he was making his preparations for the journey to Bogotá, together with Brother Bobadilla, he again practised his special vocation for service in humble tasks. Conversation with the simple brother must have roused in him again his old aspiration—to be a lay brother, giving up the idea of the priesthood. This is confirmed by the fact that immediately on his arrival in Bogotá he begged the Father Provincial, Gonzalo de Lyra, to grant him this request. The superior did not accept his view and ordered him to continue preparations for the study of theology, though permitting him in the meantime to perform in the College of Santa Fe de Bogotá those humble duties so dear to

[1] P. Ledos, *Pierre Claver*, Paris, 1923, p. 28.

his heart. Claver arrived at Santa Fe at the end of 1610 or the beginning of 1611, and he remained there only a short time, as recorded in the news from Cartagena.

Santa Fe de Bogotá, founded by the intellectual Jiménez de Quesada on a tableland nearly 9,000 feet high, has, as a city, certain characteristics of its own. It is perhaps the only town in the New World where three great *conquistadores* arrived at the same time. Jiménez de Quesada came by the river Magdalena and the Opón, and in the face of unparalleled difficulties crossed the Cordillera. He found there a native race of the Chibchas, people of an advanced culture, possessing the arts of spinning and weaving, able to use numbers and work metals and practising strange religious rites. Paradoxically the same man who arrived on the Andean plateau with a cuirass, long hair and a mighty sword was the author of a recently discovered book called *El Antijovio*, an historico-religious disquisition of high critical quality which presupposes in the writer a considerable humanistic culture. The second *conquistador* came from Quito. He followed the road of the Incas and also arrived one day at the Savannah of Bogotá. His name was Benalcázar. The third, Federmán, came from Venezuela. He crossed virgin forests with a party of half-naked men and found that the land of his dreams had already been discovered by two other men.

The tableland of Bogotá was a natural wonder, a pleasant cultivated region with great rivers and wrapped in legend. The geographical position of the city of Bogotá contributed to the local people's character. Far from the sea and without easy communications the inhabitants had to fall back on their own resources. They had no restless urge to leave their city. The journey on mule-back along stony and muddy roads and then along the hot banks of the Magdalena, over the plains, a prey to mosquitoes and crocodiles, was not at all agreeable. The distance from the sea made the man of Santa Fe a stay-at-home, fond of *tertulias*, an intellectual whose favourite occupation was to read books from six in the afternoon beside the burning logs of an open fire, and next day to exchange ideas in the forecourt of the cathedral or in some literary club. The men of Santa Fe were not much interested in military affairs, and ideas attracted them more than technical invention; speeches meant more to them than highways. In the colonial period, culture does not as a rule spring from the ports, whose inhabitants, naturally more lively and active, are less inclined to mental concentration.

Mountain cities have always been natural centres of culture. Santa Fe was a secluded height where ideas flourished. The alert shrewd temperament of its citizens, opposed to all violence, found in those old mansions, with their small shut-in *patios*, a suitable nursery for their talent. Bogotá boasts no great architecture, but the churches of San Francisco, Santa Clara and La Tercera, the convents of Santa Inés and San Domingo in their primitive style, had an unmistakeably intimate flavour. In Santa Fe there was no racial problem; the indigenous element—and even less the negro—never became an obstacle to development. Patriarchal harmony reigned among its inhabitants, and the predominance of intellectual interests among the ruling classes seems to have softened any tendency to aggressiveness among the masses. Santa Fe de Bogotá played the role of a viceregal city in the colony, the city that welcomed, as a host, all the other cities of New Granada.

Of the whole party of forty-six Jesuits who arrived at Cartagena in July 1604 under Father Diego de Torres, ten were destined for the vice-province of New Granada just formed by Father Claudio Aquaviva. Five were destined for Santa Fe and five others remained in Cartagena. Those destined for the capital were Father Martín de Fúnes, Superior, Fathers Juan Bautista Coluccini, José Dadey and Bernabé Rojas, and the lay brother Diego Sánchez. They arrived at Santa Fe on 23 September 1604 and lost no time in getting to work. The historian of the Society of Jesus in New Granada referring to the new foundation, writes with a touch of irony: 'A mental or ideal college was at once constructed, for it had only a director and one subordinate, but no building, no church, no income and no home; all its wealth the merest poverty and the essence of the college was to possess nothing.' He was right to some extent. The Jesuit fathers on their arrival at Bogotá had to be lodged, some in a few diminutive houses and others in Fontibón, a small mission residence.

In 1599 the Jesuits, Alonso de Medrano and Francisco de Figueros, came from Mexico with Don Bartolomé Lobo Guerrero, Archbishop of Bogotá. During their short stay in the city, foreseeing the possible creation of a college, they had bought the house belonging to Juan de Albis, 'the best and in the best position in the city'. The house was situated between two palaces, that of the presidents and that of the archbishops. It was the home of Judge Luis Enríquez and stood at the corner of the *Calle de la Carrera*. Economically this third college of the Jesuits was a failure. The premises were burdened with heavy mortgages; that of the chaplaincy founded by the governor Gonzalo Jiménez de Quesada for the benefit of his followers, and that laid on it by Juan de Albis himself, who sold them the property, in addition to a rental of 2,000 *pesos*.

Intellectually the college made a successful beginning. On 18 September the classes started and the young people of Santa Fe crowded into the classrooms to listen to Father Dadey. There was a great scarcity of teachers in the whole town, for only in one or two conventual chairs of grammar and philosophy were reading, writing and arithmetic taught. Father Dadey was a person of exceptional culture and great intelligence, astronomer and philologist, of the illustrious family of Mondoví, a nephew of the chief major-domo of the Roman Pontiff and connected with the nobility of the Italian and pontifical courts. Later he wrote a grammar of Muisca, the language of the indigenous inhabitants of the tableland. He taught the natives Castilian and the Spaniards the language of the Indians. The classes were a great success, and at the end of the year he had one hundred pupils. The Jesuits who went to Santa Fe were of very high quality. Father Martín de Fúnes, the Superior, of whom Flórez de Ocáriz says: 'He was a very learned and admirable holy man', attracted attention by his oratory and the encouragement he gave to the sodalities. Father Coluccini was the architect of genius whose name was to be connected with the church of St Ignatius in Bogotá and with another series of lay buildings in New Granada.

The college began with only grammar classes, to which were gradually added rhetoric and the humanities. Chairs were founded of philosophy in 1608 and of theology only in 1612. When Peter Claver arrived in 1611 there was no instruction in this subject which he needed to complete his ecclesiastical studies. So for a year and a half he acted as brother coadjutor in the college of Bogotá until a professor of theology came from Spain to New Granada. This was Father Antonio Astrain from Saragossa, who had taught philosophy and theology at Tarragona. He was a learned spiritual teacher, one of the most remarkable men who went out to the New World. Gentle and amiable in character, he had spent some time in Rome as censor of Jesuit books. He was the first to lecture on theology in the New World, in Santa Fe de Bogotá. The climate of this town broke down his health and he was sent to Cartagena and became the fourth rector of the college there. For more than twenty years he was *calificador* to the Holy Office of the Inquisition and adviser on all kinds of business. Cassani even asserts that he was 'the man of greatest authority in Cartagena and indeed in the whole of the Indies'. Humbly he devoted himself to hearing children's confessions, and his poverty was exemplary. In his room 'the furniture was reduced to two chairs, an old table, two prints hanging on the wall, his papers and the Decretals'. He died in Cartagena on 18 February 1635. This was the man chosen by the superiors to be Peter Claver's professor of theology. His friendship for Claver was deep and, while he lived in Cartagena up to 1635, he was his spiritual director. Peter Claver successfully completed his theological course at the end of 1613, fulfilling all the requirements of the Society of Jesus for proceeding to the rank of father professed of the four vows. Here too at the end of this course of preparation we learn his characteristic conception of an honour. On completion of his studies he was told that he must take the full examination in philosophy and theology with emphasis on the need to do so before going to ordination. His response was: 'Is so much theology needed to be ordained and catechize a few poor Indians?' Advised afterwards that the examination he had taken was a preliminary not only to his ordination but to the profession of the four vows of the Society of Jesus, he replied: 'If I had known that, I should have answered nothing, for I do not deserve that honour.'

Claver had ended his studies. The climate of Santa Fe did not suit him. According to the testimony of his companion, Brother González, 'the air of that town was bad for his health', and in the course of the Process one witness declared that he had heard the father say that the climate of the place was against him, and that his health suffered greatly, especially 'from colds which affected his chest, and headaches'. Did Peter Claver, who later showed such fortitude, suffer from some chest disease, as one biographer states? Perhaps it did not exactly amount to a disease like tuberculosis, yet some kind of chronic bronchitis appears to have been one of the reasons why his superiors sent him to America and now on to Tunja where the air might suit him better; for it is remarked that 'the cold healthy climate of this town had a great reputation at that time'. In Tunja there was another Jesuit house with a novitiate. Peter Claver must have left for Tunja at the end of 1614 or the beginning of 1615, for in November of that year we find him already permanently settled in Cartagena. Vásquez de Espinosa, an admirable chronicler, writes of Tunja:

About a hundred miles from Santa Fe stands the town of Tunja built on a hill in a cool climate by Captain Gonzalo Suárez in 1538 by order of the governor, Gonzalo Jiménez de Quesada, who gave him the title of lord of that territory, Tunja.

The town has six hundred Spanish householders, with a cathedral church, monasteries of San Domingo, San Francisco, San Agustín, the Society of Jesus, two convents of nuns, hospitals where the sick poor are cared for and other churches and chapels. His Majesty appoints a judge for this town in consultation with his royal Council of the Indies. It has a vast jurisdiction, and the president of the high court (Audiencia) appoints ten magistrates, i.e. Chita, Gámeza, Tenza, Toca, Cerinza, Moavita, Turmequé, Sáchica, Pamplona and Sogamoso, nine of Indians because the jurisdiction of Tunja has the greatest (Indian) population in the whole kingdom—that of Pamplona is purely Spanish.

Tunja presents the typical aspect of a South American town. In colonial times the indigenous element predominated there and was ruled by the white *élite*. Why had the Indian chiefs and later the Spanish *conquistadores* turned their eyes to Tunja? Like Castilian towns, like Soria or Avila, like Burgos or Segovia, Tunja has the gravity and depth that go with austerity. The landscape of Tunja, with its red and ochre earth, is ascetic and conducive to mysticism. It is easy to understand why oratories were erected on this cold dry height, whether the oratory of Zipa or a nun's cell like that of Madre Castillo.

Tunja is a town attuned to faith, and that is its historical significance. The churches of Tunja are the key points to which all its aspirations converge. 'Without churches and monasteries, Tunja would have no reason for existence, like Cartagena without the sea, wharves and the forts or Popayán without its mansions.'

Castellanos, the poet and chronicler, left his strong mark on Tunja, Mother Castillo her mystical spirit; and Peter Claver, who spent the year 1614 there before setting out for Cartagena, must have found reinforcement for heroic temper, a sense of detachment from the dazzle and the tumult of human affairs. After three centuries, Tunja still preserves the same atmosphere. Its heat may be less religious, its churches not so full as in those days of faith. But it is the same town.

To evoke a picture of the town we have an extraordinarily detailed report compiled for the Chief Justice on 30 May 1610. Tunja, it states:

is a town in New Granada which took its name from the most important chief living in that district when the Spaniards arrived . . . Nearly the whole of that district is a land of valleys and hills, and the valleys are flat. The atmosphere of the town is exceedingly cold and dry. Sea and land winds sweep over it, which make it cold, though not so cold as to oblige people to hug the fire but at most to keep a brazier lit; for if one is sheltered from the wind, blowing mainly from the south, one does not feel the cold, but the sun, on the other hand, is so strong that one cannot bear to stay in it. The climate is healthy rather than otherwise, and the commonest illnesses are slight head colds and pains in the side . . . The Indians find sufficient nourishment in truffles and maize. There are also potatoes and roots which they call *arracachas* that are something like potatoes. Wheat gives a tenfold or twentyfold yield and sometimes as much as forty or fiftyfold . . . The city is on a half slope lying below a ridge; it has seven streets and a main square near two small ones called San Francisco and San Agustín, because they are near these monasteries. In the main square are the cathedral church, the town hall and the notaries' offices . . . The houses are usually made of earth and stone; both suitable for building here. There are some imposing porches and finely hewn stone corners; the houses are of moderate size and have only two floors, an upper and a lower . . . Our Castilian tongue is generally spoken except among the Indians who talk to one another in their own language, but those who serve the Spaniards speak Castilian. The town of Tunja has about 300 Spanish householders. Those who hold estates (*encomiendas*) are the following: and here follow a list of names which have come to be the usual surnames in the town—Suárez, Maldonado, Núñez, Patiño, Rojas, Rubio, etc. [1]

Politically the city of Tunja is subject to the magistrate (*corregidor*) who lives in the town, and to the high court of the New Kingdom of Granada and its president in Santa Fe.

This city and the Indian villages are linked by the highroad, so the Indians of the neighbouring villages hire horses to travellers . . . In general the Indians are no lovers of work so that very few take up crafts, being content for the most part to serve on the *estancias*, a few becoming professional tailors, or practising other manual but not skilled trades. In the whole region no more than three or four Indians are known to be able to read and write, even badly, since they are by nature incapable of learning. Some religious, particularly Franciscans, teach their catechumens as part of their instruction to read and count. But they take it badly, their parents even worse, preferring to see them on their own farms than at catechism or any other occupation.

[1] Description of the city of Tunja, according to a report compiled by the juridical authority 30 May 1610, Archivo de Indias, Vol. IX, transcribed by R. B. in April 1917, pp. 153–93.

It is said of them that they have no memory of past things and that they are a shallow people and given to lying. As for food, the most usual fare of Indians in these lands is maize with some vegetables and a little salt and chili. They drink what they call *chicha* which is made from corn. Only the crafty who have some money spend it on meat and bread.

These extracts from a magnificent document enable us better than any modern account to form a picture of Tunja as it was when Peter Claver lived there. A typical city with its peasant element, simple, religious, with a melancholy characteristic of the landscape which makes it soft and pliant. The *conquistadores* found rest here in the wide porches, in the *patios* where geraniums and fig-trees grew, in those churches ornate with the gold of many penitents from the vanities of this world. A society in which masters and servants were members of one family reciting the rosary together in the evening. There were no racial problems. Not many marquises or dukes came here, but middle-class clerks, solicitors, second-hand *conquistadores*, who found there a way of life reminiscent of that they had left behind in Castile or Estremadura. Already, then, Tunja had developed that marvel of cross-breeding which is no mere superimposition of an alien culture but a fusion of races, and makes of the Indian not a creature apart but a being the same as the white—although more ignorant and poor —and a true citizen, albeit sad-looking in his copper skin.

The college of Tunja was another recent foundation. In 1614, when Claver arrived, it contained the Novitiate and the 'third probation', a year which the Society of Jesus sets apart at the end of its training, a year of trial and spiritual recollection before facing the mission field. Peter Claver had not yet been ordained. The see of Bogotá was then vacant. Chroniclers such as Andrade, Fernández and Cassani, speaking of his activities in Tunja, say that his chief reason for going there was 'in order to spend some months edifying the novices'. He must certainly have done so, but this was not his main reason for going. He went to do his year of probation and also to recover his health before leaving for Cartagena. It has been said that he acted as doorkeeper to the college, and a key which he is supposed to have used is still shown today. This is impossible to believe, despite his liking for humble tasks, since he was a student preparing himself for ordination and, furthermore, had a special ministry to exercise. It is more likely that he would have devoted much of his time to helping some of the priests in the schools and hospitals, and also to visiting some of the nearby *estancias* where the solicitors were clamouring for the spiritual education of the natives.

This house was started as a result of the visit of two Jesuits, Father Gonzalo Núñez and Father Luis de Santillán, who came to preach the Lenten sermons in 1607. They created such an impression that the mayor and the inhabitants asked the Society to establish a house there. On the Monday of Holy Week, 1611, the Provincial, Father Gonzalo de Lyra, came to the city, and an open council meeting was held in the church of Santiago, now the cathedral, when the citizens of Tunja in one day subscribed more than 6,000 gold *pesos*. The council for its part gave the fathers some houses on the south side of what is now the Church of St Ignatius. Peter Claver never knew this church, which in his day had been barely started, like the college residence later used for the novitiate.

The year must have been an unforgettable one for Peter Claver, as shortly before his death he remembered and sent this novitiate what he treasured most, the notes of his master, Alphonsus Rodríguez. One day towards the end of 1614 or the beginning of 1615 Peter Claver traversed once again the distance between Tunja and Bogotá, riding on one of the animals hired out by the Indians, and passed by those inns where Spanish-speaking Indians served maize and sometimes sold a slave or two, as history records. After several days' journey he arrived at Santa Fe in 1615. Peter Claver was now thirty-five years old. He did not make a long stay in the capital, for his apostolate called him. Once more he took the long road via Honda, the river Magdalena and Mompox to Cartagena.

Indecision had ended. Claver's mission was clear. Father Sandoval had asked for an assistant and was expecting him. Soon after his arrival that same year he was ordained subdeacon in the cathe-

dral of Cartagena on 21 December. The following year he was
ordained deacon on 23 February, and on 19 March priest, by the
illustrious Fray Pedro de la Vega of the Order of St Dominic.

He had reached his goal before the age of thirty-six. He was
the first Jesuit to be ordained in Cartagena. He chose for his first
Mass an altar in the small Jesuit church which was to be for him
through all his life a special object of devotion, the altar of Our
Lady of the Miracle. Father Alonso de Sandoval was present and
he knew the story of this picture well. One day, far off in Saragossa, in the Province of Antioquia, in New Granada, his congregation had presented him with this picture in gratitude for his
enthusiastic missionary work. It was called the Virgin of the
Miracle, because once a flash of lightning had burned to ashes the
cloth protecting the frame yet did not harm the portrait of our
Lady. This picture was the object of all Father Sandoval's love and
trust. He spent long periods in prayer before it, and never undertook any apostolic enterprise without praying before it. He was
permanent chaplain of the little chapel in the Jesuit church at
Cartagena. It was there that Father Peter Claver chose to say his
first Mass. At the elevation of the Host, surrounded by the small
community and the negro slaves his teacher was instructing, he
must have felt the full grandeur of his vocation. The crisis had
ended. *Sacerdos in aeternum.* There beside that inspired guide who
showed him the way to his approaching mission, he raised the
Host for the first time in the presence of a few negro slaves who
were greatly moved.

For the first months it was usual for the newly ordained priest
to assist in simple religious duties. Peter Claver placed himself
under the orders of Father Fernando Núñez, an energetic missionary who had great influence among all classes, and of Father Sandoval who devoted himself particularly to work among the slaves.
During this time he made the acquaintance, in all their horrifying
reality, of the huts where the slaves were crowded, and witnessed
the arrival of one or other of those galleons which carried the
black flag of the slave-trade.

Another event put the seal on his life of sacrifice. The date of
his definitive entry into the Society of Jesus was approaching—

Montserrat: The Benedictine Abbey

Galeon del siglo XVII.

A seventeenth-century galleon

his solemn profession of the four vows. Father Peter Claver wrote to the Father General of the Jesuits, Father Mucio Viteleschi, asking him not to grant him such an honour. He begged to remain without a definite grade. The latter answered him on 7 June 1619, praising his humility, but recommending him to yield to the guidance of his superiors and place himself in a condition of complete indifference. (The letter appears in a later chapter, 'Son of St Ignatius', with others from Father Viteleschi.)

For all its paternal benevolence, the letter contains a slight admonition and Peter Claver must have understood it so. Holiness in the life of a religious lies not in his rank but in the will of God expressed through his superiors. In the light of this Peter Claver made his solemn profession on 3 April 1622, the date on which Low Sunday fell that year. This event, important enough in itself, had a special aspect that was to be immortalized. On the paper on which he signed his vows with a firm hand he had placed an introduction and a conclusion now well-known to history. Preceding the formula he wrote:

'Love, Jesus, Mary, Joseph, Ignatius, Peter, *my own Alonso*, Thomas, Laurence, Bartholomew, my saints, patrons and my intercessors and those of my beloved negroes, hear me.'

It was a prayer to the dearest patrons of his heart, the Holy Family, the founder St Ignatius, Peter, his birth patron, and a person not yet publicly canonized except in his own heart: *my own Alonso*, his beloved master in Majorca, and then the patrons— not personal ones but those of his future apostolic mission— Thomas, Laurence, Bartholomew, apostles of the negro race. Then followed the usual formula by which he bound himself absolutely by his religious vows, and by one of special obedience to the Pope, for all eternity. The final formula was original. He signed thus: *Petrus Claver, ethiopum semper servus'*—Peter Claver, slave of the negroes forever.'

Perhaps when he inscribed this admirable signature he did not feel the full weight of the heroism that would fall to his lot. Forty years of complete abnegation. God accepted his sacrifice.

At that moment the hidden side of his life comes to an end. In his final vows he had laid a deep foundation for his future apostolate;

Slave of the slaves of God. He was forty-two years of age and contemporary witnesses describe him as of medium stature, with a long thin face, a wide brow, an aquiline nose, large eyes, a melancholy expression, thick eyebrows, a large mouth with a lower lip that drooped a little, a naturally pale, rather olive, slightly yellowish complexion; his figure rather bent from his habit of always looking at the ground.

Such was Peter Claver, physically and morally, when he began his active apostolic life in the Jesuit college of the city of Cartagena de Indias.

PART II

THE DYNAMIC SOCIAL WORKER
(1622—1650)

CHAPTER I

THE ENSLAVED RACE

SINCE the world began there have been slaves and mankind has been disgraced by the existence of the slave-trade. Pagan slavery was terrible. In Imperial Rome there was an Aquilian law (or *lex Aquilia*) that sentenced to the same punishment the man who killed 'a slave or any other animal'. When Varro spoke of farm implements, animals and slaves, he called them 'the mute, semi-mute and talking chattels', in that order.

The slave had no name, no known father. He was called after his country: the Macedonian, the Syrian, or by a mythological name, Eros, Diomedes . . . The slave had no rights, he was not a person. 'A slave was a chattel, a piece of merchandise. He had no right to get married.' A character in Plautus exclaims: 'By Hercules, a slaves' wedding! A slave contract marriage! That is contrary to custom in any nation.'

There were numberless slaves in that pagan world. In one Athenian census 20,000 citizens and 40,000 slaves were counted.

So great was the multitude of slaves in Rome that it was once proposed to give them a distinctive dress. The Senate opposed this suggestion for fear that the slaves, realizing they were in the majority, might disturb public order. The luxury of the great was reckoned by the number of their slaves. Pudenciana, wife of Apuleius, bequeathed to her children 400 slaves each, and the same sort of thing occurred in Syria, in Tyre among the Scythians and in the wilds of Africa.

The number of slaves in the Roman Empire was impressive, most of them as the result of conquest. Paulus Emilius sold into slavery 150,000 prisoners from Epirus. Marius brought in as slaves 90,000 Teutons and 60,000 Cimbri. Caesar brought in at least 400,000 from Gaul. Augustus enslaved 44,000 of the Salassi, and Titus brought to Rome from Palestine 99,000 Jewish slaves. And these are only a few details culled from accounts of that disgraceful pagan custom. This lasted until one day a Christian Emperor, Constantine, forbade the branding of slaves on their faces, 'because the image of divine beauty is there'. This was a symbol of the silent transformation which the world had undergone. Slavery was losing ground among white, civilized, Christian nations.

Yet history must record a new epoch of the market in human flesh towards the end of that brilliant Renaissance in which so much praise had been lavished on 'humanism'. The discovery of the New World gave rise to a new period of intensified slavery, and the enslaved race did not belong to the barbarous Saxons, Scythians or Iberians. The dark night had come for the African continent, for the negro race.

A kind of intellectual and moral blindness was produced. It is easy to launch accusations, unload the burden of our own and others' sins on the scapegoat. Father Carminati, an authority on missionary work, wrote: 'Spaniards and Portuguese added to the aforesaid crimes another more savage and cruel: the trade in the unfortunate negroes whom they tore from their homes to transport them to the countries of the New World and employ them there in forced labour.'[1]

It would be a grave mistake to believe that the slavery of African negroes began with the discovery of the New World. No one can throw the first stone. The trade in negroes was one of the crimes of that period, a sorry social phenomenon, and the theologians generally declared it illegal under certain conditions. Churches and monasteries had slaves, as did the popes and the saints. The Catholic sovereigns in 1488 made a present to Pope Innocent VIII of one hundred Moorish slaves, and he accepted it with pleasure. Pope Nicholas V in his famous Bull granted the monopoly to the Portuguese: 'It is granted to King Alfonso V of Portugal that he may claim for himself and his successors any Saracen, pagans, kingdoms, dukedoms, possessions, real and movable properties that they may possess, and *subject the aforesaid persons to perpetual slavery*.'[2]

[1] P. Carminati, *Compendio de Misiología*, 3rd edition, p. 123.
[2] Morelli, *Fasti Novi Orbis et ordinationum apostolicarum, ad Indias pertinentium, Breviarium*, p. 338.

There were slaves in Europe before 1492.

In Spain farm slaves had disappeared from the sixteenth century onward, except in Aragon, but Berber and negro personal slaves —mostly Moslems—had not. They continued as slaves obtained by purchase or in the wars of previous reigns against Turks or Africans, especially in the fights against pirates who in the seventeenth century were still a menace along the coasts. Sometimes the upper ranks of society bartered this human merchandise, and even religious institutions (convents, hospices and churches) owned slaves as in the Middle Ages, without distinction between infidels and Christians. The children of a slave mother were considered by law as slaves too, and the property of their mother's owner.

As in ancient times, those held in slavery were marked on their faces with an 'S' made by a red-hot iron, and a nail, a sign of their sad condition. Lope de Vega in *The slave of her physician* makes Ricardo, the lover of the pretended slave girl Elena, say: 'Allow me to touch with one finger the nail on your face.'[1]

In the case of fugitive Moorish house or farm slaves, these were pursued and taken by the public authorities. This service was in 1621 definitely assigned to military jurisdiction. The penalties imposed on such fugitives were imprisonment, banishment, the galleys or the gallows according to the crime they had committed in wounding Christians, theft, breaking down of houses and walls in order to escape or for conspiring to take ship.

Yet the slaves might be set free and then they were called *gacis* or *cortados* (cut or freed). Considered as merchandise, the slaves congregated especially in great towns like Cadiz where in 1654 there were more than 1,500, and they were bought and resold by certain dealers as a form of speculation. They were employed there in rough work, particularly loading and unloading ships, keeping their owners with the profit gained by the discharge of these tasks, like the Roman slave in former days.

The great number of slaves in Cadiz made a special police service necessary to avoid possible outbreaks. In many towns

[1] Lope de Vega, *La esclava de su galeno.*

slaves performed domestic service for people of certain position, including ecclesiastics.[1]

The price of slaves varied. Madame d'Aulnoy had a black girl slave nine years old for whom she paid eighty *escudos*, and she gives curious particulars as to dress and character; but according to this lady-traveller the price of these slaves often reached 400 or 500 *escudos*. They could be punished by their masters but not with death; they were generally well treated.

Yet there were exceptions of terrible barbarity: one of the most savage of these punishments was to *baste* them, i.e. to smear them with grease or pork fat and apply a blazing torch to their bare bodies.

Alluding to this cruel practice, Quevedo wrote in his novel *Negro Wedding*: 'But when the pork fat arrived for the feast there were loud lamentations, and the negro and negress who had been larded were upset for some time.'

Hartzenbusch in *Notes on Calderón* takes from a manuscript of the period the item that the Marquesa de Cañete had three of her women slaves punished by having them undressed and beaten with waxed ropes till blood came. 'It is said', the manuscript continues, 'that she took a torch and basted them.'

Yet Spaniards must be absolved of the most terrible and painful part of negro slavery.

Spaniards did not take slaves from their own country or practise the trade in slaves, which was the most cruel and appalling thing, or subject those negroes to the first slavery already discontinued in Africa. They had a great responsibility which they shared with most of the civilized nations of Europe.

Negro slavery originated from two sources: firstly, the protection of the Indian who ran the risk of being wiped out by the rough work of cultivating the land or in the mines; secondly, the greater capacity for work of the negroes—according to Herrera, 'the work of one negro was equal to that of four Indians'.[2]

In 1501 the Catholic sovereigns appointed Nicolás de Obando governor of the Spanish Territory, Indies and Mainland, and in the instructions that were given to him, it is stated that 'he must

[1] Altamira, *Historia de España*, Vol. III, p. 207.
[2] Antonio de Herrera, *Historia general*, Decada primera, Bk. IX, Chap. V.

not take to the Indies, Jews, Moors or the newly converted, but should allow negroes to be introduced if they were born in the power of Christians, which supposes them to be Christians also.'

In 1503 this same governor, Obando, asked that no negro slaves should be allowed to come in as they taught the Indians bad habits. Queen Isabella suspended all entry permits in 1503. This prohibition by the great queen, who was chiefly concerned with the conversion of the Indians to the Catholic faith, did not last long. At the time of the second voyage of Columbus (1493–96), the disembarkment began. Even Las Casas approved at this period, for he believed that it would lighten the burden of the Indians.

In 1516 Cisneros again suspended all permits; Isabella and Cisneros have not this guilt to bear. But smallpox and other diseases decimated the Indians. 'Forbid the entry of negro slaves', the Hieronymite friars wrote to the king in a letter dated 10 January 1519, 'and we certify that if this pestilence lasts two more months, the land will be completely depopulated.' And the black convoys continued to plough the seas.

After these decisions and hesitations, particularly those of Isabella and Cisneros, came Charles V who renewed the entry permits, limited at first to ninety and then increased to 400, a privilege granted to Jorge de Portugal.

From this time onward the Crown of Spain does not undertake such trade as a private or as a state policy. Its action is limited to granting entry and sale permits, contracts on which it charged a certain percentage. The first licences were granted to the Genoese and then to the Flemish. The first slave-trader was Lorenzo de Gouvenot.

Seven periods or concessions may be distinguished in what was called 'ebony traffic', or in the policy of contracts.

The Germanic traders had great influence over Charles V. Ehinger and Sayller were authorized to introduce 4,000 coloured slaves into the West Indies in exchange for a fee to the Crown. In 1595 Reinel had the exclusive right until 1600.

Particulars of this contract were found in a manuscript of the *Archivo de Indias* in Seville,[1] which reads as follows:

[1] Archivo de Indias, *Colec.* 80, Expedientes, Encomendados, g. 4.

'They are to be given permission to carry to the Indies in four years 4,000 slaves of which a third are women, to be sold at whatever price they will fetch. In these four years no permission will be given to take slaves there, except as a special favour to anyone for discovery or fresh conquest, to take one hundred slaves, and to any *conquistador* or planter to take two slaves each. For this favour they shall pay at the end of the following October 26,000 *ducats.*'

The second period is that of the Portuguese. This is the golden age of slave-traders and corresponds to Claver's time.

Juan Rodríguez de Continho, Governor of Angola, was granted the contract for negro slaves up to 1609, but as he died in 1603 he was succeeded by his brother, Gonzalo Vaez Continho. These brothers contracted to carry some 5,000 slaves to the New World and pay the treasury 162,000 *ducats*. In 1615 the contractor is Antonio Delvas or Delbas, who took there 3,500 slaves.

The Portuguese colonies in Africa were the main purveyors, and for this reason when Portugal separated from the Spanish royal authority the trade with America in negro slaves was reduced to almost nothing (1640).

The succeeding periods fall outside the scope of Claver's life. They are, in chronological order: the Sevillian in 1675, the Portuguese again in 1696, the French from 1701–13 and the English until freedom of trading in 1789. Contraband in human beings was as important and lucrative as gold smuggling, and the pirates were slave-traders.

The number of negro slaves that were brought into America is difficult to compute exactly. Humboldt calculated for the whole of the New World at the end of the eighteenth century 4.7 per cent. of the total population, a number which varies from place to place. While the Caribbean regions absorbed great numbers, countries like Chile and Argentina took only a few hundred.

The port of Cartagena is reckoned to have taken 1,000,000 slaves throughout the period; we have data from the golden age of the slave-trade showing that ten to twelve thousand arrived there yearly.

From 1680–1790, 1,337,000 slaves came to the French port of

Santo Domingo, and at the same period 2,250,000 came to the English colonies. From 1789–1819 alone, the English transported to Cuba 300,000, out of whom 50,000 died on the way.

Who can accuse anyone else? The responsibility rests on all from Las Casas to the last slave-trader. He himself recognizes this in his history of the Indies:[1]

'The priest, Las Casas, was the first to advise that permission should be given to bring slaves to these lands, not realizing the injustice with which the Portuguese take them and make them slaves; if he had realized it he would not have given them permission for anything in the world, because he considered they had been made slaves unjustly and tyrannically, as the same right should hold for them as for the Indians.'

This protest is much weakened, since we know that after his conversion and after he became a bishop he took out a permit to take four negro slaves to the Indies.[2]

As soon as he learned the cruel ways in which the African negroes were enslaved, no one condemned that trade with greater severity. He says:

> As the Portuguese, with the utmost injustice, have made it their business for many years past to steal and make slaves of the negroes of Guinea, because they saw how much we needed them and gave them good prices, they hastened—and still do so—to seize and steal them by every possible evil and iniquitous way. For example the Africans themselves, seeing the Portuguese seek them with such zeal, make unjust war on one another and by other illicit means steal and sell fellow Africans to the Portuguese, so that in this way we are the cause of all the sins they commit against one another, apart from the sins we ourselves commit in buying them.[3]

Yet shortly after these declarations he asks for permission 'to bring in four slaves'.

Kings were uneasy and took advice on the question, for they

[1] Las Casas, *Historia de las Indias*, Bk. III, Chap. 102.
[2] *Catálogo de los fondes americano del archivo de los protocolos*, Seville, Vol. II. p. 488.
[3] Las Casas, *op. cit.*, Bk. III, Chap. 129.

did not see clearly, and so we find Charles II sending the following communication to the Royal Council on 5 July 1685:

'The Council of the Indies shall inform me presently what convenience is provided by the negroes in America and what harm would result from their absence: whether there have been any assemblies of theologians and lawyers to discover if it is lawful to buy them as slaves and make a contract for them, and if there are authors who have written on this matter, who they are: and they shall tell me every single particular of which the Council may have notice and may obtain from relevant papers that may exist, laying them shortly before me.'

On 21 August the Council presented their reply, in which, as well as indicating the theologians who consider as licit—*debitas cautelis*—the trade in negroes, such as Fathers Tomás Sánchez, Molina, Palao, Fragoso, etc., the reasons are set out which justify it and the common practice of learned and pious men.

It is evident that the actions of each and every one cannot be defended. There were many abuses, but in reality the Spanish tried to mitigate them by its regulations. Treatment was gradually made milder, and so we find in 1789 a celebrated royal ordinance of great importance concerning the legal regulation of the slave-trade. This document is really rather late and is more than a century after the period under study. It is somewhat similar to the slave-trade code that was issued in France or the bills introduced by Lord Bathhurst in England.

The most impartial observers in reality are agreed that their actual treatment in the Spanish Colonies was especially mild. The testimony of Simón Bolívar, liberator of five American nations, suffices for many. It runs thus:

The Spanish settler does not oppress his slave with excessive labour; he treats him as a comrade; he educates him in the moral principles and humanity which the religion of Christ prescribes . . . The slave in Spanish America vegetates, left to himself on the estates, enjoying, so to speak, his master's inaction, his property and a great share in the blessings of liberty; and as religion has convinced him that service is a sacred duty, as he has been born and lived in this state of domestic dependence, he considers himself to be in his natural state as a member of the family of his master whom he loves and respects. Experience has shown us that even though incited by tempting inducements, the Spanish slave has not fought against his master; and on the contrary has often preferred peaceful slavery to rebellion.[1]

'The part played by the port of Cartagena de Indias in the whole of the slave-trade business was immense. We find that Cartagena and Veracruz were the only two places appointed for the reception of slaves in America, and the slaves who were required in all the other countries had to be sent there according to the regulation laid down by the Council of the Indies.'[2]

So we find in the contract drawn up with the Portuguese Antonio Rodríguez Delvas (or Delbas) on 27 September 1615, which was to be valid until 1623. He bound himself to bring every year a maximum of 5,000 negroes and a minimum of 3,500, paying a tax of 115,000 *ducats*. The limitation to the above two ports, as he himself adds, brought him difficulties.

As soon as the negroes disembarked at Cartagena and Veracruz they were kept in confinement until the purchasers came down from the provinces of the interior. The limitation of the negro traffic to the two ports shows the lack of confidence with which the government still regarded the foreigners who had permission to bring the negroes to America. As importation to any other place on the continent was prohibited, the transport of these slaves to other regions gave rise to great expense and for this reason they were sold at very high prices. The result was that either America was not provided with all the labour it needed or it was necessary to meet the demand by having recourse to smuggling which was a general practice.[3]

We find this statement confirmed by the testimony of Father Alonso de Andrade, the first biographer of St Peter Claver, who in 1757 wrote this page, which may be considered the perfect

[1] S. Bolívar, *Carta al director de la Gaceta Real de Jamaica*, Sept. 1815, Col. Lecuna, Vol. I, p. 211
[2] Abreu, *Colección de tratados de paz.*
[3] José Antonio Sacco, *Historia de la Esclavitud*, Habana 1938, Vol. II, p. 115.

picture and summary of slavery as represented in Cartagena. Father Andrade gives the following list of places of origin of the negroes who were brought thither:

> Cartagena is like a source of supply and port for all the Indies where people from all parts come to do business; from the mainland of Peru, Mexico, Quito and Potosi, as well as from the adjacent islands, from Brazil, Angola, Longo and the rivers of Guinea. As throughout the Indies negroes are employed in cultivating the ground and working the mines, they have become a common merchandise like spice, silks, and other products of the earth, and so well established that the king has sold many annuities based on the revenue from the sale of negroes, and they are none the less secure because there are so many merchants dealing in it. All who may doubt this from the difficulty they may find in buying them in their countries should know that in the countries and regions where they live, they cause wars between the different tribes and the chiefs and kings at the ports like Angola, Santo Tomé and the rivers of Guinea, seeing that the European merchants go continually to buy them and bring in exchange wine and oil and other things which their countries need. They go to war, capture and take them prisoner and sell them for a moderate price, for they barter them for half an *arroba* of wine or oil or a few glass beads. The slave who costs one or two *reals* in Angola is sold in Cartagena for two hundred. The cost of transporting them is not great, and as profit is so high, a great number of people go in for this trade, induced by greed, so that from 10,000 to 12,000 negroes are brought to Cartagena by captains and merchants.[1]

In the *Archivo de Indias* we find much documentary proof of this. We reproduce here as an illustration a number of contracts which give us an idea of the great traffic at this port and consequently of the providential mission of St Peter Claver.

'Contract made with Antonio Fernández Delbas, inhabitant of Lisbon, for the hire and general provision of negro slaves for the Indies for a period of eight years; and for each one of these 3,500 actual slaves brought to be disembarked at the ports of the cities of Cartagena and Nueva Veracruz. Madrid 21 September 1615

[1] P. Alonso Andrade, *op.cit.*, p. 24.

and the royal warrant of approbation dated in Burgos 3 October 1615.'[1]

'Contract made with Manuel Rodríguez Lamego, native of the Kingdom of Portugal, for the period of eight years that they (the slaves) be taken to be disembarked in the ports of Cartagena and Nueva Veracruz, Madrid 1 August 1623 and royal warrant (Cedula) of approbation dated in Madrid 1 August 1623.'

'Contract made with Melchor Gómez Angel and Cristóbal Méndez de Sossa, inhabitants of Lisbon (like the preceding). Dated in Madrid 25 September 1631 and royal warrant of approbation dated in Madrid on 25 October 1631. Approbation of the extension of the contract of permits for negro slaves for the Indies for six years in favour of the same. Dated in Madrid 27 April 1641.'

'Copy of the letter of the President of the High Court of the New Kingdom of Granada written from Cartagena on 4 August 1637 about the excesses caused by bringing in negroes without registration'.[2]

Why Cartagena? There must have been many difficulties to solve in that city when King Philip IV had to issue a royal decree on 8 August 1621 of the following tenor:

In the city of Cartagena are many negroes and mulattos, whose turbulence has occasioned deaths, robberies, crimes and losses, due to the fact that the judicial authorities have allowed them to carry arms and knives, as specially favoured, or slaves of ministers of the Inquisition, governors, judges, ecclesiastics or men of the military profession, under whose protection they take many liberties to the detriment of the public peace. We command that no slave shall bear arms or a knife, even though he may be accompanying his master, without our special permission, and that in no case shall it be tolerated or concealed, the governors being advised they will be required to give an account of this matter when their term of office expires and will be punished severely for any negligence or omission; and as for the negroes belonging to Inquisitors, let this agreement be observed.[3]

[1] Archivo de Indias, *Serie Asientos, Indiferente general*, Legajo 2795.
[2] *Indiferente general*, Legajo 2795.
[3] *Recopilación de las Leyes de Indias*, Tit. 5, Ley 17.

Revolts were frequent, as were also mass flights. In present-day Colombia, a few kilometres from Cartagena is a place probably unique in the world on account of its origin and ethnological interest. It is a corner of old Africa preserved and almost pure racially. In one of those slave revolts and flights, the slaves assembled at one point not far from the town and established their own private community in the midst of the forest: the village of San Basilio de Palenque. Legend relates that the revolt was led by a negro prince of royal blood called Benkos Bihojo, who penetrated into the jungle and not only formed with his runaways a separate community antagonistic to all white culture, but allowed himself the luxury of attacking the government of Cartagena in two insurrections in 1608 and 1616. St Peter Claver had to intervene. Their customs until lately had retained all the original characteristics of the African jungle, short-skirted garments, straw huts, work done by the women, dances by moonlight with drums four to six feet high and also what may be called Palenque law-giving in which the spirit of Peter Claver still lives mixed with that of the African. There are ten commandments, 'The human and divine law of our people':

1. To love and worship Almighty God.
2. Not to steal.
3. Not to kill.
4. Not to lie.
5. Not to be idle.
6. To obey exactly the Chief's orders.
7. To celebrate marriage according to the Palenque custom.
8. Not to covet another's wife.
9. To be valiant and die for one's race.
10. To respect the maiden and die for her virginity.

The primitive African language has become mixed with Castilian and has remained a special dialect of great linguistic interest.

The township of San Basilio de Palenque is a racial jewel and a reminder of the coming of Africa to America, of the mingling of two races and continents.[1]

[1] José V. Ochoa, *Consideraciones sobre las costumbres y lenguaje palenqueros*, Ex. Cultural, Cartagena, 1945.

The enslaved
race

ee sons of slaves: on the
ach at Marbella
Cartagena)

Cartagena: The fortified
city

Cartagena: Old door in the walls

As to which races came to these regions of Spanish America through the port of Cartagena, the principal lands or countries which supplied this market in negroes were: Senegal, Guinea, comprising in this name all the region of the western rivers, now Senegambia, Angola, the Congo. From there the Madingas came; the Lucumies from Nigeria; the Minas from Dahomey; the Carabalies from the banks of the present-day river Carabal. The Araraes, who were reputed to be sullen and savage, came, as well as the Minas, from Dahomey; the Mondongos from the Congo.

Fernando Ortiz, the historian of negro affairs, referring to Cuba—which may be extended to include South America, as all went through Cartagena—maintains that it was established by law that only negroes from Angola, Guinea and the Cape Verde and adjacent islands should be brought in, but smuggling and greed had no respect for race and examples might be found of all the intertropical regions of Africa—even from east Africa.

He gives a list specifying more than thirty-eight races. The principal and most numerous were the Angolas, Araraes, Apapas, Bambaras, Bondos, Carabalies, Congos, Gamgas, Iolofos, Lucumies Mandingas, Minas, Viafaras, etc.[1]

There is a curious will of Doña María Barros, which is at the same time the instrument of foundation of the Teresian convent of Cartagena, under the title of St Joseph. It is signed 25 March 1609 and today, after three and a half centuries, it gives us valuable particulars as to which were the most common races in the town.

> Trusting to the mercy of our Lord God I make donation to the above Convent of St Joseph, of the discalced nuns of Our Lady of Mount Carmel, of which I am the foundress, of the following properties:

Slaves:

Firstly.   Domingo, Creole, mason.
Item   Juan Primero of the Bran race.
Item   Greogio of the Angola race.
Item   Juliana, his wife of the Lucumi race, with a child called Marcos aged about three years.

[1] Fernando Ortiz, *Los Negros esclavos*, Chap. III, pp. 26 *et seq.*

Firstly   Gonzalo of Angola race, stone-cutter.

Item   Francisco of Arará race—old.

(Firstly)   Agustín of Angola race.

Item   Antón of Congo race—with nails in his feet.

Item   Pedro, Creole of Santome, who has a tumour.

Item   María of Arará race—old.

Item   Isabel, Biafara, and has maimed hands.

Item   Beatriz, Biojo, who serves in the convent.

Item   Clara, about seven years old, who is in the above convent.

Item   Melchora about six years old, who is in the above convent.

In all fifteen persons, among them four children and others infirm, whom the charitable lady shut up in her monastery as life prisoners in spite of their having been baptized in Christ as she was, but who had no freedom of will as they were slaves.

A strange incomprehensible mixture which founded Christian monasteries in such conditions. Here we quote Quintana: 'It was the fault of the times and not of Spain', and this is so true that His Holiness Pope Paul III had to affirm for the information of the *Conquistadores* that 'the Indians are men and have souls', and even so some doubted.[1]

What a tragedy does this world of slavery represent to the man of today! An enslaved race, millions who are human merchandise. This was the world in which it fell to St Peter Claver to live. And it lasted three more centuries, almost to our own day. Below are some extracts from newspapers taken at random. Much of this merchandise is descended from what passed through Cartagena; they are the children of those negro slaves whom Peter Claver baptized. The advertisements did not cause surprise. They were a natural thing.[2]

'A mulatto about thirty years old, a good cook, healthy and *with no defects* except that of thief; also in exchange for a negro, mules, horses or a covered trap. Inquiries at the store formerly belonging to Don Juan Rincón.' (*Periódico de la Habana*, 18 January 1795.)

[1] *Boletín Historial de Cartagena*, Vol. I, p. 28.   [2] F. Ortiz, *op. cit.*

'For sale a fine negress, twenty-four years of age, beautiful in appearance, an excellent washerwoman, ironer and cook, better than average seamstress, born in owner's house, accustomed to good manners with her master and mistress and especially good with children, has always lived in towns on the Island; has no vices, defects or infirmities, very robust and healthy; *Calle de Manique*, No. 17, Enquiries.' (*El Siglo*, Habana, 1865.)

'For sale a mulatto woman aged twenty-six married in the town of Santiago, with her baby girl of five months, for 300 *pesos*. Sales tax and indenture included, but not the baby.'

The great authority on America, Father Constantino Bayle, S.J., writes under a misapprehension in his magnificent book *España en Indias*, referring to the injustices endured by the negroes: 'There were no lamentations about their dismal lot; no cruelty or almost no cruelty on the part of their masters. These unfortunate people had a St Peter Claver who loved them with a father's love; they lacked a Las Casas to raise laments or dramatize pathetically their tragic misery, for the simple reason that this misery had no existence.'[1]

This is not true. Great misery did exist and great defenders from the beginning—perhaps without the asperity of Las Casas but with the same challenging spirit.

The early Church fought slavery, adopting various tactics to the circumstances, and the Church in the sixteenth century did the same.

Limiting the field to the Christian era the history of slavery may be divided into three periods. The first goes as far as the invasion of the barbarians and represents, as it were, the waning of pagan slavery. The second comes down to the end of the Middle Ages during which slavery was disappearing in civilized countries. In the third, slavery is initiated and intensified with the discovery of the New World.

The extent of the Christian contribution to the abolition of slavery is an all-important question. The Catholic Church co-existed with slavery, it found it in an advanced stage; no war was

[1] Constantino Bayle, S. J., *España en Indias*, p. 356.

declared against it at first, on the contrary we find St Paul himself advising Christian slaves to obey their masters.

Did he approve of this state of affairs? Was his attitude tactical? In modern times the question is again raised with the revival of slavery in the Americas for the Indian and the negro.

The enemies of the Church are harsh and explicit in their attacks. One of these, H. Havet, writes: 'The best example of believers' illusions is found in their obstinacy in doing Christianity and the Church the honour of considering them responsible for the abolition of slavery, though it is an indisputable fact that the ancient slavery persisted under the Christian Empire as under the pagan and that the slavery of the negroes was instituted under the rule of the Church.'[1]

M. Guizot, on his part, adds: 'It has been repeated a thousand times that the abolition of slavery in modern times is entirely due to the teachings of Christianity. This is, in my opinion, going too far: slavery persisted for a long time in the midst of Christian society and such a state of affairs did not seem to upset or annoy it greatly.'

As this chapter is necessarily limited to the question of negro slavery, we cannot go back to the origins of this complex problem. The reader is referred to two excellent works on the whole subject: Paul Allard, *Les Esclaves Chrétiens*, and Jaime Balmes, *El protestantismo comparado con el catolicismo*.

Before launching an accusation of toleration of injustice the accusers should ask themselves whether it was possible to abolish slavery suddenly. Could the spirit of peace and order in the Church launch on the world a general upheaval—useless in any case?

Was not the better way to influence the attitude of the slave-owners, until liberty should come, like a ripe fruit, while at the same time more energetic measures of condemnation were taken as circumstances made advisable?

The Church adopted a profoundly wise tactic. Instead of embittering the slaves by hatred, she endeavoured to soften the heart of the oppressors, and if she said to the slaves: 'Do not try to free

[1] H. Havet, *Le Christianisme dans ses origines*, 1871.

yourselves by violence,' she said at the same time to their masters: 'Love your slaves like brothers, diminish their number, recognize them as your equals and at times your superiors in God's sight, give them the right to marriage and to the family that the law denies them and grant them liberty if you wish to save your souls.'

St Paul summed up these ideas perfectly: 'Slaves, obey your earthly masters with the humility with which you obey Christ. Do not obey with servile diligence which flatters and increases pride in men, but from the heart fulfilling the will of God.'

This was the face presented to the slaves, the other is presented to the masters:

'Do not command your slaves more things, and in doing so remember that you also have a Master in Heaven.' 'Do not dominate them by fear, because they have the same God as you and that God will judge all without regarding the conditions of the persons.'

The Apostle lays the foundation of the solution in this celebrated sentence: 'There is now no difference between the Jew and the Greek, the slave and the free, man and woman; all of you are one in Jesus Christ.'

No doctrine more revolutionary in essence and application could be expounded. The development of these will come presently in practice. Paul Allard has summed up the last stage of primitive human slavery like this:

As society became gradually more Christian, the teaching of the doctors (of the Church) became more definite. Little by little the veils which hid their private thoughts were withdrawn. Ecclesiastical writers in the fourth century employ a more daring language than those of the third. Although the society in which they lived continued pagan in its customs, the Christian spirit had penetrated it sufficiently for the question of slavery to be attacked without danger. Sincere souls began to ask the leaders of the Church to tell them the origin of this strange state of things so contrary to the principles of reason and the spirit of the Gospel: 'Where did slavery arise and how did it become established in the world?' St John Chrysostom asked a popular audience, ardent, restless and enthusiastic, which crowded round him, and he added: 'I shall tell you: avarice, envy, insatiable cupidity engendered slavery.'[1] 'Tyranny it was,' said St Gregory Nazianzen, 'that divided the human race into two parts.' Lactantius at the beginning of the fourth century is even more peremptory: 'Neither the Romans nor the Greeks could make justice prevail, for they established different grades among men . . . Where all are not equal, there can be no equity: inequity excludes justice, the real force of which resides in this: making all men equal who received life in equal conditions.'[2]

St Gregory of Nyssa expressed himself with even greater energy in his fourth homily on *Ecclesiastes*:

> I own, people say, men and women slaves born in my house. What vain pride and what stupid arrogance! The phrase is a cry of defiance against God. When you condemn a man to slavery who is naturally free and his own master, you observe a law contrary to that of God. A man whom God made master of the earth and to whom he gave life that he might rule it, do you subject to the yoke of slavery, violating the divine precept? Have you forgotten what are the limits of your power? That power is limited to irrational beings. Why, forgetting what was handed over to you to serve you, do you turn against one who is free by nature, relegating him to the condition of an animal? I own men and women slaves! Tell me, how much did you pay for them? What have you found in the world which is worth a man? What price did you put on reason? . . . God has said: 'Let us make man in our image and likeness.' One who was made in the likeness of God, one who received from him power over all things on earth, tell me: who can buy or sell him? Do the slave and the master differ in any way? Will both not be converted into dust when they die? Will they not be judged by the same God? . . . Man yourself, how can you call yourself the master of another?[3]

In this way slaves came to be kings, priests and popes, whose title seemed to be :'Slave of the slaves of God.'

The Cuban writer, Fernando Ortiz, an authority on the negro

[1] St John Chrysostom, *In Epis. ad Eph.* Hom. XXII. 2.
[2] Lactantia, *Div. Ilust.* 166.
[3] Quoted from Paul Allard, *Esclaves chrétiens*.

question, is guilty of injustice when he writes the following: 'The Catalan Jesuit, Peter Claver, could be canonized without royal opposition for his virtues in mitigating the sufferings of the negro slaves in Cartagena de Indias, and for his catechetical zeal; but Spanish imperialism never allowed a modest tablet or statue in homage to the Dominican from Seville, Fray Bartolomé de Las Casas, in spite of a life completely dedicated to his untiring and wise campaigns for the liberty of the Indian and the negro. Claver wished to *relieve* the slave, Las Casas wished to *redeem* him. The Jesuit made him meekly resigned, the Dominican justified his rebellion.'[1]

St Peter Claver did not only wish to *relieve* the negro slave: he wished to *redeem* him also. But St Peter Claver did not justify useless rebellion and bloodshed for his negro slaves, his mission was not to be a Spartacus but an apostle who devoted himself passionately heart and soul to that race. Mildness for him was not a timid compromise but a creed. Exaggeration and violence were not necessary to his purpose. To the slave-traders he turned a sad and serious face. His slavery to the slaves was the greatest reproach to those who considered themselves their masters. Had St Peter Claver not possessed that mildness which has been condemned, he would not have baptized 300,000 brothers: he would have failed if St Peter Claver had put arms in his negroes' hands, he would not have been the liberator of a race but its exterminator. The decrees of political liberty which followed eventually would not have been possible in a society which had not been prepared for it by the Gospel.

The Catholic Church was not content with providing spiritual and even temporal aid by means of her ministers. Having from the very beginning attended to the task of relieving the lot of the slaves and exhorting their masters to free them, and never ceasing to raise her voice on their behalf, she also did as much as possible for the good of the Africans. Pope Pius II published on 7 October 1642 an apostolic brief against the Portuguese who made slaves of the converts in Guinea. Before

[1] José Antonio Sacco, *Hist. de la Esclavitud*, Intro. by Fernando Ortiz, Habana. 1938.

the appearance in Europe of the negrophiles and of philanthropy Paul III defended the liberty of the Indians and negroes. Urban VIII on 22 April 1639 prohibited the enslaving of negroes and separation from their country, their wives and their children. Benedict XIV on 20 December 1741 repeated the same prohibition to the bishops of Brazil for the instruction of their diocesans. Pius VII zealously intervened, using his good offices in the cause of persuading the powerful to stop completely the traffic in negroes among Christians. And Gregory XVI in a rescript on 3 December 1839, *In supremo apostolatu*, condemned as illicit and absolutely unworthy of the name of Christian the above-mentioned trade in negroes, commanding that no person lay or ecclesiastic should dare to defend it as lawful on any pretext or pretence, either in public or private. In these documents (those of Gregory XVI and of his predecessors) there will be found [says Balmes] everything that has been said and can be said on this point in favour of humanity; in them what European civilization has at last resolved to condemn and castigate will be found reprehended, condemned, and castigated . . . Catholicism has therefore fulfilled perfectly its mission of peace and love, breaking without injustice or catastrophe the chains in which a part of the human race was groaning.[1]

It would be impossible to adduce here all the American documentation which witnesses to the voice of the Church in high ecclesiastical dignitaries. There were, it is true, doubts, hesitation, but also clear and precise pronouncements on this matter.

In an appendix we shall examine later the mighty work of Father Sandoval. Meanwhile two documents—one private by Father Tomás Mercado, the other official from Cuba—prove that the Church was not silent. Father Tomás Mercado in a work published in Seville in 1587 says:

It is well known to all that in purchasing and transporting negroes from their own country to the Indies and here (Spain) endless trickery and numberless acts of robbery and violence are committed . . . Under the pretext of a just war, many and mostly unjust wars are waged, for as they (the negroes) are uncivilized, they are not moved by reason but by passion; they

[1] Jaime Balmes, *El protestantismo comparado con el catolicismo*, Vol. I.

do not examine or consider their rights. Besides this, knowing that the Portuguese and Castilians give such a price for a negro, without even waging war, they hunt one another as if they were game, and count it gain to capture one another . . .

And let no one be astonished that these people treat one another so badly and sell one another, for they are uncivilized and savage . . . Besides the fathers selling their children in extreme need, we find them in their savage way selling them without any necessity, often from annoyance and anger, for some displeasure or some disrespect shown to them . . . And they take the unfortunate boys to the market-place to sell them, and there is such a demand; everywhere there are Portuguese, or negroes themselves, ready to buy them. There are also among them dealers in this bestial and brutal trade who sell them inland to their fellow countrymen or bring them to the coasts or islands to sell them at a higher price. And I have seen many come in this way. Besides these cases of injustice and robbery done amongst themselves, a great number of other tricks are practised there by the Spaniards, attracting them, as the inexperienced creatures they are, to the posts by the offer of caps, bells, beads and pencil-boxes, and luring them by this pretence into the ships, raise anchor and set sail for the open sea with their victims . . .

Those pretexts and unjust pretences that I spoke of grow and increase at present more than ever by reason of the gain which they bring to the negroes themselves . . . Besides (though this is not the main point) they treat them cruelly on the voyage as to clothing, food and drink. They think they are saving money bringing them naked, killing them with thirst and hunger, and they are certainly mistaken for they are more likely to lose. They embark on a vessel—often not a carack, 400 or 500 of them, where the very smell is enough to kill most of them, as indeed many die—the wonder is that 10 per cent. are not lost; and that no one may think I am exaggerating, not four months ago the merchants of Gradas brought a ship from Cape Verde to New Spain, with 500, and out of them after one night 120 were found dead in the morning, because they packed them like pigs or worse below decks where the smell and stench killed them; and it would be a just punishment from God if those bestial men who took them on board should die with them; and this was not the end, for before they reached Mexico about 300 died. To tell about the treatment dealt out to the living would take me too long.[1]

In the diocesan synod held in June 1680 in Habana and approved by Royal Warrant of 9 August 1682, the following order was given in Constitution IV:

> That those who have unbaptized slaves shall take them to the parish church for holy baptism, and that the masters of those resold should teach them Christian doctrine. Our Lord God having bestowed on the untutored negroes who come to this island to be among Christians, one of the greatest blessings is to enjoy holy baptism; and because we are informed that many slave-owners have them in their service for two or three years without getting them baptized, we command all persons owning slaves who have not received the water of holy baptism, to send them to be baptized within two months and instructed in Christian doctrine; and all those who henceforward buy slaves from the hulks which bring them, shall within six months of their purchase teach them Christian doctrine with all the care and vigilance these poor negroes need, and send them to the parish churches to be baptized on penalty of excommunication and a payment of ten ducats according to the Royal Warrant of His Majesty and on the same penalty they shall inform the parish incumbents that they may register them and see to it that when these six months are up the owners are obliged to take them to be baptized; and if they are not instructed in Christian doctrine we command the incumbents that they in person or other priests shall give them this instruction and the owners of the slaves shall pay to the said clergy for their teaching a suitable fee as a penalty for their omission or neglect; and that this may take effect we command the judges and ecclesiastics to compel the said owners to pay to the above clergy the stipend which they deserve with penalties and reprimands and for this we give them due authority. And because it pertains to our office and to that of the parish priests to teach the Christian doctrine and to enquire whether the said negroes know it: we command in one of the constitutions of this holy synod that every Sunday afternoon they shall ring the bell for

[1] Tomás de Mercado, *Suma de tratos y contratos*, Lib. 2, Cap. 20, Seville, 1587.

the said slaves to go to be taught and questioned on Christian doctrine and like vigilant pastors enquire about and discover those who are missing and send for them. And we command the owners of the said slaves to take special care to send them on those Sundays without waiting for the priests to fetch them for it is their obligation as faithful and Catholic Christians to procure by every means that their slaves learn Christian doctrine and that when instructed in it they be baptized and that after baptism they do not forget it and we lay this grave charge on the conscience of each and every one.[1]

The black enslaved race. A strong, cheerful, lively race, which has suffered much and in a certain sense has conquered its conquerors, forged a new race in this New World: simple, candid souls who have forgotten their tragedies and have not sunk into the melancholy of the Indian native but delight in colour and sound, and stimulate life in the present without anxious memory of past suffering.

A black race, once the victim of slavery, walks the roads of America and swarms in its ports and along its coasts, leaving behind all sorrows with the broad smile of a grown-up child. During its time of slavery it had many friends in the Church, and perhaps the greatest friend in its history was Peter Claver; and today too when racialism has not yet disappeared from the world the Church gives them a helping hand and in its upper hierarchies are negroes with good and holy souls.

St Peter Claver never admitted any inferiority in his negro slaves, and that there might be no doubt about it he proclaimed himself, and became, *their slave* for ever.

[1] Synod of Habana, June 1680, approved by Royal Warrant in August 1682; cf. J. A. Sacco, *op. cit.*, Vol. 1, p. 165.

Chapter II

THE APOSTLE OF THE NEGROES

From the Slave-ship to Baptism

CLAVERIAN tradition includes an historical legend which epitomizes the whole life of the apostle of the negro slaves.

A few years after the Saint's death a white marble statue was erected near the ramparts, not far from the room where he died.

The salt-laden air of the Caribbean Sea soon began to darken its whiteness; it grew blacker and blacker until the white marble looked like dark bronze

The negroes watched this physical change closely, saying as they passed: 'Father Claver must have been a negro, for a white man would never have loved us so much.'

Truly Peter Claver's love for his negroes had no bounds. If it was said of his master, Father Sandoval, that his eyes followed any coloured slave he saw, we may say that the whole of Father Claver's heart went out to them. He was a willing slave in the total service of a great love.

He was the liberator of a race, because he was able above all to approach them as a brother and not as a master.

Brother Nicolás González, his companion for twenty-two years, tells us in the process of beatification that Father Claver 'showed himself full of kindness and friendship towards them, when he heard of their arrival his eyes shone and his pale face flushed as red as fire.'[1]

This love was returned. It is only necessary to imagine the condition of those unhappy creatures, victims of every misfortune, torn from their native land, chained like wild beasts, their excited brains harbouring the most terrible ideas of their future destiny,

[1] Process, No. 8.

seeing themselves confronted with a white man belonging to the same class as those who enslaved them, with no whip in his hand, no distrust or cruelty in his glance, but, on the contrary, with a kind countenance, a ready embrace, and a total sacrifice to their service. Stupefaction and love were their natural reactions.

One witness, Captain Pedro Barahona, gives us the following description: 'So great was the love the negroes had for Peter Claver that wherever they saw him they went and kissed his hand and knelt down before him.'[1]

For this Saint, work among the negro slaves was the essential. There are perhaps few saints so specialized. Everything in his life turned on the slaves. Here is another testimony from Brother Nicolás:

'I consider it certain that Father Peter Claver in this ministry exercised all the virtues because of the great spiritual devotion with which he performed it, in conditions of such mortification, humility, patience and charity combined, that this ministry would not be possible without the exercise of all these virtues especially in the way he carried it out. Peter Claver was completely absorbed in God; and for this work I am convinced that he was called by God himself and that he needed particular aid from God as all those who continued this work recognized.'[2]

We are approaching the very centre of Claver's life. The line to be followed is clear. First, to use direct sources to give an objective picture of his apostolic mission. Fortunately, we can obtain a complete reconstruction of his activity, even though we lack direct statements made by the Saint himself.

Father Sandoval's book, fundamental in its substance, is the basis of Claver's sociological action. It is the best picture drawn in America of his apostolate and the most methodical account presented in the whole of the seventeenth century. On the other hand we have the Process itself, a living source direct and magnificent, running over the whole complex scale of society at that time, white and black, and lastly the information of the Jesuits about these labours in the college itself.

In the light of these documents we can trace a realistic picture

[1] Process, No. 3.   [2] Process, No. 42.

with a definite historical background from a triple source: Sandoval, Process, private information from his colleagues.

We have insisted on these precise original documents, forgoing deliberately any attempt at subjective commentary. They speak for themselves.

In the information given by the Jesuits of the college of Cartagena in *Cartas Annuas* (1638–43), the period of Claver's full apostolic activity, of his ministry among the negroes, it is said:

One of the occupations and ministries that redounded most to the glory and service of God, to the welfare and profit of the innumerable souls in this college of Cartagena and carried out with very special zeal, work and care is the ministry to the negroes, in which all the Jesuits in this house are occupied when necesssary, but generally speaking there have been *two fathers*, fervent workers of remarkable charity and zeal for the salvation of these poor wretches so despised and abandoned, who attend eagerly to all their concerns, illnesses and spiritual and often corporal necessities, due to their extreme poverty, and this they do at the cost of infinite labours, afflictions and difficulties.

One of their chief anxieties and cares is and has been the clearing up, disentangling and examining with exactness, of the baptisms of more than twenty or thirty negro races who come to this port, because here they are all disembarked and this is the market and custom-house where they are assembled, whence distributed and sent to all these kingdoms and provinces.

Our Lord was pleased that our Society should have in this province of the New Kingdom this college of Cartagena so that it might act as a touchstone in assessing the quality of this celestial gold, where enquiry might be made to ascertain exactly the properties, conditions and circumstances in the practice of holy baptism administered to these poor slaves in the provinces of Africa, ports of Santo Tomé, Cape Verde, Cacheo, of Angola and others; confirming us more and more every day in the Lord in this holy scruple, and it is right to recognize it in the experiences of marvellous fruit and rare occurrences.

Finding many who had studied Castilian and had been stewards in their fraternities, confessing and taking communion

more frequently than pious Spaniards, already married for many
years, among some of whom baptism was unknown and in
other cases doubtful.

As God gives the accessory with the principal, his Majesty
has granted to this college from its beginning for this holy
ministry, faithful and untiring workers who needed this
quality for such excessive work and to conquer difficulties that
would daunt the mightiest, employing not only their years, life
and health in these glorious undertakings, but also their literary
ability in composing a book which as coming from such
practical masters would teach all prelates, priests and apostolic
workers not only to imitate them in their zeal and cordial love
for these miserable abandoned souls of many races, but the
necessary procedure for the revalidation of their sacraments and
exact enquiry into their baptisms, for it seemed to the author
that he made good use of the last years of his life only in adding,
making perfect and correcting this work to publish a second
edition for the service of his beloved black men, for the glory
of the Lord and the benefit of those who deal with them, and
of those who desire to save every kind of people and souls.

The second advantage granted for the same purpose by our
benevolent Lord to this his college has been to have many good
interpreters, almost eighteen of them; taking them in these
years from those uncivilized and barbarous races and preparing
them to serve and help us to catechize, teach and convert
their comrades, giving them such capability and gift of tongues
that besides being well versed and intelligent in matters of our
holy faith and in the deceits, errors and superstitions of their
own people, they know, some of them three or four and others
six or eight languages, and one of them reached the total—
worthy of Calepino[1]—of eleven languages; in which the paternal
providence of God is manifested and his great esteem and protection for this holy work and ministry; giving it as a distinctive
badge and honour to this college which for this reason and this
glorious work has won name and fame in the matter not only
in all this province but also in the others, it being well known
that some of the negroes who go to them have been thoroughly
investigated as to the validity of their baptism and are pro-

[1] Ambrosio Calepino, a famous learned Italian bishop of the fifteenth century,
whose name is used for any person of many accomplishments.

nounced capable of receiving the sacraments, and all realize the work and care spent on the negroes before they have been baptized by us, or admitted to other sacraments; we do not know that this is so with regard to those (negroes) approved by others, even though they belong to our Society in other colleges, and this very fact stimulates and obliges us to use vigilance and exactness, seeing that so many others trust in our rectitude and careful practice for the satisfaction of their own conscience.[1]

This first-hand document, simple and anonymous, makes several important points clear; before everything the primary importance assigned by the Jesuits at Cartagena to this work, so that not merely one priest but the whole house was interested in this ministry.

Fathers Sandoval and Claver are clearly indicated in those words 'two fathers, fervent workers of remarkable charity', and their extraordinary zeal recognized—'untiring'—and particular emphasis is laid on the literary work of Father Sandoval.

We have taken from the Jesuits a testimony which puts us completely in the picture.

Again we must turn to Father Sandoval for further details of the development of this apostolate. When we compare this documentation with the direct statements of Father Claver transmitted by the witnesses in his Process, we shall find a surprising uniformity.

In this chapter we propose to reconstruct the first meeting of the slave race with their white apostle. The action unfolds in various scenes; in the port, the barracks and in the two spiritual stages, the preparatory instruction for baptism and the baptism itself.

A page in the Process written by Brother González sums up perfectly the initial procedure of this apostolate. It is a truly modern type of reporting and reads as follows: 'As soon as he was ordained priest he received orders from his superiors to undertake the ministry of instructing and baptizing the negroes who came to this city'; he adds, indicating the reason for this appointment: 'Father Sandoval made a journey at that time to Peru for matters connected with the Society.'

[1] Hazañero, *op. cit.*

CITTA, SOBBORGHI di **CARTAGENA**

Plan of the city of
Cartagena in the
eighteenth century

Cartagena: Ruins of the Church of Our Lady

In this apostolate he was occupied until his death, and he exercised it with so much fervour, devotion and apostolic zeal that when he made his religious profession of the four vows—which is equivalent to the degree of master—he added that he dedicated himself perpetually to God for the rest of his life and to the salvation of his beloved negroes, and he wrote this in his own hand-writing and signed it with his name, and I know it because I had in my possession the letter in which the aforesaid Father Peter wrote with his own hand the profession as given above in the year 1622, and I gave it to Captain Antonio de Loayza, Knight of the Order of Santiago, who for reasons of devotion asked for this document.[1]

Every day he attended ceaselessly to the spiritual needs of the said negroes without regard for colour, dirt or the infirmities and sicknesses with which they were afflicted, instructing them, confessing them, helping them to make a good death . . . with as much love and charity as if each one was his own special favourite and with such zeal that every day at the collect he offered his Mass for the conversion of the negroes because this was an old custom with the Jesuits of that house.

I asked the father some years before he died how many negroes he had baptized during the time he had exercised his ministry and he replied that according to his reckoning there were more than 300,000. The number seemed to me very great, because it did not appear that so many had arrived in that port in that period, and thinking and pondering on this—for I considered Father Peter Claver a saint (incapable of telling a lie), virtuous and truthful, who would not say a thing was true if it were not or if there were any doubt—I came to know with complete certainty that the father had spoken truly; for if so many had not arrived during that time, we must take into account those who had arrived before, many years before, among whom he worked and who had not been baptized through negligence.

The first thing the aforesaid father did was to ask the negroes, whether fresh arrivals or those who were already here, if they had been baptized or not, enquiring very carefully into this question by means of an interpreter according to the language of each one, and if he found that any one had not been baptized he catechized him and then baptized him by virtue

[1] Process No. 8, 1.

of the privileges of the Society of Jesus and of the special dispensation of the bishop; this latter, after some controversy and disagreement, had a very special enquiry made as to the manner of catechizing and instructing the slaves and ascertaining that the interest of the Society was not the first consideration, but only the service of God and the good of souls, and that the said ministry was more suited for penitent and mortified relig-ious on account of the strong stench emitted by these negroes, caused mainly by the many contagious diseases they brought with them, having endured many hardships and discomforts at sea, always naked, ill-fed and ill-used.

Wherefore I believe that he did indeed baptize 300,000, both of the newcomers and of those who were in the city and its neighbourhood, seats and properties of the Society, and also in the town of Tolú and its surroundings where the Father went to hold missions, baptizing a very great number of people who had not been baptized.

The day of a slave-ship's arrival was one of great excitement for Peter Claver. His eagerness was well known and all the witnesses are agreed on this point.

'I know,' said Brother González, a witness who had been pre-sent on many such an occasion, 'that the father's joy was heart-felt when he learned of the arrival of some ship bringing negroes to the town. He offered Masses and penances, scourgings and the hair-shirt for the intentions of the first to bring the news to him; and some governors when they knew this, especially the comman-ding officer Francisco de Murga of the Order of Santiago, brought the news to him in person, and other royal officials and persons of standing did so too, some even from the Jesuits' residence, wishing to obtain such a signal reward because of his reputation for holiness.

Here Father Sandoval is again our main guide.

The first question that arose was: From what region of Africa do they come? What will their language be? The interpreters were ready to attend to their own races.

Book I, Chap. XVI of Sandoval's book is concerned with the analysis of these races and his observations on them; these are very valuable, even from the point of view of modern anthropo-logy.

Here are four main points from which negroes usually come to this port of the city of Cartagena de las Indias, which is the chief lawful place of disembarkation in the whole world.

They come from the rivers of Guinea and ports of the mainland, from the Island of Cape Verde, from the island of Santo Tomé and from the port of Loanda or Angola and any of the other out-of-the-way distant regions of western or eastern Ethiopia.

And although it is true that we commonly call all these races negroes, not all of them are black, there is among them a great variety of races, some darker than others, some lighter, others cooked-quince colour, as they call it, others dark brown or sambos, or slight colour, half-mulatto colour or sun-burned.

They call the negroes from the rivers and ports of Guinea the genuine negroes. They are much more faithful than all the others; very sensible and capable, of finer and stronger appearance; healthy negroes fit for heavy work, and for this reason they are considered more valuable than those of other races. There are immense numbers from these coasts.

Among these are the Yolofos, Berbefies, Mandingas and Fulos also called *bohotes*, Viafaras, etc., that is to say the negroes who usually came to Cartagena.

The Yolofos, Berbefies, Mandingas and Fulos usually under stand one another even if their languages and tribes are different because of their great intermingling caused by all having joined the Moslem sect. They are very difficult to convert.

Among these it is difficult to assess the number of Mandingas as they are scattered through all the regions and know almost all the languages. The best mark of recognition is that they have not pierced ears and are more distinguished and better disposed than those from Angola and the Congo.

The Viafaras usually speak a more or less elegant language, though there are very different communities and extensive groups of them. They understand other languages. A distinctive mark is that they have a circle round their bellies.

From the Cape Verde Islands a great mass of negroes also come, of the same tribes and races as we have described, chiefly from the rivers of Guinea, not because they are born there but because they are deposited there, and as from the port of Cartagena they are sent off to Peru and other parts, so from

Cape Verde they are despatched and brought to the port of Cartagena.

Three classes of negroes come from there as well as from Santo Tomé, some in their native state like those from Cacheo, others taught to speak Portuguese and called creoles, not because they were born in Cape Verde, but because they were brought there in childhood, having come fresh from the rivers of Guinea.

Others are called natives, born and brought up at Cape Verde Island and baptized as children, just as we call creoles those born and brought up in our country, where the children have received holy baptism and it is not necessary to question them about it.

The negroes coming from the island of Santo Tomé, a port from which the ships take them into slavery, are inferior in quality to those from the rivers of Guinea, but valued more highly than those from Angola and the Congo, better workers and less prone to disease, not so cowardly or inclined to flight.

The types usually brought from there are *ardas* or *araraes* which means the same, *lucumíes, caravaríes*, etc. The last named are innumerable and do not understand one another. They have a kind of special language, a mixture of African and Portuguese, which they call the language of Santo Tomé. These races are usually recognized by marks on their faces and bodies.

The *popós* are marked by a bow and arrows which encircle their temples on both sides, the arrows coming from out the sides of the eyes towards the ears.

The *ardas* have a variety of marks. Some have a band across their temples of a different colour from their faces; others have three or four deep lines on their faces below the eye-lids which give them a certain beauty.

The *lucumíes* pierce the left nostril without having any other mark. The *chavas lucumíes* have the whole body painted and in the middle of the forehead an oval, and so for all the other races.

The tribes called Angolas, Congos or Monicongos (they are the same), Malembas, etc., come from Loanda.

All these types have less value and strength and are the most useless of all the races, the most prone to diseases and least able to resist them, cowardly and more liable to die. They are distinguishable from the rest because all the men wear their hair growing round the back of their heads like a garland. And the women wear tightly twisted strands of hair. None have their ears pierced, unlike almost all the other races who have them pierced.

This account of the marks we have given for each tribe and race—although many have none, which is also a kind of mark—is very necessary for the recognition of these negroes, by which means, when there was no other system, we might summon them to instruction for baptism or confession; for ignorance of this means caused great confusion at the beginning, with the risk of damnation for many sick who were dying without the aid of the holy sacraments from not knowing their race, for if this were known it is easy to find interpreters to understand and be of use in saving them.[1]

A wonderful page in the history of negro ethnology.

It is difficult to estimate exactly how many negroes passed through Cartagena, for we have to consider the legal quota, that of the *contrato*, a word which means a contract for negro imports granted from the time of Charles V as a kind of monopoly, and the number was limited to 3,500 or 4,500 per year. This order was not complied with, for there are official licences that exceed this minimum quota.[2]

Father José Cassani mentions a year in which about 13,000 disembarked in Cartagena.

Father Fernández states that in the year 1633 alone fourteen ships arrived at the port and that the number (for each ship) was between 600 and 800. Here too the captains had recourse to fraud. Strictly speaking the entry of two slaves per ton of the ship was allowed and these ships were not over 200 or 300 tons. A calculation which included those smuggled in would give us the total of 1,000,000 negro slaves for the port of Cartagena alone in the whole of its slave-trade epoch.

Ricardo Cappa, in his *Critical Studies on the Spanish dominion in America*, gives a total of 1,837,000 slaves introduced by France into Santo Domingo between 1680 and 1790. In the same years 2,250,000 arrived in the English colonies; from 1789 to 1819 alone

[1] Sandoval, *op. cit.*, Bk. I, chap, XVI.

[2] Georges Scelle, *La Traite negrière aux Indes de Castille*, Paris, 1906, Vol. I, p. 107. This author gives the total as 20,000 per year.

the English brought to Cuba 300,000, of whom 50,000 died on the way. When the Spanish or Cartagena period ended, the French and English booms continued at their height. The total is reckoned at 15,000,000.

At the sighting of the slave galleon the port is all excitement, with that typical anticipation, blend of curiosity and mercenary spirit. In the midst of the terrible tropical heat, it is approaching slowly with sails furled; the anxious dealers wait for it in the port, not knowing how much human merchandise will arrive or in what condition.

From the hold of this galleon comes a stifled noise, cries of anguish. A representative of the Church is waiting with love in his heart for this race coming to the New World, suffering in its state of slavery. Father Sandoval writes:

> These negroes made captive with God knows what justice are thrown at once into cruel chains which they do not cast aside until they arrive at this port of Cartagena or elsewhere; they call the galley *armazón* if its load of 300, 400, 500 or more than 600 is enough to man a ship; the full cargo they call *armazones* if there are enough to fill many ships; and usually twelve or fourteen of them come to this city every year, each with this number or more of negroes; if the cargo consists of fewer negroes it is called a *lote*.
>
> Together then, and captive, if they come from Angola they are taken to the island of Loanda from which they cannot escape; and if they come from the rivers of Guinea, instead of taking them to the island, they secure each item of their cargoes by shackling them with very long chains which are called *corrientes* and with other cruel fetters and devices from which they are not freed by land or sea until they disembark at the place they are destined for.
>
> And as on the island of Loanda they endure so much hardship and locked in the chains so much misery, misfortune and ill-treatment as to food and drink that, with the bad voyage by sea, they fall into a sadness and melancholy increased by their belief that when they arrive they will be used to extract oil from or be eaten, so that about a third of those embarked die

during the crossing, which lasts more than two months; so tightly packed, so filthy and so ill-treated that the very men who bring them here assure me that they come in sixes with rings round their necks, the *corrientes* and their feet joined by fetters in pairs, so that they are chained from head to feet; below decks, with no outlet to see the sun or moon, no Spaniard dares look through the hatches without feeling faint, nor be in with them above an hour without risk of grave illness in the stench, overcrowding and misery in that place [the hold]. The only relief and consolation they have is to eat every twenty-four hours, nothing more than a platter of flour, maize or raw millet, which is like rice for us, and with that a small jug of water and nothing else but plenty of beating and whipping and ugly words.[1]

This is what usually happens with the men slaves and I incline to think that some of the ship-owners treat them better, especially in these days.

With this kind of treatment they arrive like skeletons; they are then taken out naked and placed in a great court or yard. Then there come endless crowds of people, some from greed, others from curiosity, others from compassion, and among these the Jesuits ready to instruct, indoctrinate and baptize those who arrive in a dying state. And although they make haste they always find some dead.[2]

How glad we should have been to possess documents written in Claver's own hand, describing this arrival and reception. Father Alonso de Andrade, his first biographer, quotes in his life the résumé of a letter written in 1617 and addressed to his Provincial. Here are the extracts he transcribes only three years after the Saint's death.

Yesterday, writes Peter Claver on 30 May, there came to land a great ship laden with negroes from the Rivers. We went there laden with two baskets of oranges, lemons and tobacco. We entered their house which seemed like another Guinea, piles of them on all sides; we made our way through till we reached the sick of whom there were a great number lying on the ground, which, as it was damp and liable to flooding was

[1] J. Cassani, *op. cit.*, p. 105.   [2] Sandoval, *op. cit.*, Chap. XVII, p. 71.

levelled up with sharp-edged pieces of brick and tiles, and this was their bed, where they lay naked without a stitch of clothing. We threw off our cloaks and went to fetch planks from another store-room and we laid a floor there and carried the sick in our arms, pushing our way through the rest. We collected the sick in two circles, my companion taking over one and I the other.[1]

Unhappily this is the only document that shows every sign of complete authenticity. Peter Claver is in the full excercise of his apostolate—he had been a year at work—and already all the typical traits of his social method have appeared.

In the picture we are trying to evoke, let us listen again to Father Sandoval, who presents a lifelike picture of what happened when the cargo ships arrived at the port.

Concerning the manner of examining the negroes when they arrive at the ports in the cargo ships and other necessary procedure before the catechism is taught.

When the ship arrives and the negroes disembark we must first of all go to meet them at once so as to find out how many there are, what they are like and from what lands and ports they come; what diseases they suffer from; how many and which of them are sick, chiefly those dangerously ill, and the children about whom diligent enquiry must be made to learn which of them are not baptized, for even the mothers do not dare to make known the extreme necessity of their children when they are ill. As soon as one sees them they burst into tears, and when that happens, when the boy weeps during the instruction, put a jug to his mouth and he will fill one, two or even three jugs, as has happened to me hundreds of times.

We shall also find out the state of the sick, to what house they are taken to be cared for; how many there are and the diseases from which those who have remained in the ships because they could not disembark are suffering, or those who are outside the town so as not to infect the other healthy ones, and how many healthy ones have stayed to guard and care for these sick people, and those who entered the town coming from the ship, in how many houses they have been distributed and to what houses the negroes brought in by other private indivi-

[1] De Andrade, *Vida de San Pedro Claver*, p. 54.

duals have gone, so that all may be duly attended to; afterwards they may be examined by means of trusty interpreters who can speak Spanish, according to the languages they use.

From this enquiry various experiences of baptism will be discovered among these negroes, for if they come from the rivers of Guinea, almost all have been baptized for reasons we have already mentioned; either the water has been poured over them without any understanding on their part or it had not been done at all. If the negroes come from the Cape Verde Islands, there will be the same difficulty as for those from Guinea; if they come from Santo Tomé, the Ardas, Araraes, Carabalies, Lucumies, Minas and innumerable other tribes, we shall find a great variety, for some are well-informed and others know nothing.

If they are from Loanda, Angolas, Congos, etc., they are usually sufficiently instructed to be ready for baptism and their consent is asked before the water is poured on them.

Then those belonging to the different tribes are separated, the women on one side and the men on the other, and before all else the first thing to be done is to win their confidence, giving them some presents and making their master give them something, clothing them decently and bringing them some garment for this purpose even if it is old.

At other times jugs of fresh water will be handed round, a very important thing, as they have not been able to get even salt water and they are parched with thirst, chiefly the women and children—and this is something they appreciate and are grateful for. A thing which I would have hesitated to believe if someone had told it to me, has often happened to myself; having performed a baptism from a silver dish, on giving an order for the water to be poured away decently in a corner, to be asked not to pour it away, and when I was wondering what had become of that water, to have realized that as it fell from the head of those who were baptized into the dish they were drinking it up without leaving a drop.

So great is the thirst and necessity that these miserable people usually suffer. I must also relate something which astonished me even more than what I have said and that I have several times experienced and have even made a note of as a general rule for similar occasions, and it is this, not to be able to get any answer, whatever trouble I took, to questions about their baptism. I once asked one of them, noticing that his eyes wandered to a stand for water-jars that was there, if he wished to drink and when he said 'yes', I could not give him too much water. When he was satisfied, he straightened himself, cheered up and spoke and answered and was baptized, to the great solace of those present.

From this I drew a lesson which can be taught and which I use in the course of my instruction; and it is a great help in getting them to understand what is being taught them and it is this:

'Tell me, my child, do you not remember the great pleasure your body felt when it received that jug of water so nice and fresh and cool that you drank when you were parched with thirst?' They all answer that they do. 'Well, listen, just as your body was happy because of that water, there will be much more and greater happiness in your soul which you have there inside your flesh, when they wash your head with the water which I am telling you about and which is from God and heaven, to take away your sins and make you his child.'

These things said in this rough-and-ready way are what these people need and are of benefit to them. And so this way of doing them good is one of the principal means that can be used for this purpose.

And to make this instruction easier and to find out the truth about their baptism, they should be spoken to gently, giving them to understand that one loves them greatly; being as one is father, and priest of God, whom all men respect and reverence (by reason of the tonsure he wears like a crown and which should be shown to them, for they are much influenced by these external signs), he must speak to them, caress them and tell them many things about God, great things that they must believe, take to heart and listen to with great attention.

He will tell them that their master loves them very much and does what he says, and that he will ask him to treat them well, cherish them and care for them, that they may have a good master with whom they may live happily in captivity.

He might explain to them the great mercy of the Lord in bringing them to a Christian land, where it is better to be a captive than to live as a free man in their own country; for here, though the body suffers hardship in captivity, the soul rests in the liberty obtained through the water of holy baptism.

He must cheer them by telling them that they will live in these parts among many relatives and if they continue in the right way they will have a pleasant captivity, will be happy and well-clothed; tell them to cast aside all sadness and sorrow and to be cheerful, for in that way they will have good health and satisfaction in all things. At other times if the interpreter is a good linguist and intelligent he should be made to explain this.

It is also of supreme importance that these people should be questioned and prepared to receive the sacraments with great kindness, time and patience, putting up with the slowness of their replies and their variety, very far from the point which is to be cleared up. And when it is seen that they go wrong and are disturbed and shy, they should be given time to think about the question and to quieten down, and consider it quietly, for otherwise not realizing the seriousness of the affair, they are in a hurry to answer as easily as the first time; and let them be asked the questions again.

They must be made to understand that this is a matter in which the fate of their souls is concerned.[1]

Father Sandoval deals delicately with the question of raising them to accept the Faith.

They are easily attracted to the act of faith by this comparison: My children, you see how many things I have taught you, and how much trouble I have taken to make you Christians, tell me, do you not love me?' All then say they do and they show me a lot of little attentions to prove this love in gratitude for the kindness they have received.

Then they should be thanked for such a good answer and then they must be told: 'Well, children, if you love me and show it to me for this one kindness I have done you, what love must you have for God in return for the many and great benefits he has bestowed on you and the kindness he has shown you?'

On the manner of baptizing them, Father Sandoval continues:

When these adults have been prepared and instructed they should be told to wash themselves quietly in the usual way, put-

[1] Sandoval, *op. cit.*, Chap. VIII, p. 257.

ting their heads in two or more troughs or tubs of water which for this purpose will be placed ready at one side, which is very necessary so that the baptismal water may pass through their hair to touch the skin of their heads and so that they may feel more reverence for the water that is to be poured on them to make them Christians, warning them that this washing is not God's water but is only meant to clean them for it is right that they should come with all decency for such a great occasion.

When this is done they sit down again as they were before, and those who are to be baptized unconditionally go up in groups of ten, first the men and then the women, kneeling down with their hands folded with all possible devotion and quietness round a silver dish, or a medium-sized trough when there is not anything more suitable for the water to fall into, and the priest puts on his stole and again puts to each one in particular the same questions and short exhortations that we have mentioned, by means of interpreters, so that they may be willing to receive baptism and that they may have faith, hope and charity, and contrition or at least attrition for their sins.

When this is over and the priest convinced that they are prepared, he bestows on each of the ten a name which is common and easily pronounced, making them repeat it, so they do not forget it and they may remind one another in case any one of them forgets, telling them that they are to be called by that name and known from that time forward as Christians and sons of God, putting aside and forgetting the name they had in their own country, because it was the name of a Moor or Gentile and a devil's child.

The interpreter who acted for them must be given them as godmother or godfather, or some other Spanish-speaking negro or negress of their own tribe who may be present or one they may have chosen themselves, with admonitions as to their obligations. If it is a conditional baptism no godfather is required.

Then a pretty rosary must be put round the neck of each of them, with a metal medal as a pendant.

Each one must hold his lighted candle in his hand while the priest pours the water over his head and body (observing all possible decency and decorum) pronouncing at the same time the words of the form of baptism, the water falling into a dish of porcelain or silver held by the lay brother accompanying the priest, usually kneeling at his feet.

All this is intended to induce greater reverence and esteem in the new converts.

Once they are baptized and before they rise and mingle with the unbaptized they have a strong thread put round their necks to fall down on their chests so that they may be recognized as baptized. These having sat down to one side, another ten come up till in this order those who are to be unconditionally baptized are finished.

Once the baptism is over they all show such great happiness and outward pleasure that it seems as if it is the result of the internal grace they have received from the Holy Spirit. Then they go out to meet one another and embrace each other with great happiness and joy, telling one another the Christian name they have received and they even weep with happiness.

They are also admonished with all gravity and emphasis that if in this country or any other to which they may go in the course of time anyone should propose to baptize them again even if it be in a church they should say that they have already been baptized, saying that it was to become Christians and children of God and to go to Heaven, but warning them not for this reason should they omit to go to church wherever they may be to receive salt, and the anointment with holy oils and to have their godparents.

After all this they are told not to lose their medals that have been put round their necks, explaining to them the esteem in which they must hold them because they are their badges as Christians and children of God. The esteem with which these ignorant people regard them may be seen from this instance. The father who deals with them once met a negro without a medal round his neck and, thinking that he knew him and had given him one, he asked about it; the negro smiled as if to say 'The father will think that he has caught me in a piece of negligence'; he took out a little silk purse and opening it showed him ten beads like a rosary with which he commended himself to God as well as he could and to finish it off he had in it the medal that he (the father) had hung round his neck a year before, when he baptized him during a sickness . . .

This is the manner which they use in Cartagena for examining, catechizing and baptizing, and in this way more than 6,000 are baptized every year without anything untoward occurring.[1]

Father Sandoval's conclusion seems paradoxical but it is true.

The negroes are indeed really capable of receiving the Faith. A great sign of this intelligence is to see how often and with what tenderness and joy they repeat the sweet name of Jesus when they are being punished, when they are ill and most especially when they are about to die, which I have often heard without their knowing anything more of our language, and one of them in this predicament repeated several times in his own language: 'God created me, God carries me away, what can I do?'

You should see them after being baptized, the joy they feel, especially the women, how they congratulate one another, kissing each other and telling their friends who are already Christians the names they have been given, and renew their delight and laugh if by chance they were the same as the name the other already had, making friends with them and considering them as relatives because of the similarity of their names.

From this and many other things, two conclusions follow: one that these negroes are not brute beasts, as I have heard some say, for hereabouts they try to make out that they are incapable of being Christians, nor must they be reputed childish or defective mentally, because they are grown-up men and as such they should be given baptism, preceded by an act of will on their part and the other necessary acts, etc.[2]

One of the most serious difficulties in the work of penetrating into this world that came from Africa in chains was the problem of races and languages. The slaves came from twenty to forty different races, and though in fact there were group affinities, easily surmounted, yet there still remained from ten to fifteen quite different languages.

Father Peter Claver learned to speak Angolese, the commonest language.

It was necessary to use interpreters, and the missionaries saw

[1] Sandoval, *op. cit.*, Bk. III, chap. XII, p. 285.
[2] Sandoval, *op. cit.*, Bk. III, chap. II, p. 236.

this. At first Father Sandoval borrowed these assistants from their masters and kept a list of them according to their races, but collaboration was not easy. The owners were either unwilling to consent or made objections. The need to buy slave interpreters was obvious, though this might appear paradoxical: Peter Claver, defender of the slaves, himself a purchaser of slaves.

Difficulties arose even from his brethren in religion. He had to write to Father Viteleschi, the General, who approved his attitude; otherwise his apostolate would have been paralysed.

In 1628 the college had eight or nine slaves and the rector had orders from Rome forbidding him to sell, change or withdraw them without consulting Peter Claver. In 1642 there were as many as eighteen. These slaves were real leaders and directors, and gave such great assistance that Peter Claver came to consider them as his right-hand men, treated them as his equals, bestowed on them a tender affection, and they responded well, as can be seen in the reports of the Process. The following humble friends of the Saint are known to us as from the Cartagena Process, 1657–60:

Andrés Sacabuche from Angola, in Claver's service from 1624;

Francisco Yolofo, skilled in the Mandinga language, the *yolofo* and the *bourbe yolofo*, who was in the service of Father Peter Claver for twenty-four years;

Ignacio Aluanil (or Angola), who when ten years old passed into the Jesuit College, bought by the captain of a slave-ship on behalf of Claver in 1628, together with Alfonso Angola and Ignacio Sozo, eldest of the interpreters;

José Monzolo, who spoke Congolese and Monzol;

Manuel Viafara or Biafara, called the Moreno;

Domingo Folupo, Joaquín Halu and Diego Folupo.

The collaboration of these humble assistants was admirable. A woman slave belonging to Isabel de Urbina undertook the preparation of food for the lepers of San Lázaro. Another woman slave collected gifts for the sick and poor in the towns for thirty years. There were some miraculous events.

When a merchant captain was setting off on a voyage to one of the ports where these slaves are embarked one of the Fathers (Claver) came up to him and gave him a piece of gold which had been given him as alms, to buy such goods and merchandise as are obtained at Cacheo and bring him two negroes suitable to act as interpreters for their tribes.

At the time when he handed him the gold he told him to have the greatest faith in his prayers for the success of his voyage, since the salvation and cure of more souls than he had hairs on his head depended on it, because without such interpreters it was not possible to succeed in his work of catechizing and examination.

He was caught in a severe storm in which he lost all he possessed, escaping with his life and with the small amount of gold entrusted to him. When writing to Father Claver about the miraculous event he says:

'At the very moment when all others were sinking, both ships and men, I forgot everything else and only remembered the commission entrusted to me by your reverence which I tied up in a cloth and bound round me with my white trousers, the only garment I had left. Then I plunged into the sea trusting in this commission and the many souls that depended on it.

'It was a miracle that when the royal galleons offered no security, God or the said souls provided me with a large tortoise-shell which served me as a boat; I got into it and held tightly on to the sides. God brought me alive to land and with no possession but the white trousers and the cloth in which I had put the small piece of gold.'

After this disastrous storm he went to the rivers of Cacheo and brought to the father three well-spoken negro interpreters who helped him and still help him to win many souls for the Lord who saved him so unexpectedly when all the others were drowned.

Nothing could be done without the help of the interpreters. The methods of these great missionaries of three centuries ago put into practice a basic idea of our modern social apostolate. The conversion of like by like.

The initiator of this mission to the negroes, Father Sandoval, recognized this necessity, and his disciple, Peter Claver, carried his training to the point of perfection. On different occasions he appealed to the General for permission to have these indispensable assistants, even at times in face of criticism from some brothers in religion.

All that precedes is of little use if there are no interpreters in the language of the tribe to which the sick or healthy adult belongs who, through them, is to be instructed, baptized or confessed, and the difficulty consists in the fact that usually their owners have no interpreters or have no interest in finding them, and we are virtually incapable of learning all these languages, as they are so numerous—there being no common language and no one to teach us.

I maintain, then, that those who undertake such apostolic duties must try to find interpreters, spending, if necessary, whole days in doing so.

It will be a help in this difficulty, the greatest of all, to have for this ministry a notebook or alphabetical list of the tribes, languages and interpreters written down with their names, where they live, who are their owners, how many languages they understand well and how many they speak; and so when the Angola, the Carabalí, the Madinga and many others are required—for there are more than seventy, those that come from Angola, Santo Tomé, and the rivers of Guinea and other ports, it will be possible by this means to know where the interpreters can be found quickly and easily.[1]

Let us reconstruct Peter Claver's world by the light of the Process and the preceding information.

Father Claver's face was usually serious, solemn and worn, sadness marked the great wrinkles that crossed his brow and his deep-set eyes.

He lived in a dark room apart—'the worst of them all', according to an interpreter—which had one great advantage; it was near the entrance hall of the college and they could call him at any hour of the day or night and he could come out without disturbing the others' rest.

Any day whatever a messenger might arrive breathless: 'Father Claver, Father Claver, a negro slave-ship is coming in, its great sails can be seen already near Bocagrande,' and Father Claver,

[1] Sandoval, Bk. III, chap. II.

who never used to be present at the arrival of the magnificent fleets from Spain, would run to the great hall of the residence which looked out on the sea, his face flushed and red. He reiterated his promise to offer Masses and penances for the man who brought him the news, and quickly got his preparations going.

There ready to receive his orders were the slave interpreters, Andrés Sacabuche, and Ignacio Aluanil from Angola; Ignacio Sozo and Francisco Yolofo from the region of the great rivers of Guinea; Manuel Biafara, José Monzolo . . . These companions of his apostolate were the great love of his life, his 'right-hand'.

One of them, Francisco Yolofo, tells us: 'When there were any sick he carried them to his room, gave them bed-clothes from his bed and bought the most expensive medicines for them.'

Another indispensable person was Brother Nicolás González, his faithful and constant companion: for twenty-two years he stood by him and was his confidant, his brother and biographer, for his report in the Process runs to more than 180 pages.

Peter Claver's room had the austerity of an anchorite's cell, one rickety chair, a bed and a mat; it was also a kind of fantastic larder. There were baskets of oranges and lemons, cases of sweet-meats, barrels of spirits, tobacco and wine, some women's dresses of coarse bright-coloured material, and hanging from a nail beside his bed some terrible instruments of penance, hair-shirts and scourges.

On his less busy days Peter Claver used to go out with Sacabuche or Yolofo on a delicate errand. With saddle-bags over his shoulders he called at the aristocratic portals of the rich city of Cartagena begging for the help he needed for his poor slaves; fruit, sweet-meats, presents and clothes.

Peter Claver was not the cold harsh person we might imagine, embittered towards society, something like a communist with a grievance, as a recent socialist biographer has depicted him.

He needed money and gifts from those rich families of Carta-gena. Among many sordid characters, hardened by greed and cruelty, there were other wonderful people like Captain Villa-lobos, Francisco López and Francisco Núñez de Quero, a Knight of the Order of Calatrava who used to accompany him to the

ships, and that group of rich pious ladies who considered it an
honour to help him: Isabel de Urbina, Catalina Pimienta, María
Cárdenas . . . Captain Andrés de Banquezel and the treasurer
Pedro de Estrada and Juan de Torres, a familiar of the Holy Office.

Peter Claver had very good friends and patrons. His expenses
in alms were fabulous. Claver's social apostolate cannot be understood apart from this real collaboration of classes. This point has
been forgotten, and Claver has been envisaged solely from the
heroic point of view, the misunderstood healer of the slaves' sores.
He even won over the slave-trading captains. The following
extract is from a confidential report:

> But those who are most closely concerned with this work
> and admired it were the captains and owners of these slave-ships
> themselves, who have come to feel such esteem and veneration
> for the members of the Society and especially for this college
> as is shown by the great confidence they place in us, obeying
> us in everything we ask them with regard to these poor black
> men, their salvation and good treatment, and of their own
> accord bringing them to us when we need them as interpreters
> and at times giving us very liberal alms to buy and train those
> we consider suitable and of greater natural aptitude.
>
> And this in spite of the fact that at the beginning of this
> ministry and heavenly undertaking, for lack of experience and
> real understanding of our aims, they were the most antagonistic
> and difficult to persuade, and after the priests and ecclesiastic
> persons were the bitterest opponents; and they encouraged
> each other against us, who only desired to help them to fulfil
> their obligations and obtain the temporal and eternal health of
> so many thousands of slaves, the Lord permitting this to occur
> in order that its end might redound to his greater glory and
> service and to the reputation and credit of our holy institutes.

The port was near the Jesuit College. The caravan was on the
way—Brother González and Brothers Lomparte and Manuel
Rodríguez, lay brothers from the college, his usual associates, some
outstanding person from the city or some lady who assisted this
apostolate with fervour and admiration, the interpreters with their
loads of presents. Peter Claver used to repeat: 'The slave-ship has
arrived; the hook must be baited.'

Sometimes the slave-ship did not come into port at once; there were several requirements to be met, an examination of the goods, the state of the human cargo, the buyers. Peter Claver did not wait. At first he met with serious difficulties; the owners did not view this work favourably since it implied a reproach; neither had they any desire that the slaves should find someone to speak to them of love.

Claver, accompanied by some interpreters, approached the ship in a small boat. The moment was one to excite emotion. That human cargo, enslaved and fearful, face to face with a Saint.

The first thing that he did, as we read in the testimony of Brother González and Andrés Sacabuche in the Process, was to embrace and caress all the slaves he met.

He did not know all the African languages—more than thirty; he barely understood the language of Angola, and for this reason he anxiously sought the appropriate interpreter to put him in touch with them.

Angola? Guinea? Lucumíes? Yolofos? Araraes? There stood his guardian angels and among them the one nicknamed *Calepino*, the wonderful slave who knew eleven languages.

Suddenly he found his way into the midst of the negro slaves and through the interpreters he told them he had come as a companion to them all. He welcomed them to the land of the white men. It was necessary to get this idea over to them, for the slaves believed that they were brought to be killed and that oil would be extracted from their skins for the ships. Their faces showed their joy; they were beside themselves. He asked for the sick, specially for the children who had been born on the ship.

Hung on his left arm he always carried a leather bag and in it the *Rituale*, the candles, the holy oil, everything necessary to administer the sacraments. There on board the ship itself the grace of God descended on many of those unhappy members of an enslaved race. Peter Claver was their liberator.

Father Cassani makes this comment: 'Many were those who by this means, washing their black bodies in the water, were enabled to fly from those dungeons to heaven.'

Then followed the distribution of the presents through the interpreters. Fresh water before anything else; they stared and then rushed to the water jar. A witness tells us that 'a good glass of water or spirits' cured the most despondent of their lethargy.

Those unfortunate beings who issued from the dark holds of the ships bearing with them the stench of those surroundings, naked, like a herd of beasts, who had perhaps seen many of their companions die beside them, remembering a past that had been snatched from them, with fear of an uncertain future, must have felt extraordinary surprise at the sight of this image of charity in the person of a priest. There was at least one person to smile at them and love them.

One of them, José Monzolo, relates in the Process that when he arrived in the ship with other negroes, he was won over by Claver's exquisite charity and begged him to buy him and to do what he liked with him. He was to be one of his most faithful interpreters.

The slaves came in the holds of the ships and on the lower deck like a herd of animals, inferior in price to some of them, for a slave was bought in Africa for five *pesos*; naked, with no regard for hygiene, in lamentable promiscuity as far as health was concerned, the healthy with the sick. Epidemics raged, and a voyage was considered a good one in which a third of the human cargo did not perish.

The smell was terrible, and even the captain of a slave-ship remarked that no white man could have lasted a quarter of an hour in those conditions.

There was only a short distance from the ship to the slave-sheds. These were situated in Cartagena particularly in the streets of Santa Clara and Santo Domingo—some twenty-four in all, specially assigned to this purpose; they were rectangular buildings with bare walls, a single door and a window placed high up.

The ships' captains owned most of them. There the slaves were thrown until the time should come for selling them, which was sometimes long delayed.

In this case they hired the slaves out to the government, and the ramparts and forts of Cartagena know the sweat of many slaves.

This was the favourite spot for Claver in the days following the arrival of the galleon.

The slave-interpreter, Ignacio Angola, words his testimony thus: 'As soon as Father Claver knew there was a ship in the port, he was greatly delighted. He at once ordered the old interpreters to make enquiries and to greet them and bid them welcome in his name. Joaquín Halu, Francisco Yolofo, Ventura Cocoli, Domingo Folupo, etc . . .'

Before anything else they had to enquire if there were any sick or newly born. Then he asked permission of the ship's captain and spoke to the owner of the slaves.

The father usually went to the boats at the wharves called the *Carnicerías* or *Compustistería* carrying bananas, cakes and other sweet things to give them, especially to the sick, and the interpreters were ready on the wharf to carry the injured in carts to the sheds.

Once the crowds of negroes had disembarked he used to go to their lodgings, and there he entered, taking off his cloak. But beforehand he went with his interpreters to the *Plaza de la Hierba*, to the market where he bought lemons, bananas, sweet potatoes and many other fruits of these parts and he was specially careful that they should be fruit that grew also in the homeland of the negroes, and he also got tobacco.

He went from one to another, enquiring, baptizing the dying children and hearing confessions by means of an interpreter; he always carried with him the holy oils in a silver vessel in a bag hanging from his left arm under his cloak . . . in his right hand he carried surplice and stole.

He erected an altar, and as the slaves sweated freely from heat, anxiety and sickness, he used to wipe their faces with his own handkerchief, and wiped his own with the bottom of his cloak. The cloak had to be washed over and over again.

To these valuable details Captain Vicente Villalobos, who knew the father for fourteen years, adds others: 'I saw him and heard him speak in the language of Angola'; and referring to the compounds he says: 'I found a group of slaves near San Diego and

Santa Clara and I went into one of these places. Father Claver was sitting on the ground in a dark corner and the interpreters were seated on chairs.'

'Sometimes,' another slave, Ignacio Sozo, goes on, 'this catechizing went on for three or four hours at a time.'

The memory that these scenes must have left in the Saint's mind was so deep that years afterwards when he was old and sick and his superiors did not allow him to go to the ships, he used to embrace his interpreters to infect them with his ardour and ordered them to go in his name. He recommended them to take particular care of the sick.

One day he could not stand it any longer. Some Araraes—negroes well known for their roughness—were arriving, and the old man, leaning on his interpreters, went as far as the port and received his beloved negroes.

That was a few days before his death. The witnesses tell us that the slaves who lived in Cartagena at once informed those arrivals who belonged to their tribes of the meaning to them of Peter Claver: their friend, the Saint.

He was a popular figure in the town; the children came out to the windows and balconies to see 'the Saint' go by.

He was of medium height; his expression was usually sad, his head bent down, he wore an old thread-bare cassock, a loose (unbuttoned) cloak—the miraculous cloak of Peter Claver—and in his hand he carried a staff surmounted by a cross.

On the solemn days following the arrival of the slave-ships, the interpreters carried a great quantity of provisions, scented water and spirits; also sweetmeats, fruit and tobacco.

Claver was very human in his holiness; two-thirds of the accusations made against him are concerned with this generosity to others.

On this point we must avoid exaggeration. The best description is given by the witnesses. Their words have the flavour of things actually seen and heard. They are living reports with the fragrance of three centuries. Brother Manuel Rodríguez says:

I often accompanied him to the houses where the negroes went, especially that of Captain Granzo near the Convent of

San Agustín; the house of Gundisalvo Arias de Aguilar near the *Plaza de los Gaguyes*; the house of Rafael Gómez, and as soon as he entered the house where the negroes were, he asked first for the sick; he brought a small table to the bed or frequently, for want of a table, he spread his cloak on the ground and laid the unfortunate sick man on it, and I noticed that the cloak, though particularly old and in contact with every kind of misery, had no bad smell.

As soon as he had made him comfortable with his own hands, he gave him the presents he had brought, some sponge-cakes, dipped in red wine, sweetmeats, preserves . . .

Only after that came the spiritual part of the treatment; he then set up an altar on a raised place where they could all see it, and on it he placed a picture of Christ nailed to a cross painted on cloth, with a basin at his feet into which all the blood fell that flowed from his wounds, and beside the basin stood a priest wearing a stole and cape who was baptizing with this blood several negroes who looked very beautiful after being baptized and those who were not baptized looked very ugly.

Some demons were standing nearby with their mouths open as if they would like to swallow them, and through the interpreters he (Father Claver) told them that those who were not baptized would continue to be ugly.

Then he told them that they must forget all the rites and superstitions of their forebears and tribes and he instructed them in the mysteries of the Faith with frequent repetitions.

If anyone were dangerously ill, he baptized him at once and those who were not in that state he instructed for many days, teaching them the catechism and prayers, and afterwards he made them say the act of contrition very fervently; and then when he was going to baptize them he put on the stole which was so old it had completely lost its original colour; for baptism he used a jug and a basin of very fine china, and the interpreters or others present acted as godparents; then he put the medals round their necks.

His most assiduous interpreter, Andrés Sacabuche from Angola, declared forty-five years later:

The first thing he taught them through me or other interpreters was to make the sign of the cross perfectly with the right hand. On that alone an hour was spent, because he went the rounds from one to another to see if they did it in the right way, forming a cross. Sometimes there were more than 300 or 400 of them and he made them all raise their right hands and then he showed them a perfect cross and taught them how to make it. To the one who learned it best of them all he gave a present of tobacco, and to the one who was slow about it he gave a little tap on the head with the stem of the crucifix he held in his hand and ordered the others to give him this penance. Then he taught them the *Our Father*, the *Hail Mary* and the *I Believe* and the mystery of the Holy Trinity, God the Father, God the Son and God the Holy Ghost, that although they were three persons, they were only one God, and to explain this better to them, he used to make a number of folds in a handkerchief and he showed it to them, and when they had looked at the folds he undid them and told them that it was only one handkerchief; and in this way the negroes believed easily in the mystery.

He also taught them how of the three persons of the Trinity, the second person, the Son, had become man as a remedy for the original sin with which all are born. Then he explained the incarnation and took out a book he had in which all the life of Christ was shown in pictures and he showed them one of the blessed Virgin with her most holy Son in her arms and then he explained the whole life of Christ until his death and resurrection, showing them the pictures as he explained it to them.

Then he spoke of the immortality of the soul, of hell and heaven, and showed them pictures particularly of hell, a soul in pain and also a soul in glory.

Then after the instruction he took from his bosom a wooden crucifix about a span in length that he always carried with him. Raising it up so that all might see it, he told them with great fervour of spirit and voice that the Lord whose feet and hands were nailed to the cross was the Son of God who, to redeem the human race, had become man and died an ignominious death, paying himself the penalties we all deserved. Saying that we ought all to offer baptism; and asking pardon for the sins of their past heathen life, especially for idolatry, lust and drunkenness, he suddenly made them all—through the interpreters—recite aloud the following words:

'Lord Jesus Christ, Son of God, thou art my Father. I am sorry for having offended thee. I love thee very much, I love thee very much,' repeating it many times over and striking their breasts at the same time.

Once this was done Father Claver raised his eyes to heaven, clasping his hands and remained for a time rapt in prayer as if thanking God who had used him as his instrument.

The place where the catechizing took place in those sheds was frequently the yard of the house. The method was always the same as described by the witnesses; visiting the sick and putting up an altar with a large crucifix.

Peter Claver was a great teacher and saw clearly that those untaught minds could not comprehend abstract ideas without the help of pictures.

His method of unfolding ideas was that indicated by the Archbishop of Seville and developed so successfully by Father Sandoval.

The sessions lasted sometimes from four to six hours, and Father Miguel de Ugarte, a Franciscan and a great friend of the Saint, tells of the profound impression made on him when he saw Claver opening the book of pictures of Christ's life and giving his wonderful explanation. The ceremony of baptism was the culminating point.

The way he was able to devote himself so whole-heartedly to individual preparation is astonishing. In these days there have been many hasty criticisms directed against the Saint, asserting that his work could have had only a superficial effect and that it was effaced in a short time; a like accusation was made against St Francis Xavier.

The reality was very different. It may be said that if Claver's method of procedure had been continued, the negro would have been incorporated in a living and magnificent form of Christianity. But this apostolate was difficult to carry on and necessitated great sacrifices.

He interrogated each one separately before baptism and according to the state of his knowledge proceeded with the sacrament or deferred it till later. The method of baptizing was as follows:

He [Claver] put on a rochet or surplice which he always carried on his arm. He wore a special white stole for baptism, although he had another old one in which he administered extreme unction.

He divided them into groups of ten and to each of these groups he gave the name of a saint, assigning godfathers to each one, usually the interpreters.

At the foot of the altar he used to place an earthenware half broken font—which he kept for this purpose in his room—filled with holy water, and if it were not already blessed he at least made the sign of the cross with the bronze crucifix[1] over the water.

He approached them with the godfather. He told them to kneel down and then he said that the water was holy and if they received it as they should their souls would be made as clear and pure as the sun in splendour and purity.

He asked three times in a loud voice if they wished to be Christians and when they answered 'yes' he baptized them in two forms, the ordinary and the common, and if there were any doubt about it he said: 'If you are not baptized, I baptize you' etc.

When that was finished he used to put on them a leaden medal on a string or something similar. The medal showed Jesus carved on one side and Mary on the other.

And Father Ugarte adds: 'He was so exact in ecclesiastical ceremonies and so anxious that they should be performed with all dignity and purity, not only with regard to their souls but also their bodies, that he ordered them to wash their heads thoroughly and did not permit them to be baptized unless their heads were really clean.

'When it was over he embraced them all and gave them, through the interpreters, some moral advice. Then he distributed gifts to them.'

Claver followed up those he baptized. He paid particular attention to those who were sent to Portobello or Peru, and before they embarked he himself went through the market begging alms from the stallholders; he loaded a large basket on his back and

---

[1] The cross was of wood, the figure of bronze.—*Trans.*

went with it to the ship, where he had talks with the captains about the slaves who were about to leave. These captains were to bring him later a detailed report about where they were and how they had been placed.

On Sundays he went through the streets to fetch them to Mass and confession, and we see that it was no use the upper-class white people complaining. He was before everything else the missionary of the poor and oppressed, the rest would easily find a confessor.

The sick were his favourites and he had a veritable catalogue of the hospitals and individual huts according to their needs.

There is general agreement as to the main lines of Claver's catechetical methods. More than a hundred witnesses of every social class declared under oath in the Process the profound impression he left on them. In the report of Brother Nicolás González there is one very interesting detail. It is the importance given by Father Peter Claver to the pictorial element and graphic appeal to the senses. This is his description of the final ceremony of baptism.

When the instruction was ended, he took from his bosom a bronze crucifix which he carried with him and raised it, explaining with fervour the power of redemption. He made them ask God for pardon, and he himself beat his breast with his left hand and the negroes did the same saying: 'Jesus Christ, Son of God, thou art my Father and my Mother whom I love with great affection, I am grieved in my soul for having offended thee,' and he repeated over and over again: 'Lord, I have great love for thee, great, great ...' beating his breast and weeping.

And then he said that, in the same way as the serpent changes its skin, they must change their lives and habits, forsaking paganism and its vices so as to lose all remembrance of them, and as he said these words Father Claver, replacing the crucifix in his bosom, pinched his skin from forehead to waist with his hands as if he were tearing at his skin to pull it off, and the negroes did the same, and immediately afterwards he did the same with his arms and other parts of his body, the others imitating him with such fervour that it seemed as if they were really pulling off the skin and putting on a covering of faith. This was the new man.

The work of Peter Claver did not end here in this first stage. He baptized, as he himself stated, more than 300,000 slaves.

This labour was not carried out superficially. He followed the steps of all those recently converted to the Faith.

He exercised his zeal in three main fields: In the world of physical suffering—hospitals; in the world of moral suffering—confession; in the world of ordinary life in street and market-place—by preaching.

CHAPTER III

FACING THE WORLD OF PAIN

THIS chapter too must begin with a realistic description by a witness who 'saw and whose eyes wept'. Few things make such an impression as seeing those in physical pain abandoned. St Peter Claver's initiation into this apostolate took place at the side of Father Sandoval. Claver was thirty-six years old: maturity's first encounters with reality left in his face that melancholy which stamped it all his life.

One day he was able to go with his master to one of those big barracks, perhaps the one he describes to us with a flavour of Dante, thus:

In some of the buildings of these owners of slave-hulks are several large rooms, with benches all around, where with the sexes divided, these people are locked up at night to sleep. They may be seen the following morning exactly as those inhuman creatures probably disposed them.

Such places, then, were kept for those beyond relief. There they were thrown, and in the midst of wretchedness and misery they languish, and there finally eaten by flies they died, some on the benches, others under them. I remember that once I saw amongst many living two already dead. They were stark naked on the bare ground, as if they were animals. Lying on their backs, their mouths open and full of flies, their arms folded as if symbolizing the cross of eternal damnation that was their soul's lot for having died without the holy sacrament of baptism, for not having summoned someone to administer it. If I was amazed to see them thus die in such abandon I was even more amazed by the way in which all of them were shrouded: the most worn-out mat was sought, they were wrapped in it and their bodies flung into a corner until they were buried, the latter now being done as a result of some slight reform. Before this they were left naked in the *patios*, in the yards, in the corners where their final agony had overtaken them, preventing their reaching any place of refuge. Once I found a corpse behind the door of the house, a loathsome spot, and another flung into the middle of the street awaiting burial in the shroud his mother had given him . . . All who passed were amazed and horrified.

If the healthy do not fall sick in this place, there is some alleviation of life while they are there, because they are fattened so that they may be sold more profitably. But since the poor wretches have suffered so much, nothing prevents many falling ill on arrival; indeed the food itself—for the smallest quantity is abundance after so long a fast—assists the disease, which very soon surges through the whole shed as if it were the plague so that the masters if poor have an excellent exercise for their patience, because they usually tend them. If they are rich, or the negroes are *de encomienda* (under individual Spanish patronage), their great brutality is displayed when they hand them over to evil or cruel overseers because of pressure of business. As a result the house and shed in a few days become a hospital full of the sick when the universe is peopled with corpses, some dying from severe pains in the side, some from high fevers, others from smallpox, typhoid, or measles, or a sickness they call scurvy which is incurable. It causes the body to swell and the gums to rot, so that the victims die suddenly. This sickness they catch partly in the island of Loanda from which the disease takes its name, and partly from bad diet. The sight of so many ill people arouses great sorrow and pity, so lacking in assistance they are, in care or kindness from their masters, who usually leave them naked and unprotected, without any shelter. There they lie and there they normally die without anyone caring for their bodies or their souls. One is left seriously wondering whether their sad abandonment or their sickness chiefly causes their deaths. What my eyes saw and lamented is clear proof of what I say. If I told all I should never finish, but I cannot end this subject without relating a thing which horrified me: On one occasion I was preparing one of these poor negroes so that he might die in the Lord, and on going to his side I found that he had already died in the middle of a *patio* where usually there were many people. He was naked, stretched out face downwards on the ground, covered with flies making as if to eat him, and there he was left, causing no more comment than if he were a

dog. I beseeched and begged the man responsible to cover the
body and arrange it with the decency due to his faith. What he
did was to wrench away half a mat from a poor wretch dying
close by and cover the corpse with it, leaving the other man
uncovered. Such then are the slave-sheds, such the need of these
poor negroes.[1]

Before some misery heroic souls react heroically to reveal the
phenomenon of the apparent madness of great love. Perhaps this
chapter of the life of Peter Claver is the one which most wounds
our modern sensibility. The early biographers conceal nothing.
They called things by their names. Modern writing has tried to
soften this life-story a little by distorting certain facts. It cannot be
denied that Peter Claver's behaviour in the face of those men
deprived of everything reaches superhuman levels. We have detailed this elsewhere. Some psychological realities cannot be understood without reconstructing the period and the environment.
Those were times of extremes in both love and hate, in both
cruelty and goodness, in the subhuman and the superhuman.

Let us enter a slave-shed or a slave-hospital in Cartagena between
1616 and 1654, into one of those reed huts near the harbour, half
flooded with water, open to the sky, or to the San Sebastián
Hospital in the centre of the city, stiflingly hot, or out through
the Half-Moon Gate and into the large house of San Lázaro, where
those who have lost all hope live and perish in hovels.

Some of the pages which follow may be attacked. I have heard
advice not to describe these dreadful events against which our
sensibility reacts so violently. Biographies are not supposed to
shock the reader. Readers of this type should avoid these pages
of unaccustomed realism.

The lives of the saints must be dealt with factually, both the calm
roseate aspects and the tragic aspects. Without considering the
heroic quality of his love and even his interior solitude, the figure
of St Peter Claver cannot be understood. He was the complete
man of moral power: superficially calm and controlled, basically
a volcano. He cannot be explained away through any abnormality
for he enjoyed health so robust and perfect that he was able to be

[1] Sandoval, *op. cit.*, Chap. XVIII, p. 71.

FACING THE WORLD OF PAIN 135

spendthrift with it. Confident in his faith, he was able to win the highest intellectual title awarded by the Jesuits. Claver united with an indomitable will to total surrender to his neighbour a divine love capable of superhuman follies. Apart from the imitation of the Passion of Christ there is no human explanation of his heroic deeds, apart from that bronze Christ hanging upon his bare breast no means of penetrating that labyrinth of violence. Peter Claver felt the force of his voluntary relationship of slavery to his sorrowing brother because first he had submitted in slavery to his God.

In the lives of saints there is a supreme moment when heroism bursts forth like a powder flash which lights up a section of their path. In the life of Claver heroism is the everyday normal thing. For this reason his life would be incredible if it were not told by the terrified witnesses themselves.

In these pages of a life not to be falsified we sense the awe of the superhuman, marvel at the heroic, the impetuous madness of sanctity. God raises up his saints at the moment and for the moment at which they live. In those days of roughness, of savage passions, of blood and new worlds, the personality of a saint like Claver did not arouse banal sentimental reactions. He was more of a conqueror belonging to the heroic legion of the apostles of Christ.

Before the brutal slave-owner, who attacked human beings in the hold of his ships and sold them like merchandise, without respect for human dignity, God raised up heroes of the stature of Peter Claver, who glorified in being the willing slave of those poor wretches forced into slavery and kissed their wounds until even the unfortunates themselves cried, 'Enough, Father, enough.'

That world was not ours; we cannot judge it by our sentimental standards or by our perhaps over-refined repugnances.

The picture we shall draw of Claver, sometimes in great detail, is also the firmest outline of his heroic life.

One fact has to be taken into account. Father Alonso de Sandoval in his book was not afraid to trace a spirited picture of this world of slavery with its physical and moral misery. And this book was his disciple Claver's *vade mecum*. The pages which we reproduce are the best introduction and background to all the achievements of the Saint. In this rough and cruel setting he was to move, and these were the realities which were to try his soul.

It would have been impossible to carry the light of Christ to this world with a finicky conception of sanctity. To penetrate into those wretched lives demanded all the temper of his will of steel, his terrifying power to overcome all revulsion.

Without the realism of those passages of testimony by one who lived them, we could not understand the blessed madness with which Claver confronted the sorrows of his negro slaves.

Nevertheless, there is no need to exaggerate certain aspects. To speak of the Saint and his fear, some biographers have over-emphasized physical factors of the climate, of the discomforts of Cartagena. According to these accounts the town must have been a miniature Caribbean inferno. The reality was different. Evidently then more than now, heat and dampness and nearby woods caused this scorching heat, almost unbearable at certain times and seasons, and epidemics reached there as elsewhere. But living conditions could not have been so unbearable, since the conquerors chose the town for their residence and the society growing up there was one of the most aristocratic in America.

Wealth alone could not explain this blooming of great families, or the rapid growth of the town, besieged on the other hand by enemies in the form of buccaneers and pirates. Epidemics were the great scourge of the sixteenth and seventeenth centuries. Cartagena, in its tropical situation, meeting-place of all races, went through terrible periods of plague. In only ten years four were registered: in 1633–4, 1636–7, 1639–41 and the most terrible of all in 1651.

Light is thrown on this calamity by some eye-witness accounts. Father Andrade gives this description, according to contemporary letters:

At this very time there arrived at the base of Cartagena a fleet of ships laden with more than 10,000 negroes, most of them sick. Added to the Spanish and English army of Santa Catalina, these doubled the population of the city so that there was no more room in the houses and people went to the country and the sea, living either on board ship or in the desert, at the mercy of the elements. The multitude consumed all provisions so that many died of starvation or counted themselves lucky if they could get some maize or bran bread. With the famine, ill-treatment and lowering of morale, a violent plague broke out beginning with the foreigners, spread to the natives and raged until there was no house or family untouched by the pestilent infection. The hospitals took 500 persons, all the houses of the city down to the very ships were turned into hospitals, so great was the need. Negroes, being forgotten and neglected, suffered most of all; they were full of ulcers and worms, without bed or lodging, and the pestilential smell they gave off was so violent that it went to the heads and deprived of his senses anybody who went near them. A monk tried to go in and, approaching only as far as their door, he collapsed in the infected air with such dysentery and nausea that for two days he did not completely recover consciousness. Another priest went to give the sacraments to a negro and the stench was so nauseating that it turned his stomach and for two days he could not swallow a mouthful, his head swam and he could not carry on his work. This contagion lasted for more than three months and great numbers of persons of all classes and conditions died.[1]

Father Sandoval for his part adds:

A ship arrived from Cape Verde, laden with negroes smitten with smallpox, measles and spotted fever; the authorities did not allow them to enter the city as a measure of wise policy, which added to the labour of those who had to help them but was better appreciated by the interpreters who did not want to go so far or mix with the plague-stricken.

Even so, charity was found in some of them who followed me. I found many of the negroes very sick, swollen as an effect of the plague and apparently the most dangerous; I was inclined to give them up and to try to instruct in the faith and baptize three other negroes who came out of the cabins, each of them from a different race and caste. Next day it was clear I had been right, for when I came back to visit the new Christians and to catechize the others, I found two of the baptized negroes already dead and the third died while I was there. I could tell

[1] Andrade, *op. cit.*, p. 63.

of many similar cases as they occur continually with each daily arrival of the hulks of ships laden with dangerously ill negroes.

A curious contemporary document reveals the anguish and the piety of the inhabitants of Cartagena. It dates from the very days of St Peter Claver, and it was just during those epidemics that he fell ill for the last time. The sanctuary of *la Popa* was not only the mountain dominating the great harbour but, above all, the holy place towards which all people arriving at the port from twenty miles around turned their eyes.

The city of Cartagena at the end of 1651 was attacked by such a violent plague that the number of the infected was almost as great as the number who died in the streets and the squares, even in the churches. Many fell suddenly and died as if they had been struck by a thunderbolt.

Grief and consternation prevailed everywhere; a sepulchral silence made the town like a cemetery. The inhabitants of Cartagena had a great devotion to the Virgin of la Popa and on this occasion they did not forget to implore her protection. It had been decided that the image would be carried in solemn procession from the top of the mountain, where she had a throne in the Jesuit chapel, to the town where she would be placed over a rich and majestic altar to be their consolation and hope. This was done with the consent of the Jesuits, most of whom were engaged in caring for the plague-stricken. The image of our Lady was thus carried down to the town in a well-organized and beautiful procession. The Cartagenians knelt down at the feet of the statue and implored the Virgin with tears and supplications to deliver them from the terrible plague and to purify the air impregnated with the poison which was killing them. The heavenly Lady heard their entreaties and as a merciful mother, full of compassion and love for the prayers her afflicted children had addressed to her, she caused the plague to slip away and stopped the affliction and anguish of the inhabitants of that town.

Let us re-create in the light of the records something of this heroic world facing physical suffering.

The first important document to be considered here is the

internal report of the Jesuits relating to the time that Claver lived in their house; it gives, without even mentioning the Saint, with impersonal objectivity, an impressive picture of the community.

The *Annual Letters* included in the report sent to Rome the following passage:

> The news and current reports of the copious sweat and pestilential smell which issue from the bodies and the pestilent places where these miserable dark people stayed, having almost lost their spirits, excited the curiosity of another father who wanted to accompany the priest who usually takes care of them and catechizes them, because he wanted to be an eyewitness and not a hearer only. He went up only as far as the door of the room and ward of the sick negroes and on seeing those ulcered bodies, even from a distance, being made a source of putrefaction, the food of flies and worms, and seeing that in order to prepare them for baptism and confession this companion had to get as near them as to the perfectly healthy Spaniards full of amber and soothing fragrances, he became so overcome and beside himself that with the addition of the unpleasant odours spread out and penetrating as far as the *patios*, he could not come round from a distressing swoon accompanied by nausea, nor could he bring himself to look at them again, being content from then on to admire the strength that God communicates to his workmen, and to preach everywhere these glorious works carried by holy obedience post-haste to Spain, Rome and Italy. The priest with whom he had gone to the martyrdom and holy exercise went out at eleven in the morning. He had gone there at six and when he was about to reach home and rest was called to assist another patient. He went straightway and found the man devoured by carnivorous flies that had been greedy for his flesh and he left helpless as a dog with nobody to take them off. The father picked up his biretta and using it as a fan kept them off while he confessed him with great effort and discomfort. When the confession was over, and to prevent him from dying without the *viaticum*, he set off to find the priest, who was about to begin his meal, and it was a day of fast; he begged him first to attend to the spiritual need of that poor negro and took him to the church and thence to the house of the sick man. The good priest's stomach was so turned just by the smell that for two days he could eat nothing

and begged the father not to call him again if he didn't want him to become gravely ill and die because of a negro.

The same thing happened to the fathers when they called other priests, who complained of being martyrized by the fathers of the Society wanting to take away their lives among plague-stricken untouchables. The Father Provincial ordered them thenceforward to take with them everything necessary for the last sacraments, the need being so extreme. This was agreed to by the priests with approval, gratitude and good-will, resulting in great benefit for souls, since innumerable [negroes] died without this sacrament for lack of ministers who would despise their temporal lives to secure eternal life. Thus one day there were only two priests to administer extreme unction to fifteen people from houses whose sick slaves had spread the contagion. On another occasion, there came on a vessel for negroes a woman suffering from a carbuncle on her cheek and with a deformed open mouth; she breathed through it as though it were a chimney, a difficult breathing like thick smoke, with such a pestilent smell that a big room had been reserved for her alone so that she should not infect everybody else. The father hastened to visit her, carrying a quantity of pink vinegar for her corporal health, and further her spiritual cure by instruction and preparing her to assure it by receiving baptism. He came out of this work of such heroic charity having caught the infection which drove him to bed, where he continually remembered how often the other father doing this work, the first who had charge of this heavenly conquest, used to tell him that when he noticed the vessel with negroes was coming into port he suddenly had a cold and mortal sweat remembering the inexplicable weariness and unspeakable effort which had to be endured to hasten the preliminaries that many years of experience and practice had not made easy. It fell to the same father's lot to attend to the aforementioned sick woman and then he straightway fell seriously ill and in danger of death. Nevertheless she was not neglected by the others, not only on this occasion caring for the salvation of this poor negress, but on countless others during the long time there raged an epidemic of smallpox and measles that despatched a great many of these souls to heaven since hardly a ship arrived which was not infected. There were more then twenty-four houses of *arma-*

zones where some negroes went in and others came out, all in great need of mortification, zeal and charity from our people, since their masters could not help them, while their priests either dared not or were in any case too few to deal with such a host of primitive illnesses. Therefore the fathers and the workers had their tasks allocated in their houses according to the day of the week, confessing on each day twenty to thirty of those most in need of it, administering extreme unction to those most likely to die, instructing the most ignorant and baptizing those already instructed and prepared. Marriages and baptisms were reaffirmed and different signs were put on everybody to avoid confusion. The sacraments were administered to them in cases of necessity, not forgetting the bodies when attending to the souls, but seeking among the merciful some gifts and medicines that they often applied with their own hands. Usually visited by these poor negroes, the hospital called San Lázaro is no less full of poverty and unhappiness than of poor and extremely unhappy people. Their miseries are so many and the lack of the most necessary things so acute—as well as of spiritual things— this is why our men are always busy finding presents and alms for the relief and sustenance of these poor people—though more conveniently after Lent, when they go from *estancia* to *estancia* in the neighbourhood. There they prepare the proprietors to fulfil their obligations to the Church which would not have been done for years without this assiduity and care. They are offered such alms as corn, bananas, rice, honey and plenty of *tamarains*, very useful for their illness, and so many other things they need, which cause considerable edification and profuse gratitude.

This year their house was tumbling down and nobody dared to repair it. The *father who did most to help them* reported this trouble to the rector, who gave orders for a brother of the community with all his negroes and workmen to go and repair it at once, spending all the time necessary to put it in order. In the same year the said father had given out to them twenty-five suits of clothing, fourteen awnings or poor tents and canopies for their beds to protect them from the mosquitoes and shocks from the indecencies that so often appear among invalids suffering from ulcers especially when they are so poor.[1]

[1] Hazañero, *op. cit.*, pp. 124–34.

Two facts stand out here: the great zeal of the Jesuits from the college and the particular devotion of one father, who was none other than Peter Claver.

In the light of these reports we can place his apostolate.

First to speak is his usual companion, Brother Nicolás González. In 1633 and 1634 Cartagena was afflicted with a terrible epidemic of smallpox: many died. Sick people were seen in the streets, for the hospitals could not hold so many. Peter Claver used no antiseptic, even against contagious diseases. He entered the houses or hospitals with a bright and happy face as though he were coming into a fragrant garden, saying he was comforted by the smell.

Doña María de la Maza was the widow of Captain Francisco Zevallos. She had a black slave infected with smallpox at the end of 1633. Notice was given to the Jesuit College, sending for Peter Claver. 'I went with him,' said Brother Nicolás, 'the sick woman was in a dark room, it was terribly hot and the smell was unbearable. My stomach was upset and I fell on the floor.' The pestilent smell was terrible. When the door opened the brother was fainting. Father Claver, pretending to feel nothing, said to him: 'Brother, you had better withdraw.' He knelt down before the sick woman and gave her the crucifix to kiss. 'Cheer up,' he said, 'our Lord wants to heal you.' Then gently touching her bony hands: 'Wake up, don't sleep, I want to comfort you, cheer you up, help you as much as possible.' She came round, he confessed her and administered extreme unction, at the same time wiping her with eau-de-cologne. He himself made her eat and healed her sores.

Brother Nicolás was not alone: another Jesuit, Brother Lomparte, testifies that one day he was unable to withstand the atmosphere in one of the barracks in the district of San Diego which belonged to Captain Francisco de Xenes.[1]

The sick woman was lying on some sacks. The smallpox had attacked her whole body except her eyes. Father Claver knelt down beside her, took out from his bosom the wooden Christ he always carried with him, took off his cloak and sitting on the floor heard her confession, gave her extreme unction. Then seeing that

[1] Process, summary No. 16, and Hazañero, *op. cit.*

the poor slave was complaining of the coarseness of the sacks on which she lay, helped by Ignacio Angola, his interpreter, he lifted the patient, put her with his own hands on to his cloak, applied some scent to her, tidied her bed and then put her back in her place. The black slave was soothed. The father went out after giving her the blessing. At the door he said to Ignacio, his companion, 'Don't say a word about this.' Ignacio did not keep the secret and this was one of the cases used in the Process against the Saint. Was it not contrary to religious modesty? The promoter of the faith was answered: 'Love and do what you will.'

Calls came night and day from Cartagena. Captain Francisco Caballero lived in the main street, near the sea. It was a roomy house with a yard at the back. A troop of black slaves had arrived at this house. A murmur of pain greeted the father who arrived for his usual visit. A lean and wasted man, hardly skin and bone, and ulcerous, lay on the ground in the *patio* of the house. The sun was blazing. The apostle drew near; the man moaned with pain. Out of the small knapsack on his left arm the father took some biscuits and brought them to the man's mouth. Arrived only the day before and having seen nothing but cruelty, he raised his eyes in amazement, to see somebody smiling at him. Father Claver, seeing his misery, ran to the kitchen, fetched some live coals and put perfume on them: it was one of the things he always did first.

Domestic examples continue, concrete, true examples cited by eye-witnesses. They are not legends. They are fragments of a life described both by the simple and the great. The college barber, Antonio Moreno de Miranda, describes him calling on patients, 'who didn't want to eat because they felt ill and wished to die. He then approached them, embraced and caressed them, and made them eat; for these he had in his knapsack some special pastries made by an ardent helper, a black slave who served Isabel de Urbina, the negress Margarita of Cape Verde.'

'We do not know whether the history of the Church contains any such prodigies of corporal mercy as are told of this doughty Saint', judges the great historian Father Antonio Astrain. In Claver's pocket was a small notebook. There he had a list of patients whom he visited regularly and constantly. In the city precincts, outside the walls and near the sea, in a place called the Garden of Larate after the family of Alfonso del Portillo, there was a palm-tree hut, open and half-ruined as a result of the strong sea-winds. Claver left home, sack on shoulder, went through the town's main gate close to the dock; nobody had warned him. An old negro was there, lying on the floor, abandoned by all. It was raining that day and muddy soil surrounded the hut; Claver had already been visiting him for fourteen years, taking fruit, tobacco and clothes. That day was to be the last. On going in he saw the poor wretch with his eyes burning. He confessed him and gave him extreme unction. As soon as this was done the negro died. Nobody had warned Claver except his interior voice. This happened frequently.

Here we meet the supernatural, as we shall see later. These are no gilded inventions. God, as in the time of the Apostles, was performing wonders, wholly making use of a soul given up to the heroism of charity.

A galleon had arrived with another troop of slaves. This time they came from the rivers of Guinea; they were to stay at the house of Doña Teodora de Rivera, a tall building on the right of St Agustín's church, the last before reaching the sea. A big gate with a gilded knocker, a courtyard with a well, there at the back a manor house and a door. It was the street called *de Tezadillo* and Claver arrived there without warning, without being summoned. Two hundred negroes lay on the ground. The noise made him shiver: the sound of the pain of the epidemic, the smallpox, the yellow fever. He knew these compounds very well, as he did other reduits called *del Capitolio*, a kind of sick-bay for negroes, near the city walls, where disabled invalids who lived on public charity were gathered sometimes in holes. It was moving to see, on certain occasions during the year, a procession of the sick being taken on stretchers by the father's slave interpreters on their way to the church of St Ignatius where one at a time they were confessed and given the last sacraments. On his knees Claver gave them some food, from those presents he kept on the floor of his confessional for these children of pain.

The Catalan character, austere and dry, had in Claver the mark of constancy as well as of profound delicacy. It may be easy to visit a miserable patient once, but to do it for ten or twenty years is heroic.

Magdalena was a black slave who lived in the first street of Getsemani outside the town. She was of *camba* nationality. Close to the sea, her hut was damp. She was one of those whom Claver called on every three days accompanied by Andrés Sacabuche or Ignacio Angola, or one they called Monzolo. So for ten years he arrived bringing her clothes, sweets, food . . . One day he came to give her her last Communion.

A very remarkable thing happened. His presence multiplied itself, his tireless activity wore out two or three companions and he had to go back to fetch others. Returning he was exhausted and half-fainting. Physically his health was wonderful. Often he reached home after ten hours of hard work to find at the porter's lodge a new anxious call. As if he had done nothing he said, 'You arrive just in time, I am perfectly free at the moment.'

When evening came he used to entreat the porter: 'Please, if anyone comes during the night, let me know; the other fathers work too hard and need rest, while I who do nothing sleep too much.'

This heroic life went on year after year. Some cases call for more attention than others.

Rufina came from Angola. Her mistress testifies that the father used to visit the slave during her illness, confessing her and bringing her presents for three years. Angela Rodríguez, a freed negress, took into her house, at the instance of Father Claver, another slave, Ursula de Abiler, who lived there for four years, crippled, covered with ulcers and habitually unwell. The meals were charged to Father Claver, who visited her frequently.

Then there was a blind woman living in a hut near the gate of Santa Catalina; Father Claver assisted her with particular care because of her blindness, and 'he saw to it'—as the Process specified—'that she was not in need of anything, spiritual or material'. The blind woman he visited for many, many years.

So the gay, rich, tumultous city of Cartagena used to see every afternoon a priest passing by, his eyes on the ground, and hailed by the children from their balconies: 'The Saint! The Saint?' He walked briskly, some unhappy, forsaken human being was waiting anxiously: perhaps the poor blind woman of Santa Catalina. Did he feel no repugnance? Was he abnormal? Did God put miracles in his path so that he might not be afflicted by horrors? No. He did feel repugnance and very deeply, as some facts will prove. He was not an abnormal man, for he suffered all the anguish of our human condition.

God performed some miracles through him in order to help the poor, but he left Claver all the harshness of his personal apostolic life.

Claver's charity with sick people was simple, heroic. An historian observed: 'Here, contrary to what happens in the confessional, he would not make any distinction of skin colour. Any sick person for him was a human being in urgent need of help and he gave priority to one reason alone, necessity.'

His charity was ingenious. In his cell he stocked quantities of provisions, eau-de-cologne, biscuits, medicaments and, above all, the famous dates to which popular piety attributed miraculous powers, to the point where requests quite often came from Europe for some of Father Claver's dates.

A systematic approach was needed. In a population varying between 5,000 and 7,000 inhabitants the sick formed a high percentage. Father Claver kept a notebook where he catalogued their names and needs. One by one he visited the private houses to which the owners called him. But more than once he appeared at an aristocratic house and asked for the patient, only to cause consternation. The sick person was there in a dark far-away room, lying on the floor, suffering from fever and pain. Father Claver had neither been called nor expected.

After those came the lonely huts (bohíos) lying on the outskirts of the city.

The sick lived in the most dismal poverty in the so-called popular infirmaries, Casas de Cabildo. All sick negroes infected by the contagious plague went there direct from the galleons. Their rooms, usually situated on the seashore, were damp, muddy and exceedingly hot. Father Claver visited them regularly.

There is a point at which legend has even overshadowed the

terrible reality. It might be called the epic of a cloak. Clerical persons at that period followed the Spanish fashion of wearing the kind of large cape with many pleats hanging simply from the shoulders. Father Claver's cloak was coarse, worn out, yellowing; he used it in innumerable ways and in the Process it was named more than three hundred times. He used to put it under the sick while he made their beds, covering the poor black women with it while he confessed them. It served as a shroud on extreme occasions and Claver used its edges to wipe the sweat from his face because he used the two handkerchiefs he received each week as being better for wiping the sweat off his patients. Now this cloak, which some witnesses tried to see as immune to stink and filth, was not so ordinary. One of the interpreters tells us that sometimes the cloak had to be washed seven times a day. The Saint showed no repugnance but the reality must have been hard.

'Many times this witness saw the cloak,' said Andrés Sacabuche, the interpreter, 'cover dirt and sores and it would have been impossible to go back to the college wearing it had not the interpreters promised to clean it as best they could. He wore it with great pleasure and joy, without nausea, but sometimes it was necessary to wash it many times, especially after he visited persons suffering from certain diseases.'

The possibility of miraculous effects cannot be excluded in some cases but they seem not to have been usual.

Saints must be realistically treated. Heroism must not be exaggerated or minimized. Life in a tropical harbour like Cartagena, with an average temperature of 75–85 degrees, is quite bearable, and even agreeable for anybody who does not need to work; but for an apostle like Claver, making a continuous sacrifice of his life, it was harsh and difficult. Epidemics followed one after another; he saw five major ones in his life there. A hospital is always disagreeable. His attitude must have been remarkable for the witnesses to admire it so greatly. Brother Manuel Rodríguez tells us: 'When Father Claver was praised for these things, he used to say that this was nothing but tinsel and that he does nothing.'

But the superior (prior) of the Convent of St John of God, Brother Francisco López, thinks of his work very differently.

Claver was very zealous,' he states, 'and used to say he would like to be forty people at the same time; and in truth Father Claver did the work of forty persons.'

God allowed some difficulties to arise, even in such work, and even caused by ecclesiastics. One day Father Claver was accused of interfering in business that was not his. It was a question of jurisdiction. A simple solution was chosen. Each time he was called on to give extreme unction to a sick person, he sought out the nearest parish priest.

With this and similar visits the difficulties ceased. Father Claver's superiors allowed him always to carry everything necessary for extreme unction. Francisco Núñez de Quero witnessed many scenes and gives his evidence. 'I saw the father close to those disfigured faces and repugnant ulcers which he kissed devotedly. Most admirable was that he not only cleansed these plague-stricken ulcers with the two handkerchiefs he kept for that, but did not hesitate to press his lips to them.'

These wretched victims, who regarded themselves as the scum of the earth, were in need of his profound consolation.

There is a pathetic document which in a few lines condenses a whole drama, told by an eye-witness, the doctor Adán Lobo. It happened in 1645. He was paying a visit to Don Francisco Manuel in the district of Getsemani. Suddenly he heard in the next room a woman shouting: 'No! No, my father, let me alone, do not do that!' An evil suspicion came into Lobo's mind; he was a friend of Peter Claver, he admired him, but he was suddenly afraid and he allowed himself to yield to an evil curiosity. He came into the room quickly and was as though thunderstruck to see Father Claver licking the putrid sores of the poor black slave. She could not stand such humiliation on Father Claver's part and this was the cause of her anguished scream. Doctor Lobo goes on to say during the Process that he never in his whole life saw another man who had so dominated nature. Twenty-five years later Doctor Lobo, repentant for his vile suspicion and practising then in the San Sebastián Hospital, professed such a veneration for Father Claver, such confidence, that when he was in despair about one of his patients he never gave up without previously consulting

Claver, because he knew that if Claver ordered him to go on the invalid would escape death.

Friar Juan de Sahagún, an Augustinian, testifies that in his house there was an assemblage of black slaves belonging to Manuel de Acosta. Claver arrived as usual. Almost all of them were infected with a contagious illness. Father Claver backed away, retreating several steps. His reaction was swift; as someone coming out of his surprise, he threw his cloak on the floor and the witness heard him exclaiming: 'Is that so! You are going to see!' And so saying, he knelt down and started to embrace the sick, one by one, caressing them and clearing their ulcers with his own lips.

The people who were there left the room overcome by amazement. A little later Claver came out, calm, quiet, smiling, and took his leave. The storm provoked by the rebellion of his nature had passed. He had shown them that as a man he felt a natural repugnance, but as a saint he acted with great heroism.

On another occasion he was called to the house of a rich shipowner of Lima, Peru. There was a black man in a corner, separated from all the others, as no one could stand the horror of him. Father Claver arrived as usual, a hand over his chest where he kept his wooden crucifix. He entered the dark room, followed by the master of the house and by four other Spaniards who witnessed the event. When Father Claver sensed this horrible atmosphere his head swam, he was almost fainting. His will of steel reacted; his companions could see the effort in his face dilating even more the two lines that crossed his forehead. Taking his left arm out of his cassock he uncovered his shoulders and with a whip tipped with small iron balls started to scourge himself, raining lashes upon his body, while he whispered this self-reproach: 'So you are refusing to approach your neighbour redeemed by the blood of Jesus Christ? But it is not going to be like that; you are going to pay for it and achieve by charity whatever needs to be done.' And then came the terrible reaction usual in these cases: he approached on his knees the terrified sick negro in his miserable bed, he laid his face tenderly on the ulcers and kissed them with pure and loving lips. After confessing him he left him at peace.

The witnesses went out of the room. Ten years later when

they testified under oath in the Process they still had in their ears the sound of those strokes, could still see the two figures, the miserable black man and the formidable master of his own instincts.

These two cases show that Claver was not an abnormal man. He was a saint who felt the necessity of going to extremes of sacrifice in order to save one abandoned human being from extreme of misery. It was not strange that this enslaved race, who arrived there in physical as well as moral terror, should fall in adoration before him and see him as an angel.

The exaggerated attitude of the Saint was necessary in this harsh and cruel setting. Violent reactions were needed, and they produced radical changes even among the slave-traders who persecuted Father Claver at the beginning and put grave difficulties in the way of this man who troubled their trade. Later, at the end of their lives, these hard men found themselves subjugated: they called Claver to their galleons and ships, and even more, they approached surreptitiously Father Claver's room in the residence to consult him about doubts concerning their behaviour. Claver, as before him Father Sandoval had, smoothed down their roughness, and only God knows how much cruelty was spared in that terrible world thanks to Father Claver's heroism. Those works of charity gave him an extraordinary ascendancy over the sick and over the owners.

Don Agustín de Ugarte y Saravia, inquisitor of Cartagena and later bishop of Quito, testified that he saw in his house Father Claver putting his lips and tongue over the ulcers of one of his, Ugarte's, slaves. He stood speechless with horror, and this sight impressed him vividly all his life. The same impression was received by Vicente de Villalobos who saw from a door how Father Claver was 'cleaning with a handkerchief a face covered with smallpox', and by Francisco Caballero, mayor of Cartagena, who declared, terrified: 'This action of putting his mouth to suck and lick the ulcers of the poor sick became a habit in the holy father and he did it not only in the infirmaries for the black men, but in the hospitals and more frequently in the leprosarium.'

Hagiography relates with admiration that once St Elizabeth,

Queen of Portugal, kissed ulcers, and once too so did St Catherine of Siena, St Francis Xavier and St Aloysius Gonzaga. But in Pedro Claver it was 'customary'.

To give all the particular cases would fill pages. It is enough to know that he never flinched from anything. The abyss of misery had to be filled by charity, even if the flesh crept. It was a hard thing to do, but the sick slaves who had just landed had souls heavy with sorrow. The white man was for them the scourge of their lives, the enemy who had taken away their freedom. It was difficult to penetrate their spiritual world filled with rancour. They could yield only to a white man who gave himself to them in this way. Claver, kissing the ulcers of these slaves, could speak of God, patience and love. Only this live sociology drawn from the wooden crucifix which he always wore on his chest was able to tranform these rough minds and turn them, pagans, into sons of God. If the black world departs from Christ in our modern times, it is perhaps because there are not more apostle-sociologues such as Claver.

For fourteen years he visited poor Juan in his hut. Under the direction of the Saint, Juan reached great spiritual heights. His soul was white, and when he eventually died Father Claver said to him with emotion: 'Juan, take me with you, fasten me to your feet as I am sure that you are going to see God.'

Magdalena was a slave from Biafara; she served as an interpreter and at the same time collected alms, going from door to door, for the lepers of San Lázaro. One day, seeing a terrible sickness in a brother of her race, she too wanted to escape and Claver said to her: 'Magdalena, Magdalena, do not run away. These are our fellow creatures redeemed with the blood of our Lord.' And the slave came back. Thus he formed his selected disciples.

San Sebastián Hospital was in the centre of the town and the Saint used to go there twice a week. He professed a deep esteem for the Brothers of St John of God, who cared for the sick. When he arrived 'he embraced them as soon as they met and he said that if they needed him he was there, although he was miserable and good for nothing'.

On the other hand his love was reciprocated. We have the

declaration of a witness who said: 'When the father was out on a mission the sick people missed him so badly, and the religious too, that when he came back he was received with cheers and applause by the whole hospital.'

Normally his method of procedure was as follows: most of the time he would go to the hospital without his cloak, wearing a threadbare and patched cassock just covering the calf of his leg; on arrival, his head bowed, he would immediately ask for a broom and sweep the rooms, make the beds, serve the meals and go on to do the washing up. This material business came first of all. After it appeared the priest: he would go from patient to patient, giving them the holy Christ to kiss; he brought them presents, sweets, tobacco, etc., and then confessed them.

This may seem too general and vague. Here follow some concrete cases: Juan Ramírez had gone blind; he wept day and night because of his misfortune and a terrible headache afflicted him. Calling Father Claver, he explained his life of anguish and that he could no longer practise self-control. Claver sat down on the bed and tried to console Ramírez with his special words and his earnest gaze which penetrated the soul and read in the heart. When he was about to leave he would cover the invalid's head with his cloak and give him the kiss of peace on each cheek. Thenceforward, suddenly, the blind man had no more headache and could sleep in peace.

Alfonso Salazar was a Spanish beggar who had lain in bed a long time with suppurating legs. His pride revolted when Father Claver bent over him to heal his ulcers, but all his protests were vain; and he himself admitted in the Process that he used to cry, alone, hiding his face in his hands when his friend left him.

Alvaro Barbosa Salazar tragically describes his own history. He was in the surgery ward. His right arm had caught an infection which had reached to the bone and the purulent smell was such that he had been isolated in a room upstairs, completely cut off, where he received the last sacraments. Claver went there; he used to sit down in a low small chair and used to take up such a position that his face and mouth stayed near the ulcered arm. 'Please, Father, go away, go away', the terrified eyes of the invalid implored, 'not even I can tolerate myself.' 'No, no, my brother, allow yourself to rest, it neither bothers me nor tires me.' So saying, his face was getting nearer and nearer to the ulcer, which he finally kissed.

Father Claver stayed two hours. The illness was a consequence of sin. The Saint, looking sadly at Barbosa, told him that he would be cured but that God was going to put a brake on his passions. The patient was only told later who his visitor was. 'I do not wonder,' he said, 'that he has won such a reputation for sanctity, because without doubt his virtue is even greater than his fame.'

Father Claver's visits continued and God's light illuminated this soul. One day, as Father Claver was taking leave, the sick man gave him four *reales* and asked him to say a Mass. 'Keep your money, my brother; I shall say the Mass.'

Another day Claver arrived very gay: 'Be very happy, for God loves you very much and I hope you are going to walk again through the streets of Cartagena. Always keep God in your memory and sin no more. He is going to put a curb on you so that you do not offend him any more, because he loves you very much.'

And Alvaro Barbosa became blind, but the wonder was that his soul was transformed, he grumbled no more and he recognized that his blindness was God's brake.

Such was Claver's social apostolate. Sometimes his work was multiplied. In 1636–7, the fleet commanded by Carlos Ibarra arrived at Cartagena carrying the plague. More than 1,100 sick people went to San Sebastián. Even the chapels were used as sickrooms. The father had to multiply his activities and worked eight or ten hours a day. The same thing occurred again and again during the five epidemics which broke out during Claver's life.

Work in the hospitals was one of the things which attracted most attention among the Saint's contemporaries. The superior of the hospital of San Sebastián and one of the founders of the new order, Brother Francisco López, was one of his greatest admirers. Doctor Adán Lobo, physician friend of Claver's, and many more did not cease to marvel at him.

Father Peter Claver, on his part, responded to this admiration by treating the brothers of St John of God as his brothers. 'At times on arriving,' one of them tells us, 'he embraced us and humbly consoled us, admiring our work. He begged the superior's permission in all things.' Usually he went to the hospital with a companion; when there were no brothers free in the house he obligingly helped them to wash up, fulfilling their duties so that they could go with him.

A main part of his apostolate was to carry gifts and presents. The chroniclers mention especially rosemary, dates, honey. 'Dates he picked at harvest time and put them in jars of sugar to take them to the patients.' At the same time he had plenty of tobacco and alcohol. The medicines were expensive; he begged alms from the rich families.

One scourge was as the sum of all the rest: leprosy. An extremely curious Spanish document of the sixteenth century depicts for us what contemporaries felt about this disease. It refers to a consultation which took place among some physicians in Seville in 1593, 'whose opinion is used and has been used by doctors and surgeons of the hospital of San Lázaro for the admission of leprous cases.' From this document comes the following extract: 'The sickness on which we were consulted was called *elephantiasis* by the Greeks, *lepra* by the Arabs, *gafedat* or *malatia* of St Lazare by ancient documents; what we call now the disease of San Lázaro is really the same sickness.

'Leprosy is a general or particular deformation of the body, accompanied by scabs or insensitive tumours, warts or corrosive and carious sores.'

The black population was immediately attacked by leprosy, and in the seventeenth century the focal point was Cartagena and its environs, as far as Mompox, el Socorro, etc.

Anybody might tremble at the thought of sharing meals, drinks, clothes and even the forbidden dwellings with victims of such disease at a time when it had not been mastered by science and was known to be certainly contagious. St Peter Claver, on the contrary, when he discovered the horrible reality, when he saw that the so-called hospital of San Lázaro was an old, shabby, poorly furnished building, without any resources, gave thanks to Almighty

God for the favour of being allowed to save the souls of these unfortunate people at the same time as bringing them comfort in their affliction.

Perhaps the worst suffering of these sick people—as in general for victims of contagious disease—was the terrible loneliness which overcame them, the yearning for communication, for a normal social life, and the painful sense of being abandoned on all sides. The leper feels he is the citizen of a world which avoids him, and this aggravates his suffering. He hears the cry of terror. Therefore, when such apostles as Peter Claver approach them with total abnegation, without resistance or scruple, these sorrowing people experience a marvellous, exultant reaction.

San Lázaro Hospital in Cartagena was a place of delight for Peter Claver.

In an historical account of the province of Cartagena de Indias, written in 1772, appear the following paragraphs:

'Outside the town is San Lázaro Royal Hospital with its chaplain who, besides 106 lepers whom he confesses, ministers to 218 heads of families comprising 577 souls for confession and 179 slaves scattered in various places such as works and small farms.'

The king provided maintenance for this institution as appears from the King's Rolls for 21 September.

'Not far from the mount of San Felipe outside the walls, is another centre acting as a hospital, San Lázaro Hospital, where the lepers, so numerous in Cartagena, are kept.'

'Outside Getsemaní and near the highroad running from Half Moon Gate, the municipal council bought some parcels of land where the San Lázaro Hospital was established. The terrible disease of leprosy spread quickly in Cartagena. Early in the seventeenth century there were only twelve patients, in 1627 more than seventy were admitted, not to mention another twenty-five who lived in their houses to the great danger of the neighbours.'[1]

To begin with, the hospital was no more than a conglomeration of huts, with no fence round them. At the request of a town clerk 'it was set back ten feet from the king's highway and fenced in with a stone wall ten rods in height not counting the foundation

[1] *Carta del Cabildo a Su Majestad*, 15 April 1627, Archiv. Indias, Santa Fe, 63.

and the cement finishing, but with a gateway opening on to the shore; a cross wall was put in the most suitable place, so that a lavatory could be built for women to enable them to keep the required decency and modesty'. The carpenter Juan Serrano built it for 1,500 *pesos*.

In July of the same year the clerk noted that the work was already under way and the the king was granting privileges to other hospitals of the kind.

A place where Claver liked to walk was at first an open field, with no church, near some date-palms where he assembled the lepers who were not bed-ridden. First of all he distributed the gifts which he brought: above all, honey and fruits, and in some special circumstances tobacco and alcohol. Then came catechism. He recited the prayers on his knees in the midst of them and his exhortation was always the same: 'Make of life a ladder to heaven, leprosy of the body does not matter if the soul is clean.'

Seated on a stone he heard their confessions, and when the breeze from the sea blew strong he would shield the leper penitent with half of his cloak.

He was not afraid of the disease and they knew it. There was one very disfigured man whom all shunned, but Claver took him on his lap and thus he confessed him.

Indoors they kept the most wretched for him. Some considered intolerable were shut up in a corner of the high building or in some hut in the garden; precisely these were Claver's familiar friends. In the Process are pages of realistic description of the father on his knees before the terribly disfigured, trying to put food into their mouths or tasting it himself to encourage them. So great was his renown for these deeds that many men went secretly to witness his heroic charity and could not get over their amazement. One of them one day saw the Saint's head shining as he embraced one of these unfortunates. Captain Pedro de Barahona, one of those tough conquerors who are not easily impressed, was terrified one day to see Claver carry a leper who had come out to beg alms and was too weak to return. He, who never used scents—only permitting himself a little vinegar at times when he felt faint—had a great store of perfume burners for his patients.

He, who never drove away mosquitoes that devoured him, had compassion for the torture they can inflict, especially there in San Lázaro surrounded with stagnant ponds. According to the *Annual Letter* he acquired on one occasion fourteen small canopies which were put in all the rooms, and one witness adds that after this work every patient gave him a grateful embrace, 'the lepers' hug'.

He supplied the doctors with medicines and the finest of lancets.

All the witnesses agree that 'on feasts of our Lord and of the blessed Virgin he recommended the rich to prepare magnificent dishes.' Isabel de Urbina declares that she herself often did the same as her sisters. From early hours this house of desolation was cheered by music, since all the singers of the colleges, with harps and guitars, were mobilized. They were supposed, above all, to play during meals. For Father Claver these days were wonderful. When the community went into retreat he went to San Lázaro, as he did when they had an entertainment in the college. This was one of the cases where witnesses acknowledged that his face shone with joy. 'I am going to have my carnival with the poor of San Lázaro,' he said to those he met, and so confirms the sergeant Jiménez Girolana. Gaspar de los Reyes, who lived near the Half-Moon Gate, saw him pass often with a great basket on his shoulder, followed by his interpreters, and the curate chaplain of the hospital, Don Luis Báez de Espínola, also testifies thus.

Such was the smiling aspect of the leper colony. Death was never far from the beds of the patients. Don Francisco de Ribero was archdeacon of the cathedral of Cartagena. Peter Claver's example had drawn him; he brought alms to San Lázaro and distributed them, because, he used to say, 'the hands of the priest seem as appropriate to necessities as to offer the holy Sacrifice of the Mass'.

One day he arrived to see Father Claver surrounded by his lepers, his face aflame, his head illumined like a seraph's; he was teaching catechism. Quietly waiting for him to finish, silently Don Francisco kissed his hands and begged for his prayers. Later in the Process the incident is confirmed by various testimonies from the religious of St John of God.

In 1642 the work of the hospital was threatened with ruin. It had no economic resources; Father Claver, with the approval of his superiors, dedicated himself to the work. Brother Juan de Cobalunga and the negro slaves were the builders. He spent all day in the hospital, and the food which was sent from the kitchens he gave to the most abandoned lepers, contenting himself with what was left.

The building had undergone great changes. In 1627 there were only a few huts in the open field, without walls or church. The father was 'he who during thirty years constituted himself provider, priest and patron and administered all the sacraments and catered for everything'.

In the last days of his life, Father Claver suffered from tumours. He could not walk, but this did not prevent him, a few days before he died, from going to take leave of his lepers.

At this time in the towns the dead were buried in their own parish churches or in the monastery *patios*. Thus in Cartagena the cemetery, for example, of Santo Domingo was the block of houses adjoining the convent. In the building of the Archbishop's Palace was the cemetery of the cathedral, the most usual place for burials from the city. The street was called the Cemetery of the Church. Under the cathedral high altar was also a crypt for members of the Confraternity of St Peter. The parish of the Trinity similarly used as a cemetery the *patio* behind the church. The same happened in other churches. Thus the church of St Ignatius served as cemetery for the Jesuits and there Peter Claver was buried.

A document exists, bearing the royal warrant for 27 March 1789, in which the prelates of the Andes and the Philippines are told of the advisability of establishing a cemetery outside the town. The problem of the poverty of the churches, of the subsidences and the shallow soil, must have been very serious and tended to encourage the spread of epidemics.

On 21 October 1672 the king addressed an enquiry to the bishop of Cartagena about the increase of fees paid for the burial of slaves. It read thus: 'In the name of the town, Diego Fernández

Calvo, attorney-general of this town, has informed me that it has
been the custom here for many years to bury the slaves belonging
to any inhabitant of this town when they die in the graveyard of
the cathedral and to ask a fee of two *pesos*.'

The charity of Peter Claver reached beyond life to the dead.
The following is one of the many testimonies. When news arrived
that some poor negro had died, he used to go to see parish priests
and the president of the confraternity, and he managed to obtain
their burial by charity; he personally used to find the shroud and
bring it to the dead man's house and have the corpse wrapped in
it. He gave two wax candles to be burned beside the corpse on the
way to the parish church and he invited people to the funeral,
promulgating the indulgences they won by doing this act of
mercy.

He was the first to say the prayers for the dead, and if he could
he vested himself to say the Mass for the soul of the dead man.
On one occasion he called an honest man to go with him to San
Lázaro Hospital. The man accompanied him with great pleasure.
When they arrived Father Claver took off his cloak and covered
with it the grave of a black woman who had been buried there
the previous day. Then he took four oranges, put in each a candle
and placed them at the four corners of the grave. He summoned
the poor and went out to say a requiem Mass for the dead
woman, saying at the end the prayers at the grave, with all the
rites of the Church. He did it for the deceased poor every time he
could, as was testified in the Process by parish priests and
hospital administrators. 'When the ceremony was ended, Claver
thanked the witness, who was Gaspar de los Reyes, adding: "With
that, the poor deceased is consoled." '

'A poor slave called Magdalena, of the Brau tribe, died in such
poverty that she had neither coffin nor shroud. Claver arrived,
said the prayers for the dead, spread out his cloak and laid the
corpse in it. Then he stayed, candle in hand, until the end of the
ceremony.'

Claver's heroic charity had many distinctive features but none
perhaps so touching as his attitude to the lonely sorrow of the
black slaves.

Chapter IV

PRISONS AND THE INQUISITION

BROTHER González tells us that Claver spent a great deal of time in the city prison of Cartagena.

The witnesses are unanimous on one point. Peter Claver had a special gift for bringing souls to God, especially those who seemed farthest away. Those condemned to death were always his friends, and they called him in shortly before they died.

In 1640 there was a great uproar and riot in the town. A captain, whose name is tactfully omitted from the apostolic Process—a man of some importance and consideration—was condemned to death for having issued false coinage. Don Melchor de Aguilera was at that time governor. After some disagreement with the Society he gave orders to his officials not to call any Jesuit in, when he was absent from the town, to attend those condemned to death. The captain, awaiting his last hour in the gloomy dungeon, had asked for Claver to hear his confession. Executions were carried out in various places—always outside the town walls. In this case the appointed spot was near the fort of Santo Domingo. It was four o'clock in the afternoon and the whole Dominican community was present, the friars having accompanied him to the outskirts.

This funeral scene is described in the simple language of Brother Nicolás:

> The condemned man was seated on a chair beside the gibbet from which he was to hang. Father Claver was standing near by, wearing a very old faded hat with its brim hanging down and its torn leather lining flapping against his face, his deep-set eyes set off by two dark lines of thick eyebrows. He looked graver than usual. The situation was truly dramatic. Father Claver was sprinkling holy water with an asperges brush on and around the condemned man. On his left arm he carried the bowl of

holy water together with a small basket with some glasses of scented water, wine, cakes and other good things while he recited aloud the act of contrition.

A Dominican who was present and very much edified by all this, said, pointing to the father: 'That is what being a religious means and showing what a religious should be, caring nothing for the world, going the straight road of humility.'

It was four in the afternoon. The crowd was greatly impressed. It happened that the hangman twisted the garrotte badly and the rope broke, the cloth cap fell over the face of the condemned man, who was falling to the ground when Father Claver took him in his arms and putting his face close to him spoke to him in low loving tones. As he held him like this the hangman put the cord round him again, and when the friars standing by saw it they called out to him, fearful lest he should incur irregularity, 'Take care, father, you will be liable to censure.'

Father Claver showed a trait in this case that we have seen nowhere else in his life. Shaking with emotion he said: 'No, no, I cannot incur irregularity while caring for souls,' as the text of the Process says. Another version reads: 'If I incur any irregularity by doing this, at least I have done it to help save souls.'

Another witness expresses it more clearly, putting these words into Claver's mouth, 'Well, let me do so in order to save a soul,' he replied energetically, 'but I cannot now be guilty of an irregularity.'

'The crowd was silent. The hangman went on with his task and a second time the rope broke and a second time Father Claver helped the poor culprit—horribly livid in the face—and held him like that until he died, expiring in his arms.'[1]

This event occupies a prominent place in the Process and gives the promoter of the faith an opportunity to raise objections. Why did he bring eatables to the scaffold? Was it not a time for spiritual rather than material help?

Once more Claver's delicacy shines forth and is here combined with a very interesting social trait. He shows firmness almost to

[1] Process, Nos. 16, 18.

the point of being aggressive, at the same time as a humane attitude familiar in the whole of his apostolate among the unfortunate.

Claver was well-known in the dark underground dungeons of the prison, for they were favourite places for his visits several times a week. Various accounts describe the routine. On arriving he took off his cloak and went straight to a small chapel where there was a large crucifix, a realistic sculpture characteristic of the Spanish religious images of the period. He blessed some water and then assembled all the prisoners. The matter of his sermons was direct and clear and perhaps very limited: to avoid bad language, quarrels and hatred. A witness reproduces one of them textually:

'Brothers: to escape from this torment, there is no other remedy but to keep close to our Lord, as those suffering shipwreck cling to a plank to escape from the sea. Here, brothers, you have the true plank,' and he added, addressing himself to the man condemned to die: 'Happy are you who know your last day, and happy I should be if I knew mine.'

These words must have sounded with extraordinary force in that dark cell, and he continued: 'It is a piece of great good fortune that death should come to us while we are in full possession of our senses and our reason is free to rest on that point on which our eternal happiness or misery depends. We must all come to it either by a short-cut or by a long way round in time, but what does it matter if the short-cut be the hard one of the gallows if it means that the way is the more certain.'

In the afternoon he used to recite the Litany of the Blessed Virgin with them. But the centre of attention was his wooden crucifix. Here as in the hospital, the slave-compounds and the Jesuit residence, Father Peter Claver was not merely the spiritual apostle. His social method was simple and realistic. He had doctors to look after the sick and also lawyers for the prisoners. Their names are given: Antonio Betancur and Santiago Sánchez Pareja, brother of the governor of the prison, Juan Sánchez Pareja. When the cases proceeded slowly, Peter Claver hurried them up.

Some incidents in this work stand out. Claver was coming out of the jail one day with Brother Nicolás when a negro passed by, and the father lowered his voice and said: 'I am sorry for this poor fellow, for they will cut his body in pieces.' Within a week the sentence of death was pronounced.

He saw the profound purpose of life. A prisoner who had been a great criminal was preparing for death; shortly before the sentence was to be carried out, a pardon arrived. When the news was brought to Peter Claver, he said to those who had freed the prisoner: 'God pardon you for this, for they have taken this man's salvation out of his hands and he is in danger of never recovering it.'

This anecdote is related by the Franciscan father, Miguel de Ugarte, a great friend of the Saint, who gives us the name of the condemned man, a soldier called Domingo Acebuche.

The governor of the prisons, Juan Lozano, often had difficult problems, especially during the last days of prisoners condemned to death. The judges sent word to Peter Claver as soon as sentence had been pronounced. He took, as he always did, his staff with the cross and silently passed through the two streets which separated him from the town hall. In silence he embraced the condemned man. He took out his crucifix and said: 'My brother, the day of your death is approaching, take heart.' At the same time he put his hand on the crucifix and began to prepare him for confession; when the bells of the cathedral rang for the Angelus at six o'clock, the father came out of the prison, leaving a small book with the prisoner to prepare himself for a good death, and something else which surprises us today and proves the religious atmosphere of the period, even in the sordid haunts of crime. All the witnesses declare that the father used to leave the condemned man a girdle with sharp points and a scourge, handing them to him as a matter of course, saying: 'Suffer, my brother, now that you can acquire merit.'

Every death sentence is dismal. In a small city of four to five thousand inhabitants, as Cartagena de Indias was at this time, this was the event of the day. People, as they crossed the *Plaza del Cabildo* where the prison was, stopped for a moment and ceased talking. On that day, without fail, Father Claver said a Mass for the condemned man on an improvised altar in the prison, and the prisoner received Holy Communion. After Mass, Claver recited over his head a passage from the Gospel, then with the other prisoners he said the Litany of the Blessed Virgin. A bell rang. It was time to dress the condemned man for his execution and put the noose round his neck. The father gave him a short exhortation, crucifix in hand, then made the prisoner embrace his companions and ask their pardon and prayers. The funeral procession followed —usually less than a kilometre, through the main streets of the town. The courage Claver managed to inspire in the condemned men was wonderful. On their way they begged pardon of the crowds who gathered, and Father Claver walked beside them sprinkling holy water along the streets and scented water gently on the prisoner; sometimes the latter rode on horseback. The usual sites for the execution were near the fort of Santo Domingo, or Santa Catalina or outside the Media Luna. On arriving at the appointed site, Father Claver wiped the sweat from the condemned man's face, gave him a few morsels of food and kissed him.

The gallows was ready; the prisoner, as a sign of acceptance, kissed the ladder by which he was to climb to his execution. One last embrace and a final absolution. While the man expired the father stood there, his eyes fixed on him. A witness writes: 'He was so devoted to this ministry that there was no one condemned by the courts in his day whom he did not assist. If several were executed at the same time, he attended them all, going to all the different places where they were.'

Brother Manuel Rodríguez says: 'I often accompanied Father Claver when he went to visit the prisoners, hear their confession and console them with great devotion and charity; he addressed them in friendly talks, exhorting them to patience and confession, and sitting there by the altar he heard their confessions. Then they made him their intermediary and he carried out their commisions faithfully, for he had several lawyer friends.'[1]

And his faithful interpreter, Andrés Sacabuche, adds: 'His favourite task was to help those sentenced to death; he confessed them, gave them communion as *viaticum*, and remained

[1] Process, Nos. 16, 18.

with them for days at a time . . . He paid no attention to sun or rain in going to the site of the execution. After their death he sang a solemn responsory for them with organ accompaniment and . . . I went with him as interpreter.'[1]

Father Claver had one special devotion, the burial of the poor. He wished it to be conducted with all pomp, and so we find him collecting alms and stirring up the whole town, whether for an interpreter or a man condemned to death. The prison was near the cathedral, so these ceremonies usually took place there.

Pedro Mercado, a priest in the town, describes this activity: 'On those days Father Claver mobilized all the musicians of the cathedral and all the instruments at the colleges—fifes, bass viols and horns. Among the negro slave interpreters there were good voices and artistic talent.' Their names are quoted: 'Nicolás Criollo and Antonio Congo were the tenors. Simón Biafara played the horn and Francisco Biafara the bass viol. Juan Bautista Fajardo, moreover, at one time priest in the cathedral, bears witness to this also. It is easy to understand the esteem and love that his attentions excited among these poor people who had lost everything in life and death.'

In this chapter on the prisons and the condemned we must not omit one remarkable case, described at length in the Process, which also incurred criticism.[2]

Esteban Melón, a Neapolitan, was a criminal condemned to death for murder and theft. Fernando de la Riva was Governor of the town. The condemned man refused absolutely to go to confession. They called in Claver 'who, as he usually did, converted him and prepared him for death'. The details of the case were tragic. The execution was to take place in the main square of the town. At that time there was no official hangman and they had to impose this disagreeable duty on a Moslem, Yolofo by name, a galley slave who had resided there for thirty years. He did not like the job and ran away, was pursued and caught at last three leagues from the town, near the Castle of Bocachica. On the day of the execution Father Claver did for Melón what he always did —said Mass for him, accompanied him to the place of execution

[1] Process, Nos. 18, 25.   [2] Process, Nos. 18, 19.

and in his last moments made him various gifts such as cake and wine. The hangman was a novice and trembled, not being accustomed to the job, and the rope broke three times. The hangman himself began to faint and the father had to comfort him with the cakes and wine he had brought for the condemned man. Every time the rope broke Melón fell into Claver's arms, who wiped the sweat from his livid face.

The Moslem who acted as hangman was profoundly moved by this extraordinary charity. Next day he went to the college, entered Father Claver's room, kissed him with great emotion and began his religious instruction. Having resisted grace for thirty-one years he found it beside the gallows with St Peter Claver. This Moslem, when baptized, took the name of Pedro Zapata, and when Brother González and others gave their testimony he was living in the town as a good Christian. He himself tells us of his conversion:

My name is Pedro Zapata. I became a Moslem and knew the Saint for thirty years. I was only converted ten years ago. I was the king's slave and they asked me to be Melón's hangman. I did not want to and I fled to Bocachica. The soldiers caught me. Don Fernando de la Riva was captain-general in the town. The execution was held in the main square. Father Claver carried wine in a glass which he gave to the condemned man and to me too, which gave me strength to continue. I made up my mind to be converted through Father Claver's charity. He kissed me and taught me the mysteries of the Faith; I lived all this time in the college, and Father Juan Bautista Fajardo, a priest of the cathedral, baptized me there, and Fernandino de Peñaranda acted as godfather.[1]

In his last years, old and infirm and unable to walk, Claver had himself brought to the prison in a sedan chair. Shortly before his death an urgent call came for him. It was for a Spaniard called Baltasar who had murdered his benefactor, Captain Pereira. In despair he thought of old Father Claver, the paralysed Jesuit who lived 200 metres from his prison, and he made his confession to him.

[1] Process, Nos. 13, 34.

The Inquisition

Most of the witnesses who relate these things in the Process are negro slaves or simple people. The executions were engraved on their memory in every detail. Among the most typical witnesses we find Andrés Sacabuche, Antonio de Miranda, the College barber, Ignacio Angola, Francisco de Jesús Yolofo and Dídaco Falupo.

Besides these simple people we find that Francisco López, superintendent of the prisons, gave Father Claver every facility in his work.

An official document of 25 February 1610[1] may occasion some surprise. The inquisitors are requested: 'not to proceed against the Indians but against "old Christians" and their descendants and other persons against whom in these Spanish dominions proceedings are usually taken, and in the cases that come to your notice to proceed with all moderation and gentleness and with great consideration for it is fitting to do so that the Inquisition may be held in respect and not just occasion be given for rousing hatred.'

The first inquisitor appointed was Mateo de Salcedo, a priest from the See of Valencia, sixty-six years of age, who had studied in Valladolid and held office as 'fiscal' in Saragossa in 1609. The second was Juan de Mañozca, forty-two years of age, subdeacon, a graduate in arts at the university of Mexico in 1596, who took his final examination in 1600. He is one of those about whom there has been great controversy and no definitive judgment can yet be made. Jealous of his companion, ambitious, daring, the heart and soul of the new institution, he had been inquisitor in Mexico until 1623, promoted to the tribunal of Lima and a Visitor at Quito. Fray Sebastián de Chumillas wrote a memorial against him to the Council and as a consequence a rather sharp note was sent to him. In this report grave moral and administrative accusations are made: 'his house has been turned into a centre of ex-

[1] The bibliography of the Inquisition is enormous. These are a few useful texts: Llorente, *Anales de la Inquisición en España*, 2 vols, 1812; E. Lea, *History of the Inquisition in Spain*, 4 vols, New York, 1922; J. A. Medina, *La Inquisición en Cartagena de Indias*, first published in Santiago de Chile, 1893, ed. Bogotá, 1952.

change and mart . . . he has sometimes taken great sinners, men
and women, out of the hands of justice; he is much inclined to
satirize and abuse the religious orders, as he did with regard to the
Society of Jesus and the Provincial of the Dominicans; it is public
knowledge that he gave illegal protection to the ships bringing in
contraband, and he has immoral dealings with women. To sum
up, he is one of the most licentious men I have met among Christian people.'

Of his dealings with the negroes we read:

There are in this town and surrounding district from 12,000
to 14,000 negroes in service; for this reason there is no small
danger of a rising; during the eight years I have lived in this
place I have seen it twice roused to arms on account of the acute
suspicion that they were going to rebel. As a very wise pre-
caution in view of this danger, the governors have given orders
that no negro should carry arms or a knife, nor any other kind
of weapon after dark. This law is posted up among other places
at the barracks of the regiment of guards and the watch or any
soldier who may find a negro carrying a knife or any other
weapon by night is ordered to bring him to the guard-room
and without asking the name of his owner to give him his
'fodder', that is fifty strokes. This is the law and proclamation
of this realm.[1]

Peter Claver must have known and had dealings during his
life with Mateo Salcedo and Juan de Mañozca who left office in
1623, and was probably on no good terms with them, for from
the foregoing document we see what the latter thought of the
Society of Jesus and of the negroes, the two things Claver loved
most. As a contrast to him came presently Agustín de Ugarte y
Saravia, promoted to the bishopric of Chiapa in 1629, and in his
house Claver performed one of his heroic actions for a negro
slave. Ugarte himself says in the Process: 'Father Claver heard the
confession of a negro with a contagious complaint and kissed his
sores. I stood speechless with terror on seeing him do this and I
respected him highly for the rest of my life.'[2]

---

[1] *Documentos*, Folio 81 in San Diego, Cartagena.
[2] Process, No. 8; Hazañero, *op. cit.*

Nothing special is reported about other inquisitors. Up to the death of the Saint in 1654 they were: Domingo Vélez de Asás, Martín Cortázar, Damián Velásquez, Juan Ortiz, Juan B. Villa-diego, Martín Real, Juan Pereira, Diego del Corro and Pedro Salas.

Generally the relations between the Inquisition and the Jesuits must have been fairly good, for we read in the *Cartas annuas* (*Annual Letters*) of the time: 'The holy tribunal of the Inquisition consults us on difficult matters, and they ask our opinion, and often one of our fathers undertakes the usual office and some months ago acted as interim inquisitor by special order and commission of the Supreme Council.'[1]

Shortly after Peter Claver's arrival at Cartagena a dispute arose concerning a mystery of the blessed Virgin which his aged master had deeply impressed upon him. The Inquisition intervened. This is an account sent to Madrid in a letter dated 5 July 1617:

In those days there developed in Cartagena, as never in Mexico, an extreme antagonism between the members of the various religious orders with regard to the devotion to the Immaculate Conception of our Lady, which had just reached this place. The Franciscans, Augustinians, Mercedarians and Jesuits formed a party which was opposed by the Dominicans, supported by the bishop, who had been a friar of that order, and they grew so heated that they denounced one another violently from their pulpits. The Holy Office then intervened, begging the heads of these orders to proceed in their dispute with all due modesty and circumspection, succeeding, it seems, for the moment in calming them. Whereupon a friar of the Order of Mercy preached with greater violence than ever in the cathedral, and the Dominican Fray Juan de Avalos answered him in another sermon in which he maintained that the said devotion was a Pelagian heresy, and in yet another, at which the governor was present, addressing him directly he told him that the city was seething with heresy, and appealed to him as the head of the state to make a stand for the honour of God and punish the heretics; on account of which the Holy Office had

[1] Gabriel Porras Troconis, *La Historia de la Cultura en el Nuevo Reino de Granada*, Seville, 1952, Chap. XXI, p. 465.

to intervene again in the matter and tried to bring about peace among them.

The actual building of the Tribunal was not impressive. On arrival, three houses had been rented to the west of the main square (*Plaza Mayor*) opposite the cathedral. On the same site was erected the permanent building, but not on the scale originally planned—to cost 100,000 *pesos*. In 1641 8,000 *escudos* were allotted to the work, which was completed in two parts. First of all in the courtyards and then in the buildings thirteen small prisons were in use.

Scenes took place in that building which touched Claver to the heart. In that main square (*Plaza Mayor*) great *autos-da-fé*—six in all—were held and he saw two men condemned to death. And near by in the cathedral and in Santa Domingo the less important trials took place that made a sensation in the town and became the main theme of conversation.

The life of Cartagena and of Peter Claver would not be understood properly but for this background of the Inquisition.

There is a remarkable passage, apparently unknown, as it was not used by the biographers, which throws much light on the activities and the attitude of the Saint with regard to the Inquisition and its prisoners.

The text of the statement made by Brother Nicolás González is as follows:

> He visited the prisoners of whatever race they might be, helped as far as he could to console anyone to whom the Tribunal assigned a penance, for many who sinned against our faith were punished by the Holy Office.
>
> In his opinion a procession of penitents condemned by the Holy Office was of as great benefit in saving souls as one of disciplinants in Holy Week.
>
> He felt great pity for the condemned and tried as far as he could to give them spiritual and temporal consolation, endeavouring to make them bear such penances with patience, silence and humility. I remember that in 1636 when an *auto-da-fé* was announced in the cathedral, the father went with me on the afternoon of the day before the *auto*, about three or four

o'clock, collecting alms throughout the town to give the prisoners after their sentence.

After collecting some presents and preparing others given by devout and pious persons he returned to the college. The next day I went with him to the trial and seeing that the procession of condemned persons was already on the move towards the cathedral he joined the procession and went from one to another speaking to them all. They were very glad to see him and some of them said: 'Father, commend us to God.' One asked 'Say a Mass for me.' And he said he would with great pleasure. The Mass which he celebrated later that day was for them, that God might give them patience to support the hardships they had deserved for their sins. I observed a special gesture Father Claver made for some penitents, well-known persons of the town. As soon as he saw them, he raised the forefinger of his right hand and began to bite it, showing it to the person as if he were saying with a father's loving care: 'See what a state you are in for not being good and serving God's divine majesty.' They begged him to commend them to God, and he promised it to them with kindness and love.

When the *auto* was over, the father distributed among them the presents he had collected and consoled them, which brought great benefit to their souls.

José Antonio Medina gives an account of the *auto* based on the minutes made at the time. Those concerned were Diego Lopéz, a mulatto surgeon accused of witchcraft, Inés Martín, a mulatto woman, Domingo Verdugo, a negress, Guiomar de Anaya, Isabel Márquez and Potenciana de Abreu, also accused of witchcraft, Barbola de León, a mulatto woman, Juliana de Ariza, Inés de Octavio, Elena de Victoria, Bernarda Alvarez, Sebastián de Botafuego, a negro slave, and Bartolomé Cortés, a cobbler, native of Santa Fe, accused of heretical speeches and blasphemy.

Apart from the *auto*, Fray Luis de Jodar, a Franciscan, was accused of having pronounced blasphemous and heretical opinions from the pulpit but was absolved. Antonio de Isla Liébana, from Madrid, was accused merely of fornication.[1]

We have here a concrete and definite account of the *auto-da-*

---

[1] Taken from J. A. Medina, *op. cit.*

fé of 1636. On the other hand we learn from the testimony of Francisco López Bueno, superintendent of the prisons of the Penitentiary of the Holy Office of the Inquisition, a great friend of Claver's, that:

> as soon as ever he heard that anyone was to be punished or condemned to death he went to hear his confession and to say Masses for him, give him Holy Communion, prepare him with all care and kindness to die like a Catholic and true Christian, staying by him night and day, accompanying him through the public streets without leaving him for a moment until his death, and he not only gave him spiritual but material help, giving him wine and cakes to comfort him. He also brought musicians from the college and singers (choristers) from the cathedral and as soon as the prisoner expired had a responsory sung with organ accompaniment as Brother Nicolás and Father Juan Bautista Fajardo, a priest of the cathedral, will be able to testify.

A motley crowd appeared at the *autos-da-fé*. People of all classes filed past in search of liberation, with suffering on their faces and bitter expectancy in their haerts.

One particular culprit, Luis Andrea, a *mestizo*, was accused of having a pact with a devil called Buciraco for sixteen years. He was condemned to life imprisonment and the galleys.

Diego Piñero was a professed friar of the Augustinian Order; he had dared to say Mass 'having received deacon's orders only'.

A hundred lashes were given to the carpenter, Andrés de Cuevas, who defended fasting on Saturday.

Witchcraft was much practised, especially by the negro and mulatto element. Antón Baños and Juana de Aranda, María Ramírez and the cobbler Juan de la Magdalena, were all set free after a certain number of lashes.

A curious phenomenon which illustrates the cosmopolitan character of the town was the number of foreigners. The following appeared before the Tribunal: Juan Mercader, a French pedlar, Juan Lorenzo, a mulatto from Lima, Francisco Rodríguez Cabral, a Portuguese, Jorge de los Santos, a Greek, Marco Pacio, a Neapolitan, and Isabel Noble a Portuguese.

In this trial none was condemned to the stake or death in any form. It was a spectacular *auto*.

The second public *auto-da-fé* took place on 17 June 1626. Peter Claver was present. There were twenty-two penitents.

Federico Cuperes was a Calvinist from Antwerp who had worn a *sambenito* for two years and he was condemned 'to wear it for another year, though it caused him great discomfort, and to receive one hundred lashes'. Witchcraft continued its depredations. Francisca de Contreras, Lucas González, Jerónima de León, Juan Salas, José Niño Frías and Isabel de Borda combined the strangest superstitions with a pretended piety. The punishments were: the disgrace of the gag, lashes and some years of banishment. Here too there are many foreigners; Julio César Capriano of Milan, Amaro Gómez from Portugal, and Luis Franco from Lisbon; Pedro de Abreu and Antonio Rodríguez, Portuguese; Diego Rodríguez and Domingo da Costa of the same nation. The number of Portuguese condemned is remarkable.

But the great event in this trial was the sentence passed on Juan Vicente, a new Christian, a native of Campo Mayor in Portugal, a shoemaker. He had been declared a heretic, a persistent relapsed Judaizer. The minutes of the trial state: 'His offences were very serious and so much so that in order not to scandalize pious Christains most of them were not read in public. For relapsing into such offence he was delivered to the Tribunal and he came out on the stage with distinctive marks of this relapse. After his sentence was read, he was handed over to the lieutenant of the town who ordered him to be burned.' He was the second culprit to be sentenced to death in Cartagena.

The direct record states: 'It was seven o'clock at night and the Inquisitor put on his surplice, stole and cape; the penitents were brought in and kneeling at his feet they all abjured, both those *de levi* and those *de vehementi*, and then, the ceremonies performed, according to the custom of the Holy Tribunal and with the assistance of the Cathedral choristers, the hymn *Veni Sancte Spiritus* and the psalm *Miserere mei Deus* were sung. The Inquisitor then reconciled and absolved the heretics who abjured their heresies.'

The third solemn *auto-da-fé* took place on 26 March 1634. Those accused of witchcraft were the most numerous; twenty-one witches appeared at this trial, two blasphemers and one bigamist.

A great effort is needed to penetrate this motley world of different races and countries, of religions superimposed on one another, of new converts and of fanatical adherents to religious novelties from Protestant countries, of Mahometans, and of Jews. It was a time when superstition and witchcraft were almost a dogma of the common people, and especially in cities like Cartagena, a meeting-place for every kind of person and idea, particularly among the negro slaves not yet well grounded in their new faith and still clinging to their racial customs.

Here is one example of this kind of sorcery which we find in a letter dated 19 September 1633:

As an example of these acts of sorcery we shall quote a case, in which twenty-two people were eye-witnesses, in the words of the inquisitors: A negro called Fernando Cabamoche assembled at midnight all the negroes and negresses he could find in the city of Pamplona, inviting them to join in a game with him. In the middle of the room a chest was placed with a light on it and surrounded by all the negroes the said Fernando Cabamoche began to play on a little bow which he put in his mouth, singing in his own language and saying he wanted to fly. They all answered that he should fly, and putting out the light and taking off all his clothes he kept on saying that he was flying and they again answered that he should fly. Then voices were heard up in the ceiling of the room, some saying 'How he flies!' and others telling him to fly. The door of the room where they were being shut, the voice of the said Fernando was heard outside telling them to open it for him. After a little while they heard him inside the room making a noise in the ceiling, and falling to the ground he got on to the aforesaid chest, and at the same time a number of black figures fell from above and got on to the chest, saying in their language: 'Guacolo?' which means 'How are you?' and he answered 'I am well.' Then the said Fernando and the figures in the air, moving overhead as if playing at ball, saying in their language: 'There it goes.' 'Here it is.' 'I've got it.' 'Look at it there.' They went on like this for some time, and there was a bad smell like the odour of death or graveyard earth. One of the figures touched the chest, making a gentle sound on it with hands and small sticks, and the figures could be heard catching hold of Fernando by his feet and hands, and he complaining about it. Then the figures took leave of each of the persons who were present at the game, saying: 'Stay here,' and each one giving a tap on the box they went up to the ceiling of the room making a great noise like little bells.

Crimes of sorcery caused a great deal of anxiety to the Tribunal and to the bishops of the district. These sorcerers—at least in Cartagena and its district—were all negroes brought from Angola to work as slaves in the mines.

They were so numerous at that time in the New Kingdom of Granada that in the mines at Saragossa and its neighbourhood in the province of Antioquia alone, more than two thousand of them were employed in extracting gold, and all were so stupid, according to Mañozca, that they were like horses, and it was so difficult to understand the language they spoke that their declaration could only be accepted with great reserve.

Sometimes when they were threatened with proceedings, they fled to the mountains, from which it was almost impossible to get them. Attempts to catch them were made at the expense of their owners, who found that, when the trial was over and the slaves condemned to life imprisonment, they lost the money spent in catching them as well as the price they had paid for them. The result was that very soon the owners themselves were the first to take measures to prevent them being caught.

As soon as they arrived from Africa attempts were made to instruct them in the Faith, but once they had been taken inland only half-taught they easily fell back into the devil's idolatry and denied the Faith with the same facility with which they had seemed to embrace Catholicism.

It is true that some members of religious orders came from time to time to the places where they had been sent to mine for gold; but as these

were looking for gold and not seeking the spiritual benefit of the poor creatures, and even if they occasionally preached, it was to get what they wanted more easily, because, besides being mostly undisciplined friars and dissolute priests wandering about without permission of their bishops and giving a very bad example, they never stay in these parts when once they have got what they went for. The other Spaniards who usually frequent those places are merchants who live only for gain and the slave-owners who exploit the mines only looking to the wages and tasks of each day and attending to nothing else, and even when they see a negro or negress of their gang in a poor state of health or suddenly dead, although they realize the harm done by the witches, very few of them, preferring the honour of God to their own interest, will denounce or hand over those of their gang they notice to have been affected by this pest.[1]

This world of the condemned must have constituted the strangest field for Peter Claver's life-work. A mixture of ignorance and misery, of bad faith at times and of deep-seated fear at others; priests who did not keep their vows of chastity, side by side with negro slaves who revived on the hot nights of the Caribbean the rites of Guinea; witches who were mere exploiters of others' credulity—as a way of making a living; besides these there were preachers who did not make themselves sufficiently clear in their sermons and left a disturbing impression of heresy on their audiences; bigamists who had left their legitimate wives over in Europe and sought other company in the New World; Judaizers who had one day been baptized from fear or self-interest and then felt nostalgia for the Sabbath; heretics taken prisoner on the coasts of the Caribbean Sea who had not the prudence to keep quiet and tried to discard their new ideas; innocent and foolish women who in a fit of bad temper or charlatanry made compromising statements. All these prisoners went through the houses on the west side of the main square of Cartagena where the Inquisitors and two prosecutors, grave and anxious in the exercise of their office, interrogated them and passed sentence, while the world in Europe went on its way killing one another too in the wars of religion.

Peter Claver, the Process tells us, had a great esteem for the Inquisition; he belonged to a race and nation which had made of

[1] Carta de Mañozca, 16 March, 1622.

their Faith the very meaning of their history, but at the same time he felt profound compassion for the unfortunate people who suffered in the thirteen prisons of the town.

Twelve solemn *autos-da-fé* in all were held in Cartagena and thirty-eight private ones, with a total of 767 convicted. Six persons were condemned to death, only two of them in the time of Claver, who attended them at their death—Adam Edon in 1622 and Juan Vicente in 1626.

CHAPTER V

HERETICS AND PIRATES

CARTAGENA of the Indies was perhaps unique in the world of the seventeenth century for its life of colour and contrast. The stage upon which Peter Claver was destined to carry out his social task could not have been more appropriate. It was not only the tropical background for a formidable mixture of races, it was also a city coveted both by the European rivals of Spain and by the pirate forces which sailed those seas in their dangerous search for gold and adventure.[1]

In that century the words *pirate* and *heretic* meant much as *communism*, *fifth column* or *espionage* do today. From the beginning Cartagena had been a fortified city. Claver's behaviour cannot be understood without realizing this fact. Alongside the world of the negro with its slave-ships, its hulks and its slaves are the hospital, the enclosure, the garret where the sick man lies in a litter, waiting for death from his infection; and not far away in the open sea the pirates are keeping watch, waiting for the galleons laden with gold to leave harbour, ready to fall upon the city when opportunity offered. The majority of these pirates were heretics, and fortune did not always favour them; many fell into the sea to be eaten by sharks; others were captured and brought chained into the city. There were blond Englishmen, embittered French Huguenots, tough square-built Dutchmen, Arabs and Moors lumped together as Turks. Here also was a fertile field for Catholic teaching, here also were souls to be evangelized.

[1] There is abundant literature on this subject; of the books used, the following deserve special mention: C. H. Haring, *The Pirates of the East Indies in the Seventeenth century*, Paris, 1939; *Historial de Cartagena de Indias*, Buenos Aires, 1943—an interesting volume which contains the story of the capture of Cartagena by Pointis in 1695 and the diary of Vernon's expedition; Pedro Julio Dousdebés, *Cartagena de Indias, Plaza fuerte*, Bogotá, 1948—contains original matter, especially on the invasion of 1622.

In the preceding chapter on the Inquistion we pointed out that a large number of foreign offenders were sentenced in each *auto-da-fé*. Some historians have presented a one-sided view of this problem. According to Prescott and Lea the Inquisition in the New World had no other aim than to burn heretics. Here are the exact words of Mañozca describing the ceremony on Sunday, 13 March 1622, when for the first time in Cartagena a man was to be burned at the stake:

> This ceremony was, we may hope, to the glory and honour of God, for although there were but eight penitents, there were present at it as many persons of birth and authority as have assisted at the most celebrated of *autos*. There was one only to be handed over to the civil arm, an Englishman, named Adam Edon, a Protestant heretic. This man, in spite of all the measures ordained by the law and by your Lordship, for two years has refused to repent. He persisted in the defence of his errors, and for them he died by fire, with so much obstinacy that his blindness amazed all those present, since, without being bound, he sat himself upon the bundles of kindling and remained motionless without moving even a foot. He was a man of about thirty-two, well built, with a good knowledge of Spanish. Moderate in his speech, his countenance suggested either a real or false modesty. He was taken prisoner in Cumaná and entered the public prison at Cartagena in July 1619. When he had declared himself a Protestant, he was transferred to the Inquisition's prison, where the night before the *auto* he spent many hours in discussion with two monks sent to him to attempt to convert him. They had no success.

One of these monks, it is clear from other documents, was St Peter Claver. He was normally chosen by the prison authority to deal with these painful cases of condemned men. What profound grief he must have felt in the face of this rejection of grace. It cannot have been the only case of stubbornness since we read in a letter of the same period: 'Father Claver on many occasions wrought with a certain heretic but could not incline his will because, refusing to hear a word, the man greeted him with insults and oaths, born of his hatred for the Roman Church.'

In 1617 he visited the French Huguenots from Brazil, David Mingan and Peter Hebert. These were absolved. It is worth noting that the majority of foreign heretics brought before the Inquisition and sentenced to lesser penalties were sent for instruction to the Jesuit College where Peter Claver lived. It is reasonable to suppose that this was at his own request, especially in view of the almost official position he held in these matters. Between 1618 and 1652 we have many names of Englishmen who were absolved and sent to the Jesuit college for instruction. In this latter year Claver, then paralysed, was taken in a litter to the prison to interview an obstinate heretic. He might well be called the guardian of these poor foreigners, who, far from their homes, felt upon their souls the burden of their errant lives. Possibly God made use of their misfortunes to return them to their forefathers' faith. Claver was first their intermediary and defender before the Inquisition and then their teacher. He should be called, then, not the hammer of the heretics, but their Apostle.

Perhaps the events of 1639–40 had the widest repercussions—so far as the mission of Claver to the heretics was concerned. Don Federico de Toledo, at the head of a large fleet, had captured Santa Catalina, one of the islands on the route of the galleons past modern Nicaragua. Santa Catalina was the centre of operations of the English and Dutch for their attacks against the ships returning to Spain. The authorities disagree on the order of events and on the number of prisoners taken. An account may be found in C. H. Haring's book already mentioned. But we have a report written three years after the death of Claver, which is printed by his first biographer, Father Andrade. It has the unmistakable flavour of an eye-witness chronicle:

In the years 1639–40 in a great attack there were swept out of the islands of San Cristóbal and Santa Catalina whole armies of Dutch and English. These men were brought to Cartagena. Father Claver sought out Catholic interpreters and filled a ship with monks. It sailed from ship to ship of the fleet, in which were 600 English heretics, with only fourteen soldiers to guard them. The latter begged the Jesuits to say Mass for them, saying that they had not heard Mass since they left the islands. Claver agreed, put on his vestments, and said Mass. The heretics watched attentively the ceremonies of the Holy Sacrifice which they had never seen in their lives. Claver said Mass with such devotion and gravity that they were astounded and bewildered, and argued about what they had seen. Then he asked to speak to them, and through an interpreter asked them to hear the word of God. But since it was already late they asked him to postpone his address so that they might hear him with more leisure, and they offered to go ashore and hear him. The guards invited him to eat and Claver agreed so that he might have a chance to speak with the English. These latter asked him if he would like to see their bishop. He was delighted and thanked them. Straightway there came out of the poop cabin an old man of respectable and venerable appearance, white haired, long bearded. He came forward with short steps, his countenance grave, accompanied by the most respected elder men.

Claver and his companions went forward to greet him, treating him with every courtesy. Then, on the advice of the Spanish captain, he drank his health in the English fashion. This moved the Archdeacon of London (for such was his title), and speaking in Latin he asked for private speech with Claver. The two went apart together, while the other interpreters talked with the heretics about the Faith. Claver spent many hours with the English churchman, trying to lead him to the true path of the Catholic faith and almost convinced him. As night fell he remembered that it was the feast of St Ursula (who was born in England) and to close the conversation he said: 'Sir, remember that it was on this day that St Ursula gave her life together with that of all her friends for the sake of that faith which I am describing to you, and think how contrary is the religion you profess to that which they professed, and that St Lucius, King of England,[1] was so obedient to the Roman Apostolic See and had so great a respect for the Chair of Peter, that every year he sent to Rome rich gifts and jewels as tokens and tributes of his recognition. So also did all his descendants until Henry VIII and Anne Boleyn. And consider how you and all your flock, misled, are following a road that ends in hell.' To this the heretic replied that he was persuaded of error, but that he could not at that moment declare himself, that he would do so at the

[1] Legendary King of Britain during the Dark Ages.

hour of death, reconciling himself with the Church. Father Claver contined to struggle to drag him away from heresy without the postponement he planned, but his wealth, his position, reputation and children held him so captive that he had not the strength to break his chains. He took leave of him and of the others, accepting their promise that they would see each other ashore. The heretics came to our house, where they were welcomed and provided for with all charity, and, to omit all the details of their conversion, more than 500 were received into the Church. The first of these was a wounded man who left the ship so ill that in a few days he died, having confessed and received the sacraments. Father Claver with his customary charity caused him to have an honourable burial in the presence of all the clergy and the nobility, and the singing of the choir in the cathedral. This moved many more to accept the faith, especially when they saw the fate of the dead heretics, who were buried like dogs in the open country and dragged to their graves. Many were moved when they saw the love with which the sick were treated, how they were cured and watched over with consummate care and attention. Claver spent days wrestling with a persistent heretic who was in hospital without hands or feet, and at last, making as if in despair at ever converting him, though he was on the point of death, went to look after another patient. The first, seeing his gentleness and hearing the loving words with which he comforted the man, was so moved that raising his head he made signs as if to recall Claver—being incapable of speech. Claver went to him and it pleased God to permit him to speak, and he asked forgiveness of all and was reconciled with the Church. Claver absolved him of his sins and heresies, and he died a Catholic.

Father Claver did not forget the Archdeacon of London, but commended him to God and prayed for him. On the eve of All Saints, in the San Lázaro Hospital, the said Archdeacon, carried by his companions, his face disfigured, sunken and diseased, stared at Claver, who straightway went to receive him, and speaking gently to him they embraced like brothers, and the Englishman said to him: 'The time has come for me to redeem my promises to God and to you that I would accept again the true and Catholic religion of the Holy Roman Church which my fathers professed,' and he went on to beg the Saint not to abandon him at that moment since he was very weary with sickness and wished to talk with him quietly about the state of his soul. Claver was overjoyed and gave thanks to God for the conversion of this bishop. He helped him in it with great charity and reconciled him to the Church. Having received the sacraments of the Eucharist and extreme unction he gave up his soul to his Creator at the hands of Peter Claver, who assured him an honourable burial. Many others followed this conversion, and they were so many that the commander of the fleet, persuaded by Claver, admitted them as soldiers of the king, with pay according to their rank.[1]

A witness of these events tells us: 'At the time of the sickness and death of the bishop a great number of Englishmen were in the hospital and all died Catholics following the example of their bishop. It was a consolation to hear them invoking the saints at the moment of death and calling out in Latin: "Saints of Spain, protect me", thus giving it to be understood that they died in the Roman faith professed by the Spaniards.'

On hearing news like this the healthy sailors in the ships came ashore out of curiosity and sought the Jesuit college. Christmas was drawing near, and they wanted to attend the celebrations and see again the glory of the Catholic churches. Peter Claver had the church magnificently decorated.

Once the Masses were said and the congregation out of the church, the outer doors were locked and the English were brought in through an inner door. They were astounded at the altars, the lights, the ornaments, the hangings, the jewels, the neatness and cleanliness in everything. Kneeling before the tabernacle of the Most Holy they worshipped him and listened through an interpreter to a sermon. They were so impressed by what they had seen and heard in the Jesuit college that they refused to return aboard the ships that night, and had to be found lodging and food, a difficult matter at that period owing to shortages and epidemics.

The news of these events spread among the other sailors, and every day men arrived at the porter's lodge asking for Father

[1] Andrade, *op. cit.*, pp. 56–9.

Claver.[1] He had a talk with the commander of the fleet, Don Federico de Toledo, and asked him to smooth the path of the new converts. Don Federico offered them the choice of remaining at liberty or of joining the Spanish forces with pay according to their deserts. Many exercised their choice, and it is interesting to look at the surnames later common in the city: from this period date many English and Dutch names.

The porter's lodge was another favourite spot of Claver's. He used to take charge of the keys after the midday meal, to give the porter a rest; near by lived a group of heretical prisoners who used to come to the lodge especially for water or food; their rations were scanty. Claver made use of these visits to examine their faith.

The story of the pirate attacks against the Indies is one of the most exciting of history. The names of Baal, Coates, Hawkins, Drake, El Olonés and Vernon still sound like warning trumpets in all the islands and sounds of the Caribbean. A single piece of data gives us some idea of the menace: between 1655 and 1671 the pirates had sacked eighteen cities, four towns and more than thirty-five villages, leaving a terrifying legend of robbery and violence. Two aspects only need to be emphasized here. We cannot imagine today the state of uncertainty and anguish in those towns. A sail far off at sea might be news from home or it might herald fire and battle. This sense of insecurity was peculiarly accentuated by its religious aspect. The sacking of a town by pirates meant the profanation and ruin of churches and sanctuaries. The other aspect is that of the destruction left in the wake of any military action. If the pirates won—ruin; if they were defeated— a rabble of men of all races entered the city as captives. In the days of St Peter Claver there was only one such invasion. It is often forgotten.

In 1620 Don Girón de Loaiza was governor. In June of that year he was more than equal to his task. Twenty-four hours after receiving report of the sighting he was able to surprise and defeat bitterly a large group of pirates sailing to attack Cartagena in

[1] Process; Hazañero, *op. cit.*, p. 120.

three well-armed ships, and nine launches. One of Claver's tasks
was to deal with the Moors or Turks who often took sail in these
ships, or in merchant ships or royal galleys. This work with Muslims
was difficult, but he had some remarkable successes. The major
problem was to overcome their well-known fanaticism. Claver's
way was to persevere in doing them all possible small services,
to attract them by gentleness, to win their hearts, and through
this humble constancy he gained notable victories over their
fanaticism. Two such cases are well known. He had wrestled with
one Moor for twenty-two years ... However much the Moor shut
himself up in his obstinacy Claver never tired but, always humble,
always meek, always patient, persisted in his exhortations, until
God sent the Muslim the final sickness of death. He was removed
to the San Sebastián hospital, and there Claver went to see him.
When the Moor recalled the long years during which Claver had
argued with him, when he contemplated the invincible patience
of that man who had persisted with him for twenty-two years,
and had rendered him only good, he could not resist such an
outflowing of love. He recognized the holiness of a faith which
taught men so to sacrifice themselves for their neighbour. He abjured
the beliefs of Mahomet, received baptism and died in the Faith in
the arms of St Peter Claver. A similar story is told of another
Moor. This conversion cost Claver thirty years of prayer and persistence. At the end of the time the hard soul was softened, and
Claver was the instrument of his rebirth in the waters of baptism.
The case of a Moor named Amete is famous. It is quoted in the
Process as typical. For forty years he resisted the efforts of the Saint,
but surrendered to grace through the intercession of the dead
Claver. When the Saint died this Moor was seventy years old.
Part of his life had been spent in Spain, and the last forty years in
Cartagena. He was a confirmed Muslim. Claver used to see him
almost daily as he left for the hospital, passing him in the market-
place or in the plaza de la Hierba. His friendly greetings were
received with an enigmatic and mocking smile. After Claver's
death Amete went on hanging about the college where the friend
whose friendship he had rejected was buried. On 30 November
1656 the sacristan, Brother Nicolás González, was placing the

hangings in the church for All Souls' Day when he saw the Moor in the square by the church and called him. He tried to run off, but at the brother's repeated urging he approached in an angry mood.

'Here I am. Now what do you want?'

'I want you to become a Christian.'

'This isn't the moment for that.'

'The present moment is always the proper one for God.'

'I don't want to,' he replied with an angry gesture.

A poor beggar was standing by named Alonso Nicolás, a great friend of Claver and later a witness at the Process. Claver had bequeathed the unfinished task to him. The two of them went on arguing with the Moor. They remembered what Claver used to say on these occasions: 'Christ be with me, lighten my understanding and soften my heart.' People began to gather round. The Moor, beside himself with rage, rushed away. Next day the beggar was sent to summon him. The brother, the beggar and the Moor sat together in the centre of the chapel of the Holy Saviour. Claver had died two years before. His body lay very near them. The attack continued. That soul no longer resisted so harshly. The brother pointed out a painting of hell.

'Is it possible that after a long life spent in the galleys you want to take your rest among the tortures of hell?'

'I don't want to go to hell.'

'You will go if you remain a Muslim.'

The arguments were nearly exhausted, when Brother Nicolás had an inspiration.

'Come over here. You knew Father Claver? Didn't he often advise you to become a Christian? Here he is buried, close by those sick people praying for health through his intercession.'

He took the Moor's arms and held them over the tomb. He put up no resistance: some force or other held him. Much moved he asked: 'Father Claver is buried here?'

'That is so. Beg him to pray to God for you; beg him to ask God to enlighten your mind, to soften your heart. Repeat here, by his body, what he used to say: 'Christ be with me.'

Grace came from heaven. He pressed his face to the tomb, and said in a low voice: 'If God wishes now that I should become a Christian, I wish it too; I want to be a Christian, I want to believe in Christ.'

They took him away from the tomb, put a rosary round his neck, and for the first time in seventy years he kissed the crucifix. The negroes praying close by shouted: 'A miracle! a miracle done by Father Claver. The moment the Moor came to the tomb he accepted our holy faith.' Then the Creed was recited. Rumours of what had happened penetrated into the house. The Father Provincial, Gaspar de Cugia, came down into the church, and on 21 December Father Juan Onofre baptized the Moor in the cathedral, with Captain Diego de la Torre Cantillana as godfather. The chronicle reports that Don Diego gave the Moor clothes, and his own name.

'What good work have you ever done in your life, Amete?' asked his companions.

'I remember very few. Perhaps one: every week I spared from my poverty alms for the lepers at San Lázaro.'

God had rewarded him, and the body of Peter Claver must have leaped with joy in its tomb. Six months later Amete died a Christian death, seventy years old. This is one of the dramatic stories told of the apostle. Peter Claver, like the Cid, had won the battle with the Moor after his death.

CHAPTER VI

THE JESUIT COLLEGE IN CARTAGENA

PETER CLAVER left Seville for America in April 1610 and he probably arrived in Cartagena in June or July. His first stay in the port was very short. He was still a student and had to finish his studies for the priesthood in Santa Fe de Bogotá. In 1616, his training finished, he went back to the town which was to be the centre of his labours for thirty-eight years. Apart from short missionary journeys to nearby settlements, the longest being to Sinú and Tolú, St Peter Claver rarely left Cartagena. Almost certainly he never went back to Bogotá. He might have found it necessary to attend the provincial meetings of the Jesuits there, but the reports of the meetings make it clear he did not attend. Cartagena was his town, and the Jesuit College his centre. It is important then to give a clear idea of this home which he so dearly loved.

The present church and college are eighteenth-century buildings but thanks to the Jesuit archives in Rome it has been possible to locate exactly the older structures. The Jesuits when they arrived for the first time in 1604 installed themselves in a building thus described: 'The college was founded in a house in the main square, not far from the cathedral and the palace of the Inquisition. The square was crossed by the three main streets of the town. There were seven rooms in the upper floor of the house, and the ground floor was arranged as church and sacristy.'

This Jesuit source is confirmed by a town council document which says that the Jesuits bought houses near the square for their church and residence. This church was a simple chapel and the building was soon found to be too small and too overlooked:

It was very cramped and overlooked by the higher buildings in the neighbourhood, for which reasons the Father Provincial ordered it to be sold and another bought elsewhere. This was done and two houses were bought on the road to the harbour and near the harbour. They are separated from the sea by a wall only, and from the houses there is a view of the sea, and one could enjoy the sea breezes. These houses are near a tract of land given to the Society by the town. With the money left from this transaction new houses were bought alongside, and we have a document of 1617 which reports the purchase from María de Esquibel of a 'house of slate, wood and stone contiguous with the said college of the Jesuits'.

The Jesuits moved to these new quarters in 1618 and we have the complete and authentic report of this ceremony in the *Annual Letters* for 1619–21:

Cartagena. The college moved its site because it was overlooked by other buildings. The new site is near the sea. There were difficulties, but the inquisitor Don Juan de Mañozca helped to overcome them. Near by is the town butcher. The move began on 17 September, beginning with the church. For this the most solemn procession that this town has ever seen was arranged. All the nobility and the people assembled to accompany the Sacrament. Overhead the streets were hung with awnings, the walls were covered with rich hangings and, many altars were set up along the way. The ground was strewn with flowers interspersed with fountains, and fireworks were set off. The troops in the town were divided into two squads, and as the procession passed them they saluted it with their muskets. The Franciscan monks from monasteries came to honour us, bringing their saint in procession to our church. The Father Guardian led the procession carrying the Host beneath a rich canopy carried by the councillors of the city... The church was finished in time for Ash Wednesday. It was built in the main courtyard (called 'of the butchers'), with sanctuary and choir, and at one side an aisle for men only with an altar at each end. One altar is to the crucified Christ, and the other to the Virgin of the Miracle (so called both because she came miraculously to the Indies, and because she performs miracles constantly, and is thus held in great devotion by the city).

In the light of these facts we can establish both events in the life of Claver; on arriving in Cartagena in 1610 he lived in the house already described, with the tiny chapel; on returning in 1616 he must have gone back to the same house, and in the tiny chapel of the Virgin of the Miracle he said his first Mass. This building was the base of operations for his early work with Father Núñez and later Father Sandoval. He lived in it for two years.

Claver took part in the transfer to the new site. He was one of the founders of the Cartagena college, and therefore of the present building. He was present at all the subsequent changes made in it from the time when it was 'the modest college, modest because so recently founded', of which Brother Peter Simón speaks, until it became the imposing building of 1642. He was present also at the inauguration of the chapel with its two altars to Christ and the Virgin. Alongside this church, hot within but slimy and clammy because of the sea, and in this college, being built piece by piece upon the skeleton of the three original houses, lived St Peter Claver.

The new church was still too small for all who wished to worship there, and the fathers suffered from lack of cloisters and rooms for their many tasks. Serious difficulties arose because of the construction of fortifications in that part of the city. The governor, his military engineers, the president of the high court of Chile, the viceroy of Peru and the commander of the fleet all took part in the discussions, and no final solution was found until two years after the death of the Saint. This business much embittered his final hours, so much so that he begged God to take him before he should see his college demolished. Against the wishes of the military experts, the governor gave the Jesuits permission to build upon the fortifications wall itself. This was probably in 1630, and from then dates the two-floored structure which we see today using the wall as foundation. The first floor has two arches, and the second window balconies in the Cartagena style. The fathers lived peacefully in this building until 1637-40, when the then governor announced that a house built upon the fortifications was a danger to their security. An order arrived from the court. The building was to be demolished, the walls cleared. The situation was serious. The Jesuits alleged that they had spent more than 50,000 *pesos* on the building, and that to clear the wall it would be necessary to pull down the sanctuary—that is to say, in effect, to abandon the college. The argument ended in the agreement of 1656. A second wall was to be built at the cost of the Jesuits, facing the sea, and between it and the college a street was to be left. In addition the fathers were to build the towers to reinforce the wall at that point. This was done.

A difficult question remains. Where was the Saint's cell? It can be deduced from a sentence in the Process that the porter's lodge was near the sacristy: Brother Nicolás says at one stage, 'the brother was always in the sacristy, close to the porter's lodge'. And we know from many witnesses that the dark, wretched and bare cell of the Saint—one man says it was so wretched that no negro would live in it—was above the porter's lodge so that Claver could readily help those who came for the Sacrament at night. This room must have disappeared in the construction of the present buildings.

The Jesuits use the word *operario* for those members who work in residences where there is also a church. This word implies all the usual tasks: confessions, preaching, visiting and other parochial work, and visiting hospitals. Claver was an *operario* or priest on the parish in this Cartagena college. According to the letters of the Father Provincial, Father Hazañero (1638–43) there were usually in the college twenty-four Jesuits, ten priests and various assistant brothers. As for the city itself, one must remember the two groups of inhabitants: permanent and temporary. The majority of the first group were of Spanish origin, families which had taken root there and formed the social nucleus. The second group was made up of negroes and Indians, and also by the masses of soldiers, sailors and pirate prisoners stopping in Cartagena on their way north to Panama and Vera Cruz or south to Quito, Lima or Buenos Aires. In 1573 there were 400 resident families, in 1607, 800. By 1700 there were more than 1,800, which implies a population of about 6,000.

The life of a priest on the parish was a busy one. Besides including the regular tasks, visits to hospitals and slave barracks, there was also the extra work in Lent or during crises on the arrival of slave ships, or epidemics, or enemy attacks. To all this must be added missionary journeys inland. It would be a mistake to exaggerate and think of this life that many Jesuits led alongside Claver as heroic in itself, but it is equally absurd to minimize the constant sacrifice, particularly when this life was led with the peculiar fervour of the Saint. There are many original documents which help to reconstruct the environment of Claver during these years. Among the most valuable are the *Annual Letters* of the Provincial referred to above. On the conditions in the college, after relating the figures already given:

As to temporal matters, our members continue their ordinary tasks in a state of poverty which has increased in recent years because of high prices and the cost of the new buildings. We were driven to this expense partly because of the unsuitability and inconvenience of the old building, which was irritating not only to the members of the college but also to their guests, of which latter there are great numbers, especially on the arrival of the fleet. Besides this, many of the brothers suffered extremely from the heat, and it seemed excessive that they should be expected to suffer even more in health and discomfort in order to make room for guests. The new building when finished according to the architects' plans will be large enough for all purposes, being about forty-six feet high and 466 feet long. Another improvement has been the construction of a water tank. This we needed badly in view of the general scarcity of water here. We have only one farm in the country, which also has been enlarged by an increase of twenty slaves. With this reinforcement and the great care, labour and skill of the brother in charge we are confident that it will be in the future sufficient for our supplies. We have another house in the country used rather as a retreat for rest, particularly for a day's holiday from all our cares and labour. This has been much improved in two respects; first in its structure, since the old one was almost useless from age and decay, and second in its value as a place of rest, since we begged the rector to have an orchard planted there, which will be of both practical and spiritual value. To pay for all these things we have received in alms in the years 1641 and 1642 40,000 *pesos*.

As to educational work, we begin with Latin, to which classes come not only students from the town but from all the region. We begin with the most elementary principles and continue until they leave the college complete Latinists. The classes are always full. We have founded in the college a sodality of our Lady. We have founded too a guild for the merchants and persons of higher social rank. This is in the charge of a very worthy father and one who has long lived in these parts. Every Sunday when he has leisure he busies himself with this guild.

We do not know if Claver took any part in this work of the college. In view of all his various activities, we should imagine very little. From the guilds mentioned above, that of the negroes, organized and directed by Claver, is missing, though it had a flourishing life.

A curious reason is given in the letters for poor attendance at church: clothing problems. Hazañero writes on this subject: 'the climate and the heat and its bad, relaxing effect on the human body is the general reason why throughout most of the year the churches are empty. Even pious and Christian persons stay away. After passing the days in the lightest possible clothing in the privacy of their homes they cannot face spending much time in church dressed with the decency and decorum there expected. For these and other reasons we have not been able to establish a custom that parents and teachers should send us their children'.

More serious was the shortage of priests:

So great is the number of those seeking confession that one may say without exaggeration, as there were only ten priests, that if there were three times as many they would all find themselves with plenty of work. In fact they hear confessions from dawn to dusk and sometimes later, by candle light.

Another important task is the unending service of our church, our few priests having to do the work of the many needed to supply the needs of so many people, both those resident in the city and those passing through it. And although the church is small and not even our own property (because of our many debts, the poverty of this college, and its lack of a founder) this does not militate against our providing all the services that the Society renders. When a great crowd comes to the church on popular feast days, or to hear the sermon, we use a *patio* behind the church for the men, and the women fill the building itself.

It is certain that although the city has a cathedral, a parish church, and five religious houses, more people come to us than to the others. In addition to the normal tasks of other colleges we have other duties, like teaching and preaching. Many sermons each year are given inside and outside the church, plus extra ones in Lent. There is a regular sermon in the church each Sunday afternoon, the number attending limited only by the size of the church and the *patio*. And although on that day there is preaching in all the monasteries, streets and squares, there yet remain idlers and vagabonds unwilling to listen to the word of God, so each Sunday one of the fathers goes out and collects them, leading them to the site where a sermon is to be given. In this way at least their idleness is occupied and their afternoon not wasted. On Monday, Wednesday and Friday nights many people come to listen to the moral talks, preceded by half an hour's spiritual reading. These homilies, preached by persons of authority, produce great effect. Afterwards the *Miserere* is sung to the organ and other instruments. During this, harsh scourging goes on, the bloodstains left about proving its severity. Shouts and groans and tears accompany it.

On Sunday afternoons in Lent, one of the fathers, accompanied by the schoolchildren, goes throughout the city collecting the negroes and idlers. Usually this procession ends in the little square called *plazuela de la Hierba*, a spot where all the negro women gather to buy and sell, and there a sermon is preached. The most popular sermons in the cathedral are given on Friday afternoons. Normally the bishop invites one of us to preach. In the parish church of La Trinidad also one of us preaches on Friday afternoons. This does not decrease in any way the number who flock to our own church. We visit the hospitals, such as San Juan de Dios, carrying gifts, sweeping out the wards, being available at all hours of the night. This year the plague attacked every family. It lasted months, and we were summoned endlessly from all sides. None of us, from the highest to the lowest, ever refused. We put cloth screens between the beds: in one day there were more than forty deaths. We helped with alms those who were too shy or unwilling to beg from door to door, and at our porter's lodge there was help for all the poor who came. Their numbers were increased enormously at times like that of the arrival of the vast fleet of Spaniards and Portuguese which, when defeated off Brazil, took refuge here. Or at the time of the attack on Santa Catalina to clear it of trespassing foreigners who had fortified it and ravaged the whole coast. We gave all help to the soldiers and on the day of victory a solemn Mass was sung, and our pupils gave a play before the officers.

This was the atmosphere in which Claver lived his daily life. In his life there are deeds of heroism which need no commentary; pictures of his mortification before a leper, or his work in the stench of a slave-barracks seize the imagination. But there is perhaps a more profound heroism: his silent work in the college. Fernández heads his eleventh chapter: 'Hearing confessions and Lenten labour.' He goes on:

This is the field in which he gathered the richest harvest, and he worked steadfastly to garner it, at the cost of sweat, labour, and pain. The college church in Cartagena is stiflingly hot, and damp because of its proximity to the sea. Father Claver's confessional is by the door in the full heat of the sun from sunrise till noon. It is an oven. Merely to sit in it is torture, without the toil of confessions. Every day without being summoned he was in the confessional from early Mass (five o'clock). There he stayed until eight o'clock when on normal days the task was ended. But in Lent he was there the whole day.

On this subject Brother González writes: 'So vast was the crowd of black men and women who flocked to him, that this witness does not understand how he had the strength, will, or stamina to deal with so many. Even greater is one's amazement at the austerity of his life. When I asked him once how many certificates he had given during Lent, he replied, 5,000. (The certificates were bits of paper given to penitents during Lent to show that they had been to confession.) This is the more marvellous when you consider the general character of these people, and their fecklessness.'

The interpreter Ignacio Sozo adds: 'The confessional is in the church behind the tiny door which leads to the altar of Our Lady of the Miracle. He used to take confessions the whole day and part of the night; the women by day and the men at night. He used to put benches by the confessional for the negroes to sit on. There they were till nine at night. As nine struck he would go down to the ground floor of the porter's lodge where he kept a crucifix on an altar surrounded by benches. There he made the negroes sit.'

This work must have been extremely exhausting even for a man as strong as Claver. A witness writes: 'Every day he used to spend the whole morning in the confessional, and sometimes he started hearing confessions at eight at night and carried on till eleven next morning. As a result he was sometimes in a state of collapse which prevented him from saying Mass. On these occasions he used to allow a thing which he considered pampering himself; Brother Nicolás would wipe his brow and face with a little vinegar to refresh him.'

The physical effort during Lent was overwhelming. We have a vivid picture of it from the Process, drawn by his companion, Brother Nicolás:

> The church was hot and humid. It was crowded. Claver spent the whole morning and most of the evening in his confined and stifling confessional. For the three days before Lent he had gone through the streets proclaiming the forty hours' indulgence. On Ash Wednesday he received the ashes last of all, and then entered his confessional whence he gave them to all who came until eleven o'clock when he said Mass. Straightway he went back to the confessional and knelt before the crowd, making the sign of the cross and reciting the four prayers. Then before a painting of a soul in torment which he kept fixed to the confessional throughout Lent he prepared for confession those not yet ready.

Sebastián Zapata de Talavera, in his curious way, testified in the Process that 'in the confessional he used to keep a little basket filled with delicacies, and with his own hands he would give them to negroes who were very ill. Especially dates and herbs.' This is confirmed by Manuel López, who adds that when the recipients were helpless Claver would put the food in their mouths himself. Brother Nicolás goes on:

In those days Claver used to take confessions for seven hours in the morning and four hours in the evening. When I saw him come out I used to force him to go back to the college. I used to lock the doors of the church, but it was of no avail. Claver, not satisfied with all this work during the day, used to go down to a ground-floor room near the porter's lodge, a room dark and dank, full of benches, here he would make the negroes sit in front of a large picture of Christ. In front of the picture was a candle on a table which lit up the room and a book of prints he always had of the life of Christ. It shone too on a painting of a soul in torment which he used to bring from the confessional where he always had it hanging. Then he began his teaching, followed straightway by confession until nine at night, when the doors were shut. Sometimes he was so weary that he had to be carried up to the refectory in a chair so that he could eat his frugal meal of bread dipped in water and wine, followed by a banana. This was brought to him by the college steward, Brother Lomparte.

The witness then describes a moving occasion of brotherly love: 'Andrés Sacabuche, Ignacio Angola and myself, seeing how hard Claver worked, asked the steward to bring him something strengthening, like preserves or salads (for he would ask nothing for himself). The steward did this in an ingenious way. Without Claver noticing it he increased the quantity of wine in the cup. But it was no good, there was no way of getting him to drink more. As soon as he lifted the cup he asked us if we had put in more wine. Thus he worked throughout Lent.'

In 1643 Father Bartolomé Taffier, procurator general of Lima, passed through Cartagena, and confessed on seeing Claver that he had never known such a disciple of Christ. All who knew him commented on his tirelessness. The Jesuit Brother Manuel Rodríguez says: 'There was an epidemic of smallpox, and Claver visited all the sufferers. In so doing he exhausted three or four other brothers: when one was tired he summoned another: he himself was indefatigable. When he returned with the visits finished he would tell the porter to call him in the night if help was needed, adding that the other fathers were exhausted by the toils of the day, and needed their rest. He was often called, and straightway he would appear at the lodge, saying that he was dressed and ready. He always wore round his neck two glass phials with the holy oils.'

Cartagena witnessed a spectacle which we might call the procession of the sick. 'Claver had arranged days when the blind, lame and halt could be brought to church. He had arranged too for transport for them, particularly in Lent. First he had sought permission from the bishop so that they could fulfil their religious duties in our church. When he had them assembled he taught them what they had to do in order to receive the sacraments in a worthy fashion. Then with great love and kindness he heard their confessions and said Mass for them and gave them Communion. If there were any so ill that they needed assistance he would tell the sacristan to bring wine and he himself would wait upon the sick man.' The interpreter Andrés Sacabuche completes this picture, adding: 'he did this every Sunday and every feast day when he said the eleven o'clock Mass. Before Mass he would send the interpreters to search out the baptized negroes. There were so many that all could not get into the church. So great was the heat and so strong the smell of bodies that several ladies fled from the church, unable to stand it any longer. Claver never used perfumes —at the most a little vinegar. This "pampering" he kept for the sick.'

In Claver's practical sociology one custom was invariable: his preference for negroes over the governing class. This got him into many difficulties, even with his superiors, but he remained inflexible on this point. We have evidence of various kinds on this. Doña Eleonora de Orgaz, like Agustina de Zapata and Jerónima de Urbina, was one of the leaders of society in Cartagena. She says in evidence:' He loved the negroes so much that he was unwilling to confess Spaniards, and if any Spaniard asked him to hear his confession he would reply that the negroes were in great poverty, they had to serve their masters, but that Spanish ladies never lacked confessors ready at their call, and in any case he was suitable only for blacks.' A remarkable page of the evidence at the Process deals with this point. We owe it to Brother Nicolás González:

He never granted any precedence to Doña Jerónima de Urbina (she was sister of Doña Isabel, both of them generous benefactors of his) even though he saw her waiting for hours, standing or kneeling, until the humble negresses recognized her and begged her to pass forward. The same thing happened to Don García de la Zerpa, one of the aldermen, and he used to say as a joke that if he wanted to find out where Claver was in church he looked for the largest crowd of blacks. While there were negro slaves about it was useless to attempt to confess to Claver. After the slaves came the poor, and when they were lacking, the children from the school. He did not like other people, especially people of authority, to mingle with his penitents; to the men he said that there were plenty of other confessors, and he told the ladies that his confessional was too small for farthing-ales, and that only poor negresses could get into it. (He always hated farthingales.) So if wealthier people came pestering him to confess them, he did it if they were willing to wait until he had finished with the negroes; he never bothered much about social values. Whoever he thought most acceptable to God was most acceptable to him.

Once he told Brother Pedro Lomparte confidentially that only two Spanish women confessed regularly with him, and that these caused him more trouble than all the negroes in the town. In the life of a small community this attitude aroused criticism whose effects on occasion sorely tried him. As we have said, the Saint hated farthingales. One day the inquisitor Don Pedro Calderón Gallego asked him to come and bless his house. Claver went through all the rooms, and in one of them he saw the farthingales used by the young women, and he would not bless them, saying they ought to be burned. A glance at the writings of contemporary moralists will show that he was not alone in this attitude, and that there were grounds for what appears at first sight an empty whim.

Claver by his very position and mode of life must often have met with prejudice and sectional selfishness. He represented the have-nots. 'Often he reproved the owners of slaves, he interceded for the slaves, he took them to the college, he protected fugitive slaves and sought good masters for them.' These words of Didaco de Villegas, a man of Cartagena, summarize his services to them.

He had his opponents. One witness says: 'Some, especially the ladies, were furious with him. They said that what he did was pointless, that the blacks would carry on afterwards the same as before, or worse, that they felt no loyalty. To this Claver used to reply 'that sin before marriage should be laid at the door of the owners, but that sin after marriage was the fault of the slaves themselves'. Brother Nicolás González describes a scene which might be called a domestic tragedy in three acts, with prologue and epilogue:

Some ladies of high position very much desired that Claver should hear their confessions, and since he would not agree to do so they came to me asking me to intercede for them. Because of his affection for me Claver agreed, though not without much misgiving. He said that he had neither skill nor brains for the job of confessing ladies of high birth and breeding, that his mind was tired. On saying this he struck his brow with his right hand, and declared that there were many fathers in the college who could do instead of him. Finally he agreed to do as I asked, as many ladies of the highest society in Cartagena may testify. One day in Holy Week in 1644 there came into the church a lady dressed unsuitably for the religious season, and wearing the detested farthingale. Claver was occupied with some negroes near his confessional, but as soon as he saw her he went to her and told her that she ought to respect the holy season. Thereupon she went off to the chapel of the Virgin of the Miracle shouting that Claver had insulted her in public and offended her gravely. I consoled her as well as I could, and turning to Claver told him that he ought not to meddle in these things, and that very soon because of him the church would be empty. The rector, then Father Francisco Sarmiento, heard the commotion. He came down to the church and in the presence of all severely reprimanded Claver, saying that priests were not reformers of women's dress and in any case for those purposes there existed the confessional, or even the pulpit if it were necessary. Father Claver made no reply. Next day at four in the morning while I was saying prayers in the sacristy he came in and falling to his knees kissed my feet. He called himself Judas at the feet of Christ, and I tried to make excuses for my behaviour of the previous day, telling him that I was only concerned lest fewer people should come to our church. Without saying a word Claver rose to his feet and went to his confessional.

The reader should not infer from these accounts that Claver was an anti-social man, as some modern authorities have suggested. His relations to Cartagena society were good and many of its members gave alms for his work. Best known as his benefactress was Isabel de Urbina. 'I knew Claver from childhood and I always thought him a saint. He was humble and gentle . . . he wore an old and worn habit. At home we used to cook meals for him which he gave to the poor at the porter's lodge of the college and at San Lázaro. Often he asked me for honey and wine and tobacco for his poor people.' This friendship and generosity he returned. One of the lady's slaves, Baltasar de la Cruz, tells us that 'Father Claver went every day of indulgence to her private chapel to hear her confession, and four days before he died he had himself carried in a litter to confess her and take leave of her'. The same thing happened with the family of Captain Andrés de Banquerel. For this reason we think that the priest witness Pedro Mercado exaggerates when he asserts that 'the Saint went along the streets with bowed head, and greeted very few Spaniards. He only spoke to negroes'.

Life in a religious house is full of changing colours and tiny events, a kind of mosaic in which each man can find a field for his activities and room also for his preferences within an ordered system of existence. For example, Claver did not like to go up to the huge hall on the upper floor and watch the arrival of the fleet from Spain. Nevertheless his heart leaped with joy when a messenger arrived panting at the door of his cell to announce the arrival of a slave-ship. He had one hobby: as a good Catalan he loved music. On the ground floor near the chapel he taught the children to sing with their catechists, both requiem Masses and gay songs. Later this choir sang at meals to the lepers at San Lázaro, or chanted requiem Masses for those condemned to death. Claver's asceticism had to resist a novelty which attracted him. Chocolate he did not take because he thought it an over-refined taste, a fashion for Spaniards only. Nevertheless when one day a gentleman invited him to his home, he accepted from a negro a cup of chocolate. In the routine of college life one day was set aside for going to the country, in the direction of Turbaco or El Tejar de Tierra Bomba. Normally Claver did not go, but knowing about the fruit trees there he used to ask an interpreter to bring him some baskets of fruits to furnish welcome gifts for the sick. During the hours of recreation he was often grave and silent. Sometimes this silence was misinterpreted as the result of ignorance. One day a well-known father said, 'Claver won't know anything about this; he's only an expert on blacks,' knowing nothing of the capabilities of the Saint who read Greek and wrote it elegantly, who was a master of casuistry, often consulted in difficult cases. Another day when he appeared in the recreation room silence fell on the other brothers. They knew that that morning as he absent-mindedly went along the street the governor's coach had almost run him down. He had known nothing until he felt the arm of González which pushed him forcibly into a doorway. Claver had his own entertainment. When the recreation hours dragged on in the hot Cartagena nights he would take from his pocket tiny sheets of paper which he covered with his clear writing. These were the certificates of confession which he sent to his friend, the parish priest in the cathedral, as well as to the priest of La Trinidad. At his death few valuables were found in his cell, but there were thousands of these scraps of paper which the eager crowd carried away as relics. Some of them were the occasion of miracles.

One day the doctor, Bartolomé de Torres, found him very weak and pale, with deep shadows under his eyes, and a temperature. He warned the Father Provincial, Gabriel de Melgar, and Claver was ordered to bed. When they tried to undress him he resisted, but he could not prevent the doctor and the negroes Domingo Folupo and Sacabuche seeing the terrible marks of the scourge on his body. The Father Provincial already knew of them. Claver's cell in the porter's lodge was already well known. When the porter went off to get a meal or rest Claver used to take his place. This was the hour for the poor to seek alms and advice. Some heretic pirates, driven by hunger, came from time to time. For many that lodge became the anteroom to conversion. The soldiers on patrol at night would hear as they crossed the empty square strange sounds from the lighted room on the second floor. It was Claver scourging. Very soon they took no notice. Claver himself suffered three scourgings at nightfall and one at dawn. He undertook few administrative tasks. One day, Father Juan Manuel, rector of the college, put him in charge of the residence. Disaster resulted. One of his subordinates said: 'How could he take charge of the brothers when he could not even impose his will on black slaves, for these latter he obeys implicitly and humbly.' His first action was to set aside for himself the heaviest and most menial tasks: it was shrewdly said of him, 'to put him in charge was to make him the slave of those inside the residence, adding a fresh servitude to the one he had already accepted under those outside the residence'. They soon had to relieve him of the post. Claver was not born to rule. Nevertheless he was considered a saint, and so great was his reputation both inside and outside the residence that when he was ill in 1634 and had to be bled, the brothers and the rector himself soaked cloths in the blood and distributed them as relics. Claver was then forty-four. It was possible to argue—as people did argue—about his prudence, his gifts, his value in practical matters, but there was no argument about his heroic love and self-sacrifice. We can imagine that melancholy smile so characteristic of him. He must have seen so much misery and degradation during his endless search for opportunities to express his love. For many years he was the Father Spiritual. During his nights of torture Brother Nicolás turned to him; he crouched in a corner of the room while Claver prayed in his customary attitude; prostrate with his face to the ground. Often epidemics struck down those within the residence, sometimes two-thirds of them were ill. This was Claver's opportunity. Let a witness speak:

He gave them medicine, he swept their cells, he washed their dishes, he was by their sides night and day. He laboured thus not only with the veteran fathers and brothers, but also with the least of the novices and with the servants and even with the blacks who worked our land. On one occasion a novice fell ill and Claver took charge of him and acted as his nurse. He gave him his own bed and waited upon him and took care of him.

In the same way they used to bring to him the blacks who worked on the farms belonging to the residence. He arranged their rooms, made their beds, brought them delicacies and medicines. Many of them thought their sickness a cheap price to pay for Claver's love and gentleness. Although he behaved in this way to all, when any of the black interpreters on whom he relied so much fell ill his concern knew no bounds. At his own expense he brought them the best doctors in the town, he bought them the finest medicines, however costly, he sought out chickens and other delicacies for them. Often he gave up his bed to them and slept on the ground. Sometimes he did this not for a day or two, but for months. While they slept he watched over them, when they were awake he kept them calm and tranquil, telling them stories of the saints to pass the time. He fanned them, and kept the flies from them.

The influence of Alphonsus Rodríguez was so profound in Claver's life that it seems Alonso's post of porter had a special attraction for him. Whenever he could, he acted for the porter while the latter ate or rested. These moments were some of the happiest of the Saint's life.

While the porter was resting and Claver had the keys he gathered together the beggars and spoke to them of Christian teachings. Then he distributed food to them, and often he would sit down and eat with them, holding himself poor and a beggar, as indeed he was. He did the same with the sick negroes, eating with them not only at table or on the floor, but even sharing their dish and food in order the more to please them . . .

The sensitivity of his love did not end there, because before they arrived he would arrange with cook that the stew for the poor should be prepared with care, and he sought alms to make it richer. If the toil of confessions allowed him he would cook it himself, saying that God was merciful to him in making him a cook for Christ, whose face he saw in that of the beggars. On the days of our Lady there was a banquet for the beggars and good-for-nothings. He arranged for music while they ate, he sat and ate with them, he served the food and handed out presents with a father's love. It seemed that God increased the food as it passed through his hands, because there was always enough and more, however many came to eat.

One of his great friends was the beggar Alonso Nicolás, who acted as a missionary among the other beggars. Margarita of Cape Verde was Isabel de Urbina's slave: she undertook the exceptional task of preparing the special dishes for these banquets in the porter's lodge. Brother Nicolás adds further details: 'Many heretic prisoners and slaves used to come to the lodge. He gave them to eat with his own hands, he sometimes knelt and washed their hands, said his rosary in front of them, took a broom and swept clean the *patio*. There was a well in the *patio*, from which he drew water to wash the dishes of the poor. On Holy Thursday he washed their feet.'

One of the Saint's interpreters, Ignacio Angola, deeply moved by these attentions to his coloured brothers, says: 'On important feast days, such as Easter, Christmas, Lady Day or the feast of St Ignatius, there were splendid meals in the lodge . . . there was music while we ate, and my heart was stirred to see Father Claver sitting on the ground while the beggars sat in chairs.'

These are a few pictures, all taken from original and authentic documents of this practical sociologist living his motto, *slave of the slaves*, in that Jesuit residence by the sea.

CHAPTER VII

BY HIGHWAYS AND BYWAYS

IN modern times it has been said that Claver's apostolate was superficial, its effects transitory, as if the Saint had done nothing more than baptize his converts without preparing them, and without continuing their subsequent instruction. Exactly the opposite is true. A study of the demands he made before baptism, his careful preparation in catechism and, above all, the care he took in following closely the development of his converts, arouses only wonder. If faith waned later among large sections of the negro population, if today there are non-Christian regions— almost a regression to paganism—the fault is not Claver's. We have seen how this work began in the very port of arrival in the Indies—even in the very slave-ship. His work went on in the gloomy slave-barracks, in the masters' houses, in the hospitals and the prisons. It radiated from these centres into the streets and squares, along the tracks to distant *pueblos*. It was not a simple task. To change a pagan outlook into a Christian outlook, to banish a whole complex of superstitions, of rites and magic, was slow work. The negro slaves came from a primitive and frightening world. Claver, because of his character, demanded much of himself, and he demanded much from others. On his public work in the streets (as distinct from his work within the residence) we have several witnesses. Captain Dídaco de la Cruz Arzona says:

> Among their other rites and superstitions, the blacks used to dance all night around their dead to the sound of drums. Claver went to the bishop to seek a decree against this practice. He used to go out into the streets himself and disperse these groups of dancers and confiscate the food prepared for their midnight sacrifices. Sometimes he threatened them with a whip. As for their other dances, he used to go and watch them;

it they were unobjectionable he went away. If they were immodest he used a language which—from its simplicity and his air of authority—they readily understood. He used to take out from under his cloak a scourge, and stand with that in one hand and a crucifix in the other. The blacks behaved as if their well-loved priest were a wild bull bursting into their amusements. From time to time he would take one of their drums—in spite of its size and weight—and leave it in a shop as a pledge, and redeem it only when the blacks had collected two *reales* for it. These he gave as alms to the lepers of San Lázaro.

Many of the negro customs in the New World were relics of their old religions and superstitions in Africa. Claver took great pains to combat this pagan recrudescence. The mayor Antonio del Castillo reports that Claver was especially anxious to prevent the ceremony the negroes called *lloros*.

'For this men and women gathered together by night to lament their dead to the accompaniment of pagan ceremonies. At this time they ate and drank to excess. In 1652 a widow kept a shop where she sold an intoxicating drink called *guarapa*. I went there with Manuel López and we found a great crowd of blacks round the shop. I had the place closed and Claver was most grateful—so much so that he said a Mass for me.'

Cartagena, like all cosmopolitan cities of the period, was a hotbed of superstition; not only among the negroes but also among the Europeans. The notes of the Inquisition trials are full of reports of these practices, and probably about eighty per cent of the *autos-da-fé* deal with witchcraft and divination. Claver was much concerned about this problem. He was conscious of the natural tendencies of his new converts and of the danger their new-found faith ran of shipwreck in the stormy cross-currents of mingled Christian and pagan beliefs. The future of the faith he had implanted with so much labour was constantly in jeopardy. His Christian sociology faced yet another question: public morality. The climate, the mixture of races, the high degree of sexuality of the mulattos, the abuses made possible by slavery and the licence of a cosmopolitan port—all these factors made morality a major problem. It was exacerbated by the negro craze for dancing.

Cassani with his usual vividness describes Claver's attitude to this:

He was moved to stop the dances which the negroes were trying to introduce. Constant work and slavery forced them to seek recreation and the devil tempted them to introduce into Cartagena the dances of their native Africa. They succeeded so well that the drums to accompany the dances were publicly on sale, and one negress went so far as to open a public dance-hall and tavern where she sold *guarapa*, the intoxicating drink. Claver learned of this and decided to stop it. On his way to the hospitals he chose the streets where these dances took place, and confiscated the drums, as already related. At first the negroes, taken by surprise, obeyed him, but soon they repented of this submission, and opposed him. With no intention of vengeance, but seeking the glory of God, and remembering the example which Christ gives us in the gospel, he used to draw his scourge which he always had beneath his habit and just as Christ with the whip chased out those who bargained in the temple, so the servant of God dispersed the offenders against modesty. The negroes, thinking themselves safe behind locked doors in the dance-hall, took refuge there. Claver learned of this, and straighway, furious, sped to the house (or rather brothel) and wasted no time in forms of courtesy. As soon as he got in and saw the crowd of both sexes, the drum, and the dances, he drew his scourge, dispersed the crowd, threw out the negroes, and took away the tabors. As soon as he was alone he searched the house and emptied on the floor all the *guarapa* and smashed the earthenware containers. Not content with this, and determined to avoid future trouble, he begged the governor to warn them all and punish the negress owner.

In sexual matters Claver was severe. The negroes were accustomed to great sexual liberty, and it was difficult to lead them along the road of Christian monogamy. Brother Nicolás says: 'If he saw a negro speaking to a negress in the market square he reproved them. He would take their basket of vegetables and carry it publicly through the square to some shop and hand it to the owner, telling him to keep it until the negress gave a *real* or two as alms to San Lázaro. If the pair chatting insisted that they were relations, he used to tell them that at the very least they were setting a bad example to those unaware of the fact.'

As he went through the streets his presence alone imposed respect. It happened once that a negro passing through the *Media Luna* gate met a negress who made as if to chat with him. Straightway the terrified man hissed: 'For heaven's sake keep away. Don't you see Father Claver across there?' She ran off, but a passing friar of San Juan de Dios heard and noted the remark. The power Claver had over his converts was amazing. The reason was simple—his social work was not merely negative, his association with the negroes is full of examples of extraordinary delicacy and sensitiveness. They looked for his figure in the market-places and gates of the town. Often the wretched stall-women found that their accounts would not balance at the end of the day: they were short of money. Terrified of the expected punishment from their masters, they went sobbing to Claver. According to the character of their owners, he either interceded for them or collected alms on the spot to make up the missing sum. He took great care that the negro women should not work on Sundays, and if he found them spinning he took away their bobbins. Occasionally he would return to the residence with ten or twelve, and he would not return them except under promise of reform. The women well knew that if they alleged that they could earn nothing to eat, his answer would be a ration of rice and other food. His net was cast wide. He was the father of the wretched in many senses of the word. Slaves were often punished severely for mere peccadilloes. Rumour of these barbarities always reached his ears, and without warning he made for the houses concerned. As he went in the screams of pain ceased. The slaves' confidence in him was unbounded: so much so that once a woman slave, driven by the cruelty of her owner to the desperate decision of flight to the hills of the interior, felt that it would be base ingratitude not to say good-bye to Claver. She went to him and asked his blessing on her enterprise. The men were often punished by solitary confinement in the dark, chained to the walls of their cell. Claver would appear at the door with tobacco and food and spend the evening with them. As a result of all this, it is not surprising that he could make demands on them. Both black and white used to come out on to the wide balconies of the *Calles de Candilejo* and *de Bandillo* and whisper to each other as he passed, 'The Saint is coming.'

In that epoch of the mingling of races he undertook an important task: he was an intermediary between two worlds and two peoples. His work was not confined to the negroes, he cared too for the souls of the whites. There arrived at Cartagena from September to Christmas fleets from Spain, ships from Peru, caravans from Potosí and from Quito with loads of silver. Vast numbers of merchants entered the town: it became a changed city, full of moral dangers.

From the ships landed lawyers and soldiers, governors and future *conquistadores*, merchants and beggars. But as Fernández comments:

> As they bring riches, the ships also bring their cargo of vices. At sea danger and lack of opportunity kept them concealed; ashore absence of the former and an excess of the latter give them free rein without fear of divine justice. Postponed duels are fought, anger, long controlled, bursts forth, gluttony and drunkenness seize their chance, pride and the heat of lust come into the open day. Loose women hasten to take their profit. Concubinage is established and marriage at a discount, money is lent at exorbitant rates and cheating at cards is called skill. All this laced with oaths . . . sin and trickery flow out in a vast current which is breasted and opposed by the soul of Claver.

This is not empty rhetoric. All the personality of a bold and disinterested saint was needed to challenge this wave of wickedness. Claver was first feared and then respected by the slave captains. He did not hesitate to favour the underdog, but simultaneously he sought to soften his persecutors. This is the key to his social work. He had to fight against the whites in two major fields: cruelty, and the immorality which perverted both institutions of slavery and marriage. The Process is full of cases like the following: a Spaniard well known in the town was leaving Cartagena with a loose woman. Claver's words, 'I am sorry to see you travelling with the devil', checked him like an arrow to the heart. He got no farther than Turbaco. That night he was knocking at Claver's door. He fell on his knees and told the story of his disordered life.

On another occasion Claver was in the main square inveighing against sexual vice. A Spanish woman of the streets laughed at him and yelled insults when he began his customary reading of the Gospel. The Saint held up his crucifix and said: 'Since you wish to go to hell, here is the Divine Judge to pronounce judgment.' The woman, terrified, was overcome, and brought her repentance to Claver. This conversion caused a great stir.

When Portugal recovered her independence from Spain, the slave traffic in negroes practically ceased, since the majority of the exporting regions in Guinea were Portuguese. Claver thought that the moment had arrived for him to join the African mission. His letters seeking permission have not survived, but his petition was refused. Perhaps his age and the opposition of his superiors in New Granada were against his transfer. As an alternative plan he suggested going to the harbours of Caracas, Santo Domingo, Cumaná, Maracaibo and Santa Maria. Many negroes he knew were stranded there on their way to Cartagena, and he wanted to be sure they were baptized. This too refused, he planned to get to Cotoca, near Urabá, where the natives were notorious for their barbarous cruelty. Claver laboured as a travelling missionary in spite of these setbacks. He had learned from his master, Father Sandoval, that to the east and the south there were fertile tracts where the negroes worked on the plantations round Turbaco and Tolú and Sinú. Ignacio Sozo, the interpreter, in his evidence says: 'Every year after Low Sunday he went through all the outskirts of this city and the city of Santiago de Tolú, taking confession from Moors, marrying . . . he was the usual refuge of the slaves in their sorrows and their labours, he gave them corn, fruit, dates, and medicaments.'

We find constant evidence of Claver's care in following up those he had been able to influence. Witnesses tell us that he had a veritable card index of his slaves which covered not only Cartagena but as far as the mines of Antioquia, up to the Magdalena river, over the frontiers of New Granada and as far as Quito and Lima, and to the north as far as Portobello and Vera Cruz. Ships' captains knew this, and that on arriving at Cartagena they would have to face the inquisitive eyes of a saint who would not be deceived by lies since he read their hearts. He would ask them about Ignacio Mandinga and Juan Yolofo and José el Ararae . . .

Here is a picture of Claver as a missionary:

> When he set out on these missions he used to carry on his arm a leather bag containing some images, the holy oil, his surplice and stole, some candle ends, holy water and perfumed water, and a tiny flask of wine and some biscuits; these last so that he might be ready for any eventuality. In spite of this load he travelled so fast that in one afternoon he used to wear out two or three companions. He did not pass the night in the mission houses or the priests' houses, but on a bed of beaten earth in the hut of the oldest or sickest of the negroes, his food a little rice boiled in water with sometimes, as a great delicacy, a banana cooked or roasted in the ashes of the fire. He would never accept a dish specially prepared for him, even if it were merely a thin stew.

Cassani writes these comments on the above notes from the Process:

> Whenever the slave-ships were late, and no unusual epidemic filled the hospitals, and if the multiple tasks in Cartagena gave him any respite, Claver would go on a missionary journey to the estates and villages of the district, although the fear that he might miss the arrival of a slave-ship kept him within call of the town. Every step he took reflected a Christian example. All day he busied himself with his negroes, patiently putting up with their lack of civilization. Since they knew something of Spanish he was able to instruct them, and on these journeys he found many titular Christians as yet unbaptized. These he baptized at the cost of immense labour. When night fell he preached, in a church if he was in a village, or in some room of the estate house, or in the yard, if there were one.

It is possible to get some idea of the limits of his wanderings. We have information that he went to Turbaco three times. He got to Tolú, and there are some indications that he reached lower Sinú.

There is no news of him going Goajira way, nor to Antioquia or Mompox. These were the districts of the missionaries led by Father Sandoval, who from the day of Claver's decision to make himself responsible for the city's negroes decided to make the rural regions inland his mission area. On one of the missions to Tolú, when he arrived he found the people dejected by the threatened loss of the harvest through drought. Prayers had been said without effect. They beseeched Claver to pray for rain. He did so, and the following morning rain began to fall. It continued for three days.

CHAPTER VIII

HEAVEN UPON EARTH

HAGIOGRAPHERS in the past insisted perhaps too much on what was out of the ordinary in the lives of their subjects. Sometimes the descriptions of miracles filled so large a part that these external manifestations of sanctity might appear to the reader to be its essence. This is an error. God can, and normally does, concede to his servants these graces in greater or lesser degree, but they are not indispensable. On the other hand, a modern rationalistic interpretation of history makes some fear to write of miracles. This too is an error. Facts must be scrutinized critically, but a margin left wherein the power of God may pass the frontiers of the normal and the logical.

St Peter Claver was rich in graces both interior and exterior. When we come to discuss his inner life we shall concentrate on the former aspect. The present chapter deals with his gifts from their social and apostolic viewpoints. His mission called him to be the bond between two worlds and two races. In some ways the primitive apostolic mission was repeated in his day. There was a parallel paradox in his own life. He sought to conceal whatever it might hold of glory and exaltation; his slogan being the slavery of the humble victim offering himself in silent sacrifice. But God raises him up, letting his own majesty shine through the humble life. Historically one might say that few saints were better prepared for these gifts: his very soul rested on a foundation of slavery. On the other hand, there can be no doubt about his personality. Healthy in mind and body, he had a clear, direct and sensitive brain, seeing life realistically, unexcited by a fevered imagination. Without morbid sensibility, his asceticism was built on the traditional severe lines of the Castilian plain, inherited from Alphonsus Rodríguez. Education had brought him to the highest intellectual standard of the Society of Jesus. Morally he was sincere, an enemy

of exaggeration, restlessness and passion. He was the living pattern
of the rules laid down in his time by Pope Benedict XIV for the
canonization of saints. In this part of his biography we have insisted
upon Claver's social message. Had he been only a human philan-
thropist we should end this section with these words: he left
behind him a thankful multitude and an established organization.
Another modern biography has emphasized this aspect alone: his
fascinating personality—a little embittered and misunderstood—
but a will of iron. This view, being one-sided, is totally false. If
you separate Claver's life from contact with the supernatural, all
that is left is a paradox, a failure, a quixotic and abnormal existence.
There is a profound mystery of more than human vitality in this
life. In the earliest portrait of the Saint, that of Orozco, the inscrip-
tion reads: 'The Venerable Peter Claver, illustrious in holiness,
prophecy, and miracles.'

In Cartagena, during his life, all recognized his holiness, and
called him a saint. As he crossed through the gate of *Media Luna*
on his way to San Lázaro the children shouted: 'The Saint is coming.' In the report of the Process there are 150 pages which
recount evidence of miracles. The gift of prophecy fills twelve
pages, knowledge of secret matters fills seven pages, miracles
during life twenty-four, miracles after death until the opening of
the Process, forty-six. Such a mass of material has its effect on the
reader. We are not dealing here with a legend which has grown
through the centuries. We are in the seventeenth century, the more
than 150 witnesses are living witnesses, they are describing what
they have *seen*. On 7 September 1657, three years after Claver's
death, the *calificador* of the Holy Office of the Inquisition was
named commissioner for the Process, with Juan Téllez as secretary.
The taking of evidence lasted three years. Most of the witnesses
were men, they gave their evidence under oath, and it was given
independently so that it would be simple to discover discrepancies
or collusion. It was no light matter to offer lies or fantasies to the
inquisitors. Moreover, the documents were sent to Rome, and
Benedict XIV had just issued the instructions on canonization
mentioned above. What was sought were not second-hand reports
of miracles, but historical facts.

Two kinds of miracles are attributed to Claver: some blazing and magnificent, and the others like tiny shining lamps called by Cassani 'miracles of endearing delicacy'. In the selection which follows are a few of each kind. Many more may be found in the reports of the Process. None is mentioned which is not in these reports: none, that is, which might have originated in later ages.

Evidently no scientific proof is available in the three cases of resurrection from the dead, and the strong personality of the Saint may well have had an enormous influence in the events reported as supernatural. In the second type—the 'darling' miracles —legend may have added additional touches. But one fact remains incontrovertible: the miraculous floated about the life of this man; his life itself was a miracle. It was impossible to have lived thus without the especial help of God. His blessing on Claver's mission is as clear as in the missions of St Francis Xavier and St Francis of Assisi.

In 1649, when Claver had just finished the confessions of his negroes, a young Spanish woman sought his advice. She was engaged to Gabriel de Mencos, governor of Santa Marta, and she asked Claver's blessing before her marriage. As she entered the visitors' parlour she noticed that Claver was staring fixedly at her. On taking leave of her he said: 'Go with God's blessing. Go to Spain, but see that Don Gabriel has all his affairs in order, because after that long journey a much longer will follow.' The frightened girl asked him what he meant. He replied, 'The journey of death.' They married and, the governor's term of office ended, they set out for Spain. On the way the girl told her husband of Claver's remarks. Bitterly disappointed that she had not told him before in Cartagena, because he believed implicitly in Claver, he prepared himself for death and made his confession. Mencos himself left a description of this scene. Thirty days later he died.

León was a slave belonging to Doña Mariana de Bellido. One day Claver called at the house to see him. He was not there, and the priest left a message asking him to call as soon as he returned. León was a powerful, healthy negro, in the prime of life. When he called at the college, Claver told him to confess and prepare for death. The man replied that he felt completely well but, nevertheless, was ready to obey. This he did in tears and sorrow. As he returned home he felt ill, and the same night he died in Claver's arms.

Antonio was a young Italian from Padua, who had joined the Jesuits. Full of enthusiasm he was setting out from Cartagena for Bogotá in the company of Father Alfonso González. He was on horseback at the door of the college when Claver came out and, going up to him, said, 'Brother, you will not persist in your vocation.' He repeated this three times. Antonio laughed at this old man's foolishness. Five months later, on reaching Bogotá, he confessed himself overwhelmed by melancholy. He sought permission from the Provincial, Father Gaspar Sobrino, to leave the order. He no longer remembered Claver's words. Only much later, when he returned to Cartagena at the age of forty-four, a layman, did he offer this evidence.

Then there was the affair of Captain Pedro de Barahona, whose father Claver visited on 30 April 1647; he was very ill, and very pious. Claver heard his confession, and remained one and a half hours with him. Alarmed by this his wife ran in, and was amazed to find the priest kneeling by the bed and begging the sick man to remember him when the following day he should give up his soul to God. Barahona promised this, and Claver insisted on an embrace as pledge. The weeping family was consoled by the Saint, who told them that Barahona was a great man, who would find heaven. The next day he died.

Gaspar was an old slave belonging to Doña Juana de Simancas. One day Claver appeared at the door and asked to be taken to the sick man. He confessed him, and on leaving said to the family, 'Take care of Gaspar.' Worried by this, they went to his room and found him dead. No one had summoned Claver. The owner and all the servants testified to Claver's prophetic spirit.

In a tiny town such as Cartagena then was, rumours soon spread. Faustino de Rutinel had gone to Spain. He was the husband of Mariana de Bellido, a prominent local lady. Rumour grew that he had been killed during the wars in Catalonia. A letter received from Spain lent colour to this. Through her slave Francisca, the worried wife begged Claver to ease her fears. After a moment's thought he announced: 'What purpose would it serve if I went to your mistress's side, since I can say nothing to console her?' There was no longer any doubt. Shortly afterwards letters from Spain confirmed the news.

This insight of the Saint's became proverbial. Captain Pedro de Arriola, chief constable of the Holy Office, had sent his son to Salamanca to study. Some days later he came anxiously to Claver to ask him to remember his son in his prayers. Claver replied: 'I was doing so, because the galleys are in the midst of a great storm, but they will survive.' The captain took a note of the day and the hour, and a letter from his son confirmed the exactness of the Saint's vision.

The freed slave Jacinto de Medina testifies that once he went to the river Sinú, to an estate belonging to Antonio Sanz on the river bank. A ship designed for the river traffic lay half built there. A few days before his visit Claver had been down preaching and hearing confessions. The negro captain of the boat was lax in his observances, and Claver looked into his eyes and said, 'Make your confession quickly, and mend your ways, for you are to die very soon.' The next night the crocodiles were excited. The captain had disappeared into the river. Only some bloodstained rags remained as a proof of Claver's prophetic power.

The future held no mystery for him, and it is not surprising that a mere look from him was enough to move souls profoundly. The slave of Micaela de Monterroso relates that he was very ill and Claver was called to him, for he thought that he was about to die. Claver said, 'Take the sacraments, they will not hurt you, but I shall die before you do.' So it happened, and the slave was a mourner at the funeral of his friend. Other persons of more worldly importance came to him. He paid no deference to them, and made them wait, but their trouble was repaid. Antonio Betancur was planning to sail for Jamaica, but he hesitated because of the coastal pirates. He consulted Claver. 'Go in complete confidence and take your children. On no account leave them here.' Don Antonio said no more, and obeyed implicitly. During his absence the plague flared up and many died. He and his family were safe in Jamaica.

Claver was very reserved and scarcely greeted anyone in the street. He walked with his eyes cast down, as if lost in thought. One day he was sent to say Mass in the castle at the Punta de Judío. There came out to greet him Don Antonio de Subiza, a knight of Santiago, recently arrived, and a stranger to the Saint. Scarcely had Claver seen him when his eyes shone and he threw his arms about his neck saying that he held him in great esteem, since there ran in his veins the blood of St Francis Xavier. This reading in the heart was so characteristic of him that witnesses tell us that when he asked questions the interpreters lowered their eyes.

On the eves of solemn feasts, José de Villalobos tells us, he used to walk through the streets and into the shops and work-rooms and houses inviting people to come to Mass. One day he went into the house of the lieutenant Juan de Gramedor, which was in the square near the crossroads. It was a feast of our Lady; all the workmen promised to attend Mass. Claver went back there the following day and they all said that they had fulfilled their promise. A young man named Juan Galindo joined the chorus. When he heard his voice Claver turned to him and said: 'Do not lie, go and confess immediately.' When Claver had left, the man confessed the truth: he had not gone to Mass. Claver had read the truth in his heart.

A Carmelite, Sister Isabel, was ignorant of this insight. She summoned Claver to the convent (a few steps from the college) to discuss a personal problem with him. She herself relates that she went trembling into the confessional, discussed irrelevant matters, and was getting up to go. Claver gently led her back to the intended subject in all its details. Light entered her soul, and she realized that for him there were no hidden corners. On another occasion Claver came to the same convent to preach there to four negress slaves, and to them alone. A nun, Blanca María de la Purificación, tried to eavesdrop, and said to herself that what he was saying did not seem appropriate to negresses. She might as well have announced this aloud, for immediately she heard Claver say, 'I come to preach here not to white women but to black.' She listened no more; her curiosity was satisfied.

On dealing with the subject of supernatural gifts, Cassani writes: 'When I reached this point in all the biographies that I have written my pen begins to stumble and hesitate, but in this life of Claver the opposite happens. This is because I have before me the documents of the Process. This strengthens my heart and chases away fear.'

Using the same Process as our guide in separating fantasy from reality we propose to begin with the great miracles, and continue with the lesser; these latter as it were framing the life of the apostle to the negroes.

The year was 1628. The people concerned were young Francisco López, son of Francisco López and Juana de Mercado. She was the sister of the priest Pedro Mercado, who gave the details in the Process. López was a pious young man, he belonged to the Brotherhood of the Blessed Sacrament, and one of his tasks was to go from house to house collecting wax candles for the altar. Going about in the heat he suffered severe sunstroke, which threatened his life. The news sped through the town that he was dying. His uncle the priest ran to Claver and begged him to visit the youth. Meanwhile they heard that he had died; the slave Manuel, who worked at the hospital, brought the news. Claver took the youth's little finger, and squeezing it tightly said with complete confidence, 'The Lord will return to you the health you lost in his service.' Then—an amazing thing which was often repeated in Claver's life—he used a means which seems completely inappropriate to the end sought. He told them to wipe the body with a sponge. The negro Manuel said that it was pointless, the man was already dead. Claver replied sternly that he was not, that the remedy was to be tried. He returned to the college to pray for López. Shortly afterwards Pedro Mercado, disconsolate, came again to Claver. The youth showed no sign of life. The Saint smiled and said, 'Why do you weep for your nephew as if he were dead? The sponge has lost its effect, we must try with another.' They offered him five, he chose one, dipped it in water, and applied it to the youth. Immediately he breathed deeply and sat up. Claver crept away, and all those present cried, 'A miracle, a miracle . . .'

Here he used a sponge, at other time bananas or dates, 'the

famous dates of Father Claver, whose fame reached Europe', or
a rough-hewn cross or the relics of saints. This is how Andrade,
his first biographer, describes these facts three years after the
Saint's death:

> There was a miraculous wooden cross which Claver used. It
> is now in Madrid in the hands of the Marquesa de Mancera, who
> received it as a precious gift when she was vicereine of Peru.
> She considers it of great price, and in order to write this I have
> examined it and held it. It is of walnut wood, a little over six
> inches long and hollow. Within it are some relics and a piece of
> the true Cross, and three tiny bone nails on the surface. Claver
> always wore it on his breast, and performed amazing deeds with
> it. Two of them are related in the *Annual Letters* for 1628 as
> follows: the subject of the first was Father Antonio Agustín,
> who contracted a mortal illness for which the doctors could do
> nothing. They ordered him to be given the last sacraments. This
> was done on the eve of Ascension day, and the whole town wept
> his certain death. Claver, who was in the college, had with him
> relics of Brother Alphonsus Rodríguez, his beloved teacher, and
> the rector had others which had been brought to him from
> Mallorca. The sick man commended himself to Brother Rod-
> ríguez, Claver touched him with the relics, read the Gospels to
> him, and within a few days he was well again.

The affair of the slave Agustina, who served in the house of
Captain Vicente de Villalobos, was one of the strangest in the
life of Claver. Villalobos was the chief constable of the town. His
wife was Micaela Heras. It is possible to argue in this case whether
there was a real resurrection or not. The witness in the Process
tells us that the attack from which the slave suffered was so severe
that she was taken for dead. Andrade asserts that 'when Claver
arrived she was dead'; Fernández agrees in this particular. When
Agustina was in her last agony Villalobos went in search of Claver.
When the latter arrived the body was being prepared for the shroud
and he found it already cold to the touch. His expression suddenly
changed and he amazed everyone by crying aloud, 'Agustina,
Agustina.' He sprinkled her with holy water, he knelt by her, and
prayed for an hour. All in the room waited, upset and fearful, for

something to happen. Suddenly the supposedly dead woman began to move and vomited a large quantity of blood. All fell on their knees. Agustina stared at Claver, and as if awakening from a deep sleep said, 'Jesus, Jesus, how tired I am!' Claver told her to pray with all her heart and repent her sins, but those standing by, moved by curiosity, begged him to ask her where she came from. He did so, and she said these words: 'I am come from journeying along a long road. It was a beautiful road, and after I had gone a long way down it I met a white man of great beauty who stood before me and said, 'Stop, you cannot go any further.' I asked him what I should do, and he replied, "Go back the way you have come, to the house you have left." This I have done, but I cannot tell how.' On hearing this Claver told them all to leave the room and leave him alone with her because he wished to hear her confession. He prepared her and told her that the complete confession of her sins was of immense importance if she wanted to enter that paradise of which she had had a glimpse. She obeyed him, and as he heard her confession it became clear to Claver that she was not baptized. He straightway ordered water to be brought, and a candle and a crucifix. Her owners answered that they had had Agustina in their house for twenty years, and she had behaved in all things like themselves. She had gone to confession, to Mass, and performed all her Christain duties, and therefore she did not need baptism, nor could she receive it. But Claver was certain that they were wrong and insisted, baptizing her in the presence of all, to the great delight of her soul and his, for a few moments after she had received the sacraments she died in the presence of the whole family.

Don Vicente was so deeply impressed with the sanctity of Claver that whenever he met him he knelt before him to kiss his hand as if he were a saint on earth. Anything of Claver's he held as a relic. He fell gravely sick of a fever, which damaged his brain so that for twenty days he could not sleep. In his extremity a relation told him that a slave of his, suffering from the same illness, had been cured when Claver had had his head poulticed with hot banana. As soon as he heard the name of the Saint he ordered the same cure for himself. This was done, and the heat in his head diminished and he was able to sleep. It seems clear that not the the hot poultices but his faith in Claver was the source of his cure.[1]

The subject of another curious and marvellous event was a slave just arrived in a barracks who rejected the mission of Claver and died unrepentant. When he was told of this the Saint was deeply moved and hastened to the yard where the body, as that of a pagan, had been thrown. He insisted that it be taken to the cell where the man had died, and Claver closed the door. Shortly afterwards the Saint left, holding tightly his wooden cross, and at his side leaped the slave, crying out for baptism. This event could not be concealed and the Father Provincial heard of it, and asked Claver for the details. Claver said nothing but 'they called me saying that the slave had died. I went to him and it was the will of God that he should recover.' The news of the miracle reached Rome and it was published without names in the *Annual Letters* of 1628. Andrade saw the original documents in the library of the Imperial College in Madrid when he was writing his biography in 1656.

A similar account is given of a young negro aged fourteen who was suffering from tuberculosis. He was a slave in the Duarte Bravo family. Suddenly he died, and as they were about to en-shroud his body Claver arrived and asked for time to pray for him. He sprinkled the body with holy water, placed his famous cross on the boy's lips and called his name three times. At the third, as if awaking from a deep sleep, the young man sat up exclaim-ing, 'What amazing things I have seen!' Claver heard his con-fession, administered extreme unction, and the slave died in his arms.

There was a well in the square of Santo Domingo round which the young negro children played. Some of them on this occasion had been baptized a few days earlier by Claver. As they leaped about on the coping, one of them fell in. The well was deep, and when they dragged him out he was dead. They took him to the doctor, Mendo López, who made every effort to revive him. Claver passed the door, was told of this, and straightway took off

[1] Process, No. 42; Andrade, *op. cit.*, p. 150.

his cloak, laid it on the ground, and wrapped the corpse in it. He knelt before it and clapped his hands loudly several times. A great crowd assembled, and a freed slave, Alfonsa Mora, remembers that it was St Matthew's day, and two in the afternoon. The dead child began to move, and, as always on these occasions, asked those about him where he was, and told them that he had come from a far country.

These are mere excerpts from the miraculous life of Claver, who, when he besought his God, could bring down heaven to earth.

It is with some hesitation that I include in this biography the stories which follow. The question is ever present: are they miracles or legends? After careful scrutiny and rejecting all information which does not appear in the Process, I was forced to realize that what Cassani calls the 'darling miracles' (*milagros de lindo gusto*) of Claver appear at every step. They possess a reality more mystical, more profound and beautiful than the great miracles. The hyper-critical are permitted their smiles. Since it seems to me a miniature masterpiece I transcribe word for word what Cassani writes, then I shall modify some details in the light of the Process.

Once when Claver was walking through the streets, announcing a feast day (at the time when, because of his age, he was using a crutch), there happened that miracle of the eggs, which if it was not of great importance was at least of great delicacy. He saw a gang of boys dancing round and mocking an old Indian woman whose whole wealth and means of existence was a basket of eggs. As she carried it on her head it had been knocked to the ground by a low balcony. Claver went up to her and attempted to console her; but words, however compassionate, were of no value to one who saw her living ruined. The boys laughed at the scene of Claver's useless encouragement, while the woman, with her clasped hands raised to heaven, cursed the balcony and lamented the smashed eggs on the ground. At last the servant of God said to her gently, 'Don't be so miserable, daughter, God helps the poor.' He began to stir the eggy mess with his crutch, clearly the best way to smash even the few that remained whole. But behold, as he stirred that soup of yolks, whites, and shells, slowly the shells grew together again, each with its yolk and white within, leaving the basket spotless, and the ground clear of eggs. Then without delaying further, Claver said to her, 'Learn, daughter, how God consoles the poor when they earn their bread by the sweat of their brow.' He went away, leaving the woman collecting the whole eggs. As she did so she looked at each one and held it against the sun; since they were new-laid they were obviously all fresh; she looked at them again and again, she saw what she could scarcely believe, and the incident was to her benefit in many ways, since the boys published with their shouts what had happened, and all who came bought eggs from her, calling them the miraculous eggs. In this way Claver did a double miracle, because her earnings were doubled.

Isabel de Mieres was a witness of this event. She was a parishioner of Claver's and she begins her evidence by saying that he was a perfect priest. Her story adds details to that above:

> One day I was going along the *calle de las Carretas* with a young negress, a slave belonging to Doña García de la Serpa. She was carrying on her head a basket of eggs. A man recently arrived from Spain collided with her and the eggs fell to the ground. The negress burst into tears, and begged God to help her, since she feared the anger of her mistress. At that moment Claver appeared and I knelt before him to kiss his hand. He asked me what was the matter with the slave, and I told him. He went up to the basket and righted it with his stick. Then he collected the eggs together and told the slave to replace them in the basket. This she did, and each one was unbroken. The slave herself is dead, and since it happened some time ago, and the crowd which gathered was large, I do not remember the names of other people who saw the miracle.

The Carnations

Don Francisco de Silva y Castillo's house was one of the oldest in Cartagena. It had wide balconies and a *patio* with a pool and flowers. One of the negress slaves was found one day inert on the ground, and the chronicler adds 'without breath, pulse, or motion of any kind'. Don Francisco was a friend of Claver, and ordered that the body should not be moved until he had seen it. She was not baptized and at Claver's appearance she sat up and demanded baptism. 'Do not be afraid,' said Claver gently, 'she will live for many years; bring me some water.' Let Cassani continue the tale:

At this point a lawyer or a doctor may interrupt my story; the former because it is his office to contradict, the latter because of his greater knowledge, because there is no proof that the girl was dead; some accident may have rendered her unconscious, and she may have recovered by chance as Claver stood by. I, since I am not arguing a case in court, do not want to insist on a major miracle, but none can deny the extraordinary nature of the sequel, which I find asserted by two eye-witnesses; a sequel which could not have been produced naturally. The water which Claver used was left in a bowl, he having ordered that since it had been used for a sacrament it should not be merely thrown away. The servant allotted the task could think of no better place to pour it than into a flower-pot on the window sill. This pot had in it roots which had been dried up for the past four months. In a short while new life appeared in the pot. It cannot be said that the old roots revived, for the flowers which grew were of a kind not seen before, and with a scent never before experienced: God thus multiplying his marvels in order to accredit his servant. When Don Francisco saw this new growth, he had all the other flower-pots watered, but abundance of water produced no effect on them. It had been produced in the first either as a fruit of the merits of the Saint, or as a reward to him, or as the effect of using the water of a sacrament.

The Stained Chasuble

This is a domestic scene which took place on the second day of Easter. Those concerned were Claver and his usual companion, Brother Nicolás. The most prized possession of the tiny chapel of the college was a white chasuble which was used at the most frequented Mass, that said by Claver at eleven. Brother Nicolás tells us that on ordinary occasions Claver insisted on the plainest vestments, but on feast days and special occasions he made an exception. He even delighted then to wear the white woollen chasuble lined with scarlet taffeta. On this day as he turned to offer Communion he knocked against the sacramental lamp, and oil was spilled on the chasuble. The witness goes on: 'I was very upset because it was the finest vestment that we had, and when Claver came back to the sacristy I told him that I was very angry, that it was quite clear that he hadn't the expense of buying these things. Claver made no reply, but received my admonitions as humbly as a child. I put the garment aside so that it should not stain others. After some days I noticed it again and I was astounded to see it without any kind of mark, not only on the wool, but even on the taffeta which takes a stain so easily. I witness to this on oath.'

Lemons and Pomegranates

The scene changes. We are in the hospital of San Lázaro. Claver has taken off his cloak and has begun, as always, to sweep the floor. Let Andrés Hermosilla speak: 'We needed lemons in the hospital, and there were none to be had. I told Claver and he told me not to worry. He went out and shortly afterwards returned with a huge basket full of lemons. All in the building were astonished and considered it a miracle.' On another occasion a sick man longed for pomegranates, and was certain that he could be cured by eating them. They were very scarce in Cartagena. The prior of the Brothers of St John of God had all the market-places searched but none were found. Claver went to him and said, 'Rely on me, I shall go and get some.' In half an hour he came back with a basketful. Was it good luck or miracle?

Warm Water

With members of the Inquisition in question it was not prudent to have much to do with superstition. One of Claver's daring miracles happened in the house of the grand inquisitor of Cartagena. María Fonseca was the wife of Andrés Castro, rector of the Holy Office. The little child of a slave was dying in the house and Claver asked for a little warm water to baptize him (cold water might have killed him). There was none available and there wasn't much time. In an urgent tone Claver told them to bring what there was, and the witness says that when it was brought, Claver without attracting attention put his hand in the basin and then went on with the ceremony. This action aroused her curiosity; she examined the water and found that it was quite hot. The mistress of the house and all present held this as a miracle.

PART III

THE INTIMATE SAINT

CHAPTER I

A FLAME IN THE NIGHT

O N a night of dreadful heat in the Jesuit residence, especially in Claver's gloomy comfortless cell, where one of his slaves had found it almost impossible to live, the Saint would be praying as usual, kneeling by his bed, face in hands. His character, formerly prone to anger, had changed, and people now found him melancholic. The bed would not be used, he had a mat in the corner with a stone underneath for pillow. On a stool near by lay an open copy of Father Ricci's book full of engravings from the Gospels. Claver's favourite pictures were of subjects such as Christ lashed to the column. He said once that the only book which ought to be read was that of the Passion. Another night, in the early hours of the morning, the rector sought confession from Claver and found him wearing a crown of thorns, his body hung about with the instruments of the Passion.

Claver's system of prayer was a secret between himself and God and his superiors, to whom he gave an exact account of his spiritual life. Since his youth they had considered him wise in spiritual things, though they disputed his wisdom and experience in earthly matters. As a student he had felt the movements of ecstasy which had tortured his flesh in Barcelona. He had spent hours of contemplation by the side of St Alphonsus Rodríguez in Montesión. Continuous prayer for forty years, unabated by the heat and languor of the tropics, is in itself heroic. For forty-five years, 154 witnesses repeat on oath, his nights consisted of five hours of prayer, three hours of sleep and three scourgings. Biographers of Claver have not emphasized enough the contemplative nature of his mission.

In Claver's inner spiritual life St Alphonsus Rodríguez appears at every turn. Brother González asserts clearly in the Process: 'Father Claver was very conscious of being a follower in things spiritual of Brother Alonso Rodríguez. He told me this many times, and I have frequently seen him reading his notes on mental prayer, the presence of God, mortification, humility and self-abnegation, notes taken down from Brother Alonso Rodríguez.' The latter left writings in the third person in which he describes his mystical experiences. These, without perhaps touching the profundities of St Teresa or St John of the Cross, analyse excellently the states of the soul. His ideas helped to form the soul of his pupil, in whom we find the same high estimate of prayer, the same methods, the same themes for contemplation. Without any doubt St Peter Claver must be placed among the great contemplatives: contemplation was the secret of his immense practical activity.

Fernández adds: 'In his humility Claver never revealed to which degree of contemplation he had attained, but it may safely be assumed that he reached, if not the highest, at least one of the most perfect.'[1]

The incident in Barcelona, when Claver appeared rapt in ecstasy on reaching the spot where St Ignatius had been beaten up, has already been told. Many years later, in Cartagena, he confided to a companion, without relating the incident, that merely the memory of Barcelona moved him; and when he said it he burst into tears.

Another case of ecstasy is told by Don Francisco de Ribero, archdeacon of Cartagena, who used to go once a week with alms to the hospital of San Lázaro. One day as he entered a ward he saw the servant of God preaching in the midst of a group of patients. When he looked at Claver's face it was radiant, as if flames were darting and rays of light shining from it. His gaze was fixed on a distant point, and a gentle smile softened that face crossed by a deep line in the broad forehead. One of the interpreters gives the following description, which is reported by Father Andrade:

Some fathers and negroes who lived with him and went about with him swear that when he prayed he rose in the air. There is alive today a negro interpreter who was with him in his last illness. He asserts that at the end of August, a few days

[1] Fernández, op. cit. p. 488.

before he died, the candle in the room went out, and he went
down to relight it from the lamp in the transept. When he came
back light shone from within the room through the cracks of
the door and the window. He was surprised, since none but
himself could have brought light. He went in and saw a lighted
candle in the wretched clay candlestick which he had provided
for Claver. He went to ask Claver who had brought the light,
but the bed was empty. He looked for him behind an old awn-
ing and saw him raised in the air, holding a crucifix in his hand,
absorbed in prayer. The negro was much upset, and wondered
what to do, whether to wake up the other slaves or the other
Jesuits. Finally for fear of annoying Claver he decided to make
no noise, but when the ecstasy was over helped Claver into bed,
for he was very weak. The latter, in his humility, begged the
slave to mention nothing that he had seen, and the negro obeyed
until the death of his master.

These few cases draw away a little the veil concealing the inner
life of Claver. There is no autobiography, and we have to rely on
witnesses. Brother Nicolás, for example, is quite explicit on the
frequency of his prayer: 'All the time when he was not hearing
confession, or preaching, or teaching, he spent in prayer.' The
same witness goes on: 'For eight years I had the cell next to his,
with only the thickness of one plank in between. When there
were great thunderstorms at night I often ran into his cell, and
always I found him praying at the foot of his bed, his hands over
his eyes, the light on all night. I heard him say verses from the
Psalms and the Gospels.'

Andrade writes: 'Since he kept the favours God granted to him
secret, we cannot say to what degree of contemplation he attained,
but we know most certainly that every day he spent *five consecutive
hours* in prayer before going out on his duties. As night fell he
slept for a short while, then from midnight to one he got up, to
enjoy, so he said, the silence and peace which God granted him
when all slept. Then either kneeling or prostrate on the ground
with a rope round his neck and the crown of thorns on his head,
a crucifix in his hands, he prayed from one until six. When there
were confessions to be heard, he began the whole cycle earlier.'

Cassani adds other details: 'We owe a good deal to the curiosity or incredulity of a father provincial of Lima, who, hearing these stories of Claver passing the night in prayer, invented reasons to visit him by night, and always found him in the position we have described. It was quite clear that he was rapt in prayer or contemplation, because on occasions the visitor walked in front of him, or strode up and down in the cell, or made other noises; but he was unnoticed by Claver, who, his whole attention on God, noticed not the noises of this earth.'

His usual theme of meditation was the Passion. Brother Nicolás reports:

> Claver had in his cell an illustrated text of the life of Christ, and whenever he prayed he chose the picture of the mystery upon which he intended to meditate, so that it might inspire him. His most frequent subjects of meditation were the prayer in the garden, the column, the crown of thorns, and the Crucifixion. When the subject was this last, so great was his fervour that his eyes dwelled on the picture the whole day. He used to leave the book open at his place on a little table, and it was so worn and battered that it revealed its constant use. It was never out of his hand or out of his sight. This I saw throughout my life.
>
> Shortly before his death Claver gave me the book, but having regained a little strength he struggled down to the sacristy where I was, and although he could no longer read, he asked for the book, if only so that he might see the pictures again. I returned it to him, and for the rest of his days he kept it open by his pillow. At his death, as had been arranged, I took possession of it.

This book was the life of Christ by Father Bartolomé Ricci: *Vita Domini Nostri Jesu Christi*. And the book which he used for meditation was *Meditations upon the Mysteries of our Holy Faith in the practice of Mental Prayer*, by Father Luis de la Puente. This was a new book, and from its first appearance it was the favourite book of prayer among Spanish Jesuits, and its use spread to the whole Church. Also in the Saint's library Andrade mentions as used by him *The Book of the Guide to Virtue, and of the Imitation of Our Lady*, in three volumes, published at Madrid by Maroto in 1642–46, and commentaries on the spiritual advice of St Teresa of Jesus, published in Madrid, 1647. These few books, and the fundamental manuscripts of his teacher Alphonsus Rodríguez, were the sources of the spirituality of Claver who, like St Teresa, did not disdain to use a simple picture to concentrate his attention. He had pictures on his *prie-dieu*, in his confessional, in the wards of the hospital. But his greatest book of all was the crucifix. 'He always carried it with him, as a constant friend, an image of Christ in metal upon a wooden cross, and he had a notebook in which were written salutations, taken from the meditations of St Bernard, to the body of Christ crucified.'

In the form of his prayer he followed the method of St Ignatius, and he had a high opinion of them. Things he saw on his walks became objects of contemplation. A witness who asserts that he never noticed flowers exaggerates. He saw them and praised God for them. A companion describes a scene of this kind: 'If he saw a lovely flower in the field he would say: "O God, how gracious is the earth, and how ungracious am I to the gifts which God gives me, since I do not repay them in flowers of virtue."' Sometimes the symbol was more unpleasant. Like Alphonsus, who used bare and direct expressions in his writings, 'if he saw a dead animal rotting on the ground he would say that it was an image of himself . . . But God on the cross was the key-stone of his devotion and his heroism.' If there appeared at his confessional candidates who were recalcitrant and difficult to move, he would take them into the chapel and show them the image of Christ crucified, he would talk to them and perform with them the act of contrition, saying, 'Lord, I love thee beyond all things,' and all repeated it after him. Both Andrade and the reports of the Process mention many other cases: 'If he went to visit a sick man, and saw no cross, he would make one with two sticks and put it at the head of the bed. On his missions he carried a stick mounted with a cross and he used to lean it against the confessional. Without the cross the life of Claver is inexplicable. All his "holy madness" is explained by Christ crucified. When because of his age and infirmities he could no longer kneel he used to sit on a low stool near the altar and ask for alms for the work of the church. When he could not toil with his own hands he sought to carry on the work through the hands of others.'

After his long hours of prayer in the hot nights of Cartagena, Claver would come forth from his cell and go along the narrow corridors of the college, on his head a crown of thorns, a huge cross on his shoulder, his body covered with weals. He would walk to the choir stalls and then down into the church (he had the keys): this was the *via crucis* of his soul eager for pain and expiation.

In the spirituality of Claver there are two other major devotions, learned also from his teacher. He was asked as an old man if he had been to Montserrat. He burst into tears. For a Spaniard, a Catalan and a Jesuit, devotion to the Virgin was fundamental. The Virgin was with him throughout his whole life. In Verdú there was a carved image much venerated by the peasants. The Virgin patroness of sailors saw him leave Seville. The Virgin *de la Popa* greeted him at the entrance to Cartagena harbour and the Virgin of the Miracle awaited him in the tiny chapel of the college: there he said his first Mass, at her feet he placed his confessional, near to her his body lay in death. Andrade emphasizes his devotion to her. At all the great festivals he made public penance, kissing the feet of all the other brothers. This he did on Saturdays also. Every day he said a complete rosary. He regularly had brought from the hills large quantities of a fruit like cinnamon. With this he made with his own hands vast numbers of rosaries which he distributed free, especially to the negroes and slaves. He organized a brotherhood of negroes and mulattos under the patronage of the Virgin to keep her feasts. One of the interpreters, Andrés Sacabuche, says: 'One of Claver's pastimes was the making of rosaries out of a fruit called *iaconcillo*, and we helped him to thread the stones. It is calculated that he made each year 9,000 rosaries. He said the rosary on his knees each day in his cell, and when he was out he said it as he walked along, holding the beads under his cloak. On Mondays and Saturdays he said the Office of the Virgin from the text which Alphonsus had given him. On Saturdays he said Mass at the altar of Our Lady of the Miracle, and on the great feasts of the Virgin the banquets he gave to the poor in the porter's lodge and in the San Lázaro hospital were famous. Before going about his work he always passed through the chapel of the Virgin, and retraced his steps through there when he returned. He founded a Congregation of the Virgin for coloured people, which flourished during his lifetime. He composed a prayer which Brother Nicolás found among his papers:

'O Virgin Mary, Our Lady, full of grace and mercy, in my unworthiness I humbly pray thee that I may not die a violent death so that my soul shall not leave this world without a perfect confession and without making satisfaction for my sins. O Holy Virgin, pray for me through the love of thy Most Holy Son. Amen.'

The Virgin heard him; his death was not sudden. He was able to prepare for it for four years, and she took him away on the early morning of her feast of 8 September.

The other great devotion of his life was the Eucharist. Until his last days he managed to draw near to the altar, and so great was the change in expression of his face that witnesses in the Process declared that they returned to God through hearing Claver say Mass. One who went regularly to his Mass said that he said Mass 'with great calm, devotion, attention and contemplation.' He adds, however, and reveals the human sympathy of the Saint, that he always tried not to exceed half an hour because 'in that heat an over lengthy Mass killed devotion'.

This sketch of his religious personality would be incomplete if we did not mention what might be called its *apologetic* aspect. He had a great devotion to the souls in purgatory: he said a Mass for every slave who was dying, and a penance upon which he insisted was that they should do some good work in return. He had a devotion too for holy water. He made great use of it—at the bedside of the dying, in the prison cells, with criminals on their way to execution. A devotion to the saints, too; especially to St Ignatius, St Peter and St Alphonsus. These he especially invoked, their names preceded the formula of his complete surrender to God. Prayer, sacraments, the holy Virgin, the pontificate, the cult of the saints, holy water: it is not difficult to see in this systematic intensification of Church practices something like a living apologetic sermon against the errors of the age. Here St Peter appears as a great defender of the whole Faith. It is interesting to note that he appeared to insist most on those parts of the Faith singled out for especial attack by the heretics. His devotion to the Eucharist led him to adopt practices which aroused opposition. In some ways he was in agreement with modern views on Holy Communion. Brother Nicolás says in the Process:

> He readily gave permission for Indians and negroes to take Communion. A moderate preparation was sufficient for him. He bothered so little about this, that some criticized him for it. Then he would use the words of the parable: 'Go out into the highways and byways.' He would say, 'If they are brutes and savages it is my duty to civilize them; it they are ugly, it is not the ugliness of the body, but sin, which befouls the soul. Repellent souls may be found in handsome bodies, and if from without my negroes are the dregs of nature, within they are beautified by grace.' Then with great emphasis he would demand: 'Why, if they are Christians, should they not obey the demands of the Church, and why should they not enjoy the blessings of the Sacrament, whose glory is to feed the poor and humble?'

He met with opposition on this point even from within the college, though in general his fellow Jesuits supported him.

CHAPTER II

A BODY ON THE CROSS

'PRAYER and mortification are the two wings by which, with the grace of God, the soul rises and reaches the summit of perfection.' These words of St Alphonsus, which Claver must have heard again and again in his youth, touched his heart.

For the ordinary mind there is an almost complete identification of sanctity and mortification, especially if it is thinking of external penitence. The view has a basis of truth. There are no saints without mortification, there is no sanctity without a cross, although perfection does not lie in this element alone but in loving God. Claver carried mortification to heroic lengths.

That lean and almost fleshless body, bent towards the earth like a twisted vine, was forced by an iron will to submit to cruel treatment: cruel from a human point of view. In body and soul, Claver was a man crucified. It is impossible to list all the mortifications in his life, we are forced to select, but the selection may help to suggest the complete picture. Here, too, his teacher was St Alphonsus, who is called by Casanovas the 'Mystical Doctor of Mortification'. His views on mortification may be seen in Vol. III of his complete works (the Nonell edition). He insists on the inner light and strength from God, which alone make mortification saintly. Without these it may be sin. We have already noted Claver's scourgings, commented upon by the town watch as it made its rounds. Brother Nicolás offers more details:

He had three kinds of scourges, a veritable museum. They had tough lashes, iron tipped. He did not wear a shirt; his cloak was in direct contact with the hair shirt which covered his body. Juan Manuel, the rector of the college, ordered him to wear a cloth shirt during the hot season. His body was enclosed in a shirt made of knotted horse-hair. This horse-hair shirt was so tight that it pressed upon him as if it were a load hoisted upon his back for a journey. I used to see this shirt when I helped him to dress. If I commented upon it, he replied, 'Leave me in peace.' One day in 1650 Claver fainted. It was in the house of the Father Provincial Rodrigo, and Father Sandoval, then his spiritual guide and confessor, came to see him. He called the doctor. Sandoval and the negro Domingo Folupo undressed him, and they were appalled when they saw the hair shirt which he wore right down to his toes.

Andrade adds more details:

From the top of his head down to the tips of his toes he wore a hair shirt or similar garments. He took them off neither to preach nor when he was ill, nor to sleep or walk. Round his toes he kept fastened coarse knotted cords of hog bristle, and under his instep a thicker cord of the same material—about the thickness of a finger. When he was still or seated this was very painful, but when he walked it tortured him. He wore a steel-tipped cord round his neck in memory of the halter worn by Christ: this hung down and across his breast as far as his waist, rather like a stole. He wore also another bristle sash, about six fingers wide, from his neck to his waist. This was discovered when a doctor was summoned to him after an accident. On another occasion the doctor made a further discovery: he was taking Claver's pulse, which was more rapid than he expected. He uncovered his arm, and found it bound to the coarsest bristle thongs, the whole arm skinned and sore. Only with great difficulty did they make him promise not to use these again during illness. For many years he used no other shirt but a hair-shirt. Even his hands and head were treated in the same way. For reading, studying and praying he wore a tightly fitting crown of thorns. He never used mattress or sheets or pillow for his bed. This bed was an old mat thrown on the floor. In later years, because of his age and other weaknesses, even this was rejected, and he slept on the bare floor with a piece of wood as a pillow.

Claver helps to explain his severity with himself in some lines he wrote: 'In order to follow our Lord Jesus Christ in the love of souls, we must persecute ourselves, in order to be his we must cease to belong to ourselves, we must accept what is bitter as if it were sweet. Of all the adversities which fall upon us for his sake, there is no higher path for life, nor anything more grateful to God, than to suffer willingly for Christ.'

The college servant, Manuel Moreno, who caused Claver so much suffering in his last days, confessed later that he was amazed by the way Claver's hand trembled as he continued to scourge himself even during his last illness.

Ordered once to wear woollen shirts, he did so for twenty years until his superiors realized the deception which he was practising. Once Brother Pedro Lomparte said to him: 'Why do you go on, Father? For how long is the mule to be in harness?' Claver replied coldly: 'Until he dies, brother.' The college doctor, Bartolomé de Torres, when he saw the poor shattered body on the day when Claver fainted in the church, could not prevent himself falling on his knees beside him and saying: 'My dear father, how can you fail to be ill if you torment yourself like this? Don't you understand that this is an excess of mortification, and even suicide?' We may ask ourselves what was the purpose of this austerity to Claver. Is it another symptom, as in his behaviour in the hospitals, of an abnormal mind? This has been suggested by a modern biographer. He is wrong. Claver belongs to the category of the saints of terrible austerity, to the family of Peter Alcántara, whose body, says St Teresa, was like the twisted roots of trees. The austerity of the Saint was no greater, though its motive was distinct, than that of the early *conquistadores*, who forced their way through the jungle with incredible sufferings. He was of an austere generation. As to his abnormality, he was a Catalan peasant, temperate, healthy, of sturdy stock, pertinacious in effort. In character he was silent, calm, withdrawn into himself, although beneath this exterior he concealed strong emotions. His health was robust: no sickly man could have lived his life for long. He was a realist, without great power of imagination . . . These are not the marks of an abnormal man, of a masochist. On the other hand—and this is the vital point overlooked by non-religious biographers—he had a powerful reason which explains this crucifixion of the flesh. A vast love inflamed his soul. God moved him with the power of his grace, and these mystical interior movements were exteriorized as a desire to copy his Beloved. He knew this colloquy of the soul enamoured of Christ, written by his teacher: 'Most sweet Jesus, the love of my soul and adoration of my heart, who is there who will not willingly suffer pains and torments for thy love who didst suffer so many for love of me? I long for sorrows to make my heart their dwelling place, so that I may take delight in them, and go with them to dwell in the heart of Christ crucified . . . Come, then, all kinds of travail that are in the world; that is my consolation, to suffer for Christ . . .'

There was another complex of motives for his mortification. He lived in a world of extreme moral barbarity, surrounded by physical and spiritual wretchedness. And his zeal for souls was immense. He was the brother who stretched out a hand to the thousands of slaves who reached those shores, abandoned and wretched, and he tormented his body in order to approach the sufferings of those he served.

But we must beware of exaggeration among the early biographers. They loved the words *never* and *always*. Many of their sentences begin with one or the other. Such generalizations are false, there is often other information which contradicts them. It is one thing that he had a tendency to reject the pleasant things of life; quite another that he *always* rejected them.

Claver was a saint of terrible austerity, he carried out his duty to the limits of heroism. His very daily tasks were a source of constant sacrifice: there is no point in overloading the picture and producing an inhuman caricature. Indeed, this tendency produces the opposite of the desired effect; it makes his heroic life appear beyond belief.

The horror of the Cartagena climate had been made much of by this kind of biographer. But Monsignor Brioschi, who lived there many years, can put us right on this point. In his biography of Claver he writes: 'The unpleasantness of the climate of Cartagena has been much exaggerated. Almost all those who write about Claver provide us with horrific descriptions of the weather there. No doubt their aim has been thereby to exalt the qualities

of the Saint who worked there so many years.' Father Fleuriau
is an example of the vivid imagination at work:

> The heat is excessive, the rain so frequent, the air so un-
> healthy that only extreme greed or sublime zeal can make the
> place supportable for foreigners. From the beginning of Decem-
> ber until the end of March a cold wind blows from the north.
> During the other eight months of the year the sun is a blazing
> fire, which even the Spaniards themselves find hard to bear.
> Sudden changes in temperature upset the health of many. The
> heat penetrates to the most protected rooms and makes them
> like stoves. Newcomers fall slowly into a heavy langour, and
> completely lose their appetites . . . thus becoming subject to
> frequent attacks of illness. What is worse is that during the heat
> it rains heavily, and from these two causes proceed extra-
> ordinary and unheard of maladies, which quickly undermine
> the strongest constitutions . . . there were great numbers of flies
> whose bites raised poisonous sores . . . many of the inhabitants
> perished in hurricanes and thunderstorms.

All these things there are in Cartagena, but none of them in so
terrible a form as the poetic mind of Father Fleuriau would have
us imagine. After all, Claver, leading a life of great toil and hardship, managed to live there for forty years. In fact, the newcomer
does feel a strange lassitude in the early morning, but this normally
disappears soon after eating one's first meal of the day. In fact,
too, the heat is suffocating for those who have to work, and especially if their work is in enclosed premises or wretched quarters like
Claver's.

He was a man of great abstinence: the witnesses are unanimous
in this. Brother González, for example: 'At midday he would eat
a plate of rice, and a piece of bread dipped in water or wine.
At night a little rice. There were days in which he ate only bread
and water. He used to attend the second sitting because he had a
late Mass, and he used to bring to the dining-room a bitter herb
which he chewed to make him lose the taste of what he was about
to eat, and sometimes I saw him throw ash into his food. This the
Superior later forbade.'

Antonio de Betancur adds that on feast days he would not eat a single olive. Olives were looked upon as a delight in Cartagena, because they did not grow there. Claver probably did it as a special mortification, because in Verdú he had been born and brought up among olive groves. He used to ask to be given maize cakes because they were better for his stomach. Here the exaggerators insist that he did this because the cakes were slaves' food. But all ate them, and in America maize is a normal part of the diet.

The following is a selection of what might be called 'holy tittle-tattle' from the Process:

In spite of the heat, he always drank lukewarm water, never beer or chocolate. He never sought little luxuries, like jams and cakes and blancmange; he never put salt on his food, nor oil and vinegar on his salads, nor did he eat lemons or oranges. Once a brother asked him when he was ill and without appetite whether he would like a thin olive soup, thinking that it might revive his appetite. Claver said neither yes nor no, so he brought him some. After much persuasion Claver dipped a piece of bread in the soup and ate it. He then told the brother to keep the rest safe, for it had tasted good. The brother went to replace it in a jar from which he had taken it, and as he poured it in he saw that it was full of dead and rotten cockroaches. He tasted it, and a bitter flavour like gall upset his stomach. Merely one drop on his tongue produced violent retching. He was astonished at the mortification of Claver who not only tasted it, but swallowed it, and said it was good enough to preserve.

In the heat most people in Cartagena were obliged to seek protection in cool rooms and baths, and the use of fans. Claver was never seen to use any of these means, and those who knew him say he never wiped the sweat from his brow however tired he was. Andrade asserts that in spite of the constant plague of flies and mosquitoes, with their stings which penetrated through clothing to the flesh, Claver was never seen to brush them away from face or body, suffering their stings for the love of God. He adds, too, that Claver practised the mortification of curiosity, for he never sought any news when the fleet arrived but whether there was peace in Europe, and whether there were any sick on board to look after. This, of course, refers only to the arrival of the galleons from Spain: the arrival of slave ships he awaited impatiently.

Claver's mortification by mosquitoes attracted popular attention. He used to say smiling to Captains Rocha and Lozano who were amazed at it: 'I gain the advantage, for I am bled without a lancet.' Sometimes, when on mission journeys, he went down to the banks of the rivers where the mosquitoes were most abundant, and stripped himself to the waist, and one man heard him say gently to the insects: 'Go away, you have had your ration, make room for the others.' Claver recognized what a torment these would be to others, for one of his acts of charity was to beg for alms to purchase mosquito nets for the sick in San Lázaro. A last example of his search for bodily pain: The college barber, Antonio Montero de Miranda, asserts that Claver insisted on being the last to be shaved, so that by his turn the razor was blunted. Another three witnesses add to this. They say that often he would come into the barber's shop and say smilingly to all of them: 'Is there an old sword anywhere about?' He would not have his chin or head shaved but by the newest apprentice there, who sometimes made such a slaughter of it that on one occasion a priest intervened, to the sorrow of Claver.

Such stories can be endlessly multiplied. He adored the Cross and sought suffering. Not the sterile selfish suffering of the abnormal, but the desire to accompany Christ in his suffering and thus redeem souls through sacrifice. This chapter might well end with a quotation from his interpreter, the slave Ignacio Angola: 'One day after he collapsed on a table near his confessional, Sandoval reproved him, saying that penitence was good, but not the rigorous penitence practised by Claver, that Rome was not built in a day and it was not right that he should tire himself so much in the confessional and by saying Mass so late. He advised him to moderate his efforts, and treat his body with greater gentleness.' And the slave adds: 'This had no effect on the Father. He went on in the same way.' The mule was to stay in harness until death.

CHAPTER III

THE SOUL'S SOLITUDE

THE chronicler Fernández speaks of Claver's invincible patience, his courage which passed human limits, and goes on: 'His constancy was seen as obstinacy, his zeal as capriciousness, his austerity with himself as coarseness of character, his solicitude for the slaves as lunacy, his silence as ignorance, his holiness as delusion.' Capriciousness, coarseness, lunacy, ignorance, delusions—these words summon up a clear picture. What was the final judgment of him by his contemporaries, those who knew him best? As elsewhere, the truth may lie between the extremes. He was neither as despised and misunderstood as might appear from some documents, nor was he above criticism.

Claver, as we have seen, suffered all tortures in his body, but the tortures of the soul are more keen. The interior world of private bitterness, of misunderstanding, is infinitely more painful. The friends of his youth show us a Claver full of energy, silent, prompt to anger. Forty years of time and testing add melancholy. Suffering has overcome illusions. All that remains is an iron will to work and self-sacrifice, and an immense love for God in the souls of his brothers the slaves.

The early biographers insist on the episodes of misunderstanding, of contradiction and of difficulty which tested and strengthened the patience of Claver. He wanted to be like the silver which is shaped by the hammer. His wish was heard and he suffered in silence. Sometimes the hammer took the shape of a slave, of a slave-owner, an angry woman, a fellow priest, a colleague in the college or a superior.

In Claver's notes we find the following maxims: 'Every time I do not behave like a donkey, it is the worse for me. How does a donkey behave? If it is slandered, it keeps silent; if it is not fed, silence; if it is forgotten, silence; it never complains however much

Part of a letter from a contemporary, Father Melgar, referring to Cartagena in the last years of St Peter Claver's ministry

'The people of this town are so different in their Christianity and so pious that they, who scarcely seemed Christian before, can now serve as an example of righteous living to those of other parts. Confessions and communions are many, and they show great zeal in attending Confraternities, meetings and lectures. Every day a large part of the town gathers together to say the Rosary of the Most Blessed Virgin, and the town that everyone shunned on account of the uncleanliness and unpleasantness of its people, is now one of the most flourishing in the vicinity.'

Cartagena:
The Church of
St Peter Claver

Interior of the
Church of St Peter
Claver

it is attacked or ill-treated because it is as long-suffering as a donkey. This is how the servant of God must behave; I stand before you, Lord, like a donkey.' These ideas are not the product of sentimentality and lack of knowledge of the world. A man who served for thirty-eight years among slaves necessarily had difficulties with their owners. Fernández notes this: 'Many owners were bitterly opposed to the work of Claver. They objected when he kept the slaves for a long time at catechism or confession, and alleged that this made them idle and no better. Others objected that he treated them too gently: this made them not pious but insolent. Others objected when he married those living in concubinage; this they said was against their interests and cured nothing; and finally all agreed that the time they spent with Claver was stolen from their working hours.'

To this, Andrade, mentioning the same basic complaints, adds that the owners insulted Claver and railed at him, saying that he was ruining the slaves. They shut their doors against him and sent him away with contempt. All this he bore with patience until he finally achieved permission from these very owners to reveal to their slaves the road to heaven. This was not the case with all owners. There were some like the Villalobos, the Banquerels, the Urbinas who were deeply interested in the spiritual life of their negroes. Claver's refusal to consider any precedence in his confessional other than that of the negroes and the poor caused him a good deal of trouble. Many benefactors of the college and other persons of birth flocked there so that Claver might hear their confession. We have already mentioned the incident of the woman who came into his church wearing a farthingale. It was then that his friend Brother González said to him: 'Do you want to close the church with your exaggerations?' The words must have wounded deeply. One thing should be clear. Claver was not attacked because he took the confessions of negroes: humanly speaking it was not an enviable task, and he pointed out ironically that the well-born could find confessors without difficulty. The problem was created by his zeal, and the enemies which it might arouse against the college. It is, in fact, easy to understand the anger of the rector, Sarmiento, imprudent in his turn for reproving

Claver publicly—and the anger of the sacristan. In their human judgment they feared that the church might be left empty. Nobody could tell them that even after three centuries the church would still be visited precisely for the sake of this rejector of worldly women.

What his brother Jesuits in the college thought of him will be studied in detail in a later chapter, entitled 'Son of St Ignatius'. Here we are interested only in the difficulties he faced in what Andrade calls 'domestic upsets, which are often the worst because they arise more secretly, and from persons who think to serve God when they persecute his servants, and who call their fussing zeal for the glory of God and the good name of his religion. Claver suffered a good deal from this kind of trouble, which at times might even be called persecution.' Andrade goes on:

Many thought that he offended against the norms of prudence and criticized his evangelical methods, especially in his catechism and baptism of pagans. They tried to persuade his superiors that they should stop these excesses and punish him. This caused Claver great sorrow, but he bore it with patience and bowed to the will of God, accepting this opposition as an expression of his will, and praying for those who persecuted him. Many times he suffered bitter reproof, expressed in angry words, from some of his superiors impressed by his critics. Among them was a priest who disapproved of what Claver was doing, and of the publicity his ministry received. He said so in public, and the rector of the college ordered him to write down his arguments, so that all might see them. The priest seized his opportunity, and used phrases so crude and unreasonable that they revealed rather the strength of his feeling than the sins of Claver. The latter suffered this attack in silence. In public he humbled himself and confessed himself a great sinner, worthy not only of the punishment received, but of greater castigation. He prayed for his persecutors, for when the hearts of those who are aflame with the love of God are struck, sparks of charity like these fly off. Many, taking advantage of his patience and gentleness, despised him and treated him shamefully, calling him ignorant, stupid, presumptuous, without learning or prudence or Latin. On one occasion a priest arguing with Claver before other clerics on the rubrics of the Mass, lost his temper and said hurtful and insulting things to him. Claver was silent. He suffered these insults for the sake of those which Christ had suffered. This patience impressed the other clerics who were present. He shewed similar restraint with a brother who accompanied him on his missions, and who served him rather as St Catherine of Siena's companion served her. This was an ill-tempered man without much sincere religion, who by word and deed pestered Claver, taking advantage of his patience to tell him that he was a hypocrite, and begging that God might rid him of 'saints' like Claver, for if the true saints were like him, he no longer believed in them. This man was insufferable: when they were to leave the college, he always kept Claver waiting, and through the streets he always hung back, walking slowly when there was need for speed, and letting Claver go a long way ahead. Both inside and outside the college he gossiped, always speaking harshly of Claver. Once the latter had to go and hear a confession. He called this companion but the latter said he was busy and could not go. Claver called him a second and third time, urging him for the love of God to come with him. But Claver's gentleness had no softening effect on his stony heart, until Claver knelt before him and humbly begged him to come because there was no one else available, and a soul was in danger. The heart of flint was moved to come, but its hardness remained, and finally this brother was expelled from the Society, his superiors losing all hope of improvement in him, since even with such a companion as Claver he remained incorrigible.

Father Juan de Arcos was a superior who did get on with Claver. One day he summoned him to his room and admonished him severely. Claver had accepted responsibility for a dispute between a negro interpreter and another member of the college. Juan de Arcos used the opportunity to tell Claver that he wasted too much of his time with negroes who were too retarded to profit in any way; that he was too considerate with them, that he wasted the time of the servants in the college, that it was difficult to understand how the defender of the slaves could himself have slaves, and finally he forbade him to keep wine or spirits in his cell. Claver was ordered to kneel in the refectory until further orders.

Without a word he went there and prayed for three hours. Juan de Arcos had forgotten about him, and he was only released through the intervention of other fathers.

A rector finally forbade him in teaching the catechism to use images and pictures which appeared to the rector childish. The Saint obeyed, but the subsequent failure in explaining a mental concept without visible aids soon persuaded those in authority to reverse their ruling. Father Sandoval, himself an intellectual genius, had used them. Simple methods like these, and Claver's habit of concealing his intellectual powers, occasioned much ignorant criticism. One day a discussion arose about various liturgical uses. Claver intervened and one of the fathers turned to him and said harshly: 'Be quiet, and busy yourself with your blacks. You don't even know Latin.' Father Fernández mentions that the speaker several times was in charge of the college, and at these times Claver's patience was sorely tried. One of the complaints against him was the noise he and his negroes made, especially within the college, 'As if,' Fernández writes, 'he could control and manage so many negroes in complete silence.' To this charge Claver humbly replied: 'It is a sad thing, my father, that I cannot do a little good without causing so much evil and disturbing the whole house. But one might expect this from a worthless fool like myself.'

The whole subject of the slave interpreters was taken so seriously that criticism reached Rome, and Father M. Viteleschi was made cognizant of it. We can read in his answer the drift of the accusations: he writes to the Provincial in 1628, Father Gabriel Perlín, that Father Claver must not be disturbed, that he should keep his negro interpreters, who should not be employed on other tasks while he had work for them to do. But that when they were free they should not remain idle but be found other work to do. In this same letter a very curious accusation is dealt with. The Father General writes: 'Claver should not have money at his disposal; if a certain quantity is necessary to assist in the relief of the poor negroes, it should remain in the hands of the procurator of the province or someone else selected by yourself, ready to disburse it promptly whenever necessary. It is also seemly that Claver should not keep in his cell the two casks of wine, which are not fitting in the cell of a member of our Society. Have them kept in the foodstore, and arrange that the wine shall only be used for the needs of the negroes.' Other things which witnesses tell us were in his cell—a store of food, fruit, sweets, clothing and so on, for giving to the ships and hospitals—are not mentioned. A Father Provincial once overheard a slave addressed as the 'little negro of Peter Claver'. Disturbed by this he reprehended the Saint severely. As always, the latter heard him in silence.

These are the facts, from which it has been inferred that Claver was misunderstood and persecuted by his own Order. Several circumstances must be remembered. In his forty years in the college he lived under more than ten superiors, who had under them from twenty to twenty-five colleagues. The work in which he was engaged was difficult and apt to bring about unpleasant clashes with others. He had to take the side of the weak and the wretched. On the other hand, as prefect of the church during almost all his time there, he was able to impose certain attitudes and practices with which all did not agree. To fill the church with negro slaves and their stench, to prefer these to persons of wealth and power, who contributed to the church and its work, to crowd the *patios* with negroes and the din of their instruction and baptisms—all these actions aroused criticism from those who valued peace and quiet. Many, too, were provoked by his very character, retiring but direct, to react strongly against him. But those who defended him most firmly were his senior superiors. We have five letters from the Father General, all full of praise and encouragement. The same is true of the fathers provincial, and most of the rectors held him in high esteem. As direct evidence of what his immediate superiors thought of him we have *four* of the triennial reports sent to Rome; for the years 1616, 1642, 1649 and 1651. They thus cover his whole life. These are the opinions expressed:

1616. *Mental powers*, less than mediocre. *Prudence*, lacking. *Instruction*, slight. *Character*, choleric. Ability for mission work, useful for hearing confessions and dealing with the natives.

1642. *Mental powers*, mediocre. *Judgment*, mediocre. *Prudence*, lacking. Good progress in instruction. *Character*, very melancholic.

1649. *Mental powers*, good. *Judgment*, mediocre. *Prudence and experience of the world*, nil. *Instruction*, good. *Character*, melancholic. *Missions*, outstanding in his dealings with the negroes. *Advance in spiritual matters*, excellent.

1651. *Mental powers*, good. *Judgment*, mediocre. *Prudence*, lacking. *Experience of the world and its affairs*, mediocre. *Advancement in instruction*, good. *Character*, melancholic and sanguine. *Ability in mission work*, good. *Advance in spiritual matters*, excellent.

The unanimity on his lack of prudence and faulty judgment, his holiness and skill with negroes, is obvious. Many of his actions already related here are seen from the human point of view only, and will explain the low valuation of his prudence. He was always careful not to display his scholarship, and a man who knew Greek and held a degree in philosophy and theology accepted the charge that he knew no Latin. His virtue of patience was extraordinary, and on two occasions his superiors made use of it when there was no other solution but to have recourse to the imprudent, unintelligent but saintly Claver. Andrade writes:

> His superiors made use of Claver's patience on many occasions, and often to his great cost. One occasion was in a lawsuit of great importance which the college was fighting in Cartagena. The judge was opposed to the Society and showed this in his constant bias against it, so that finally none dared present a petition to him, and so our interests suffered. It occurred to the superiors to send Claver, trusting in God that the judge would respect him because of the reputation for sanctity that he had throughout the town. They were certain, too, if he were harsh to Claver, the latter would suffer it in patience. When Claver presented his petition to the judge the latter received him furiously, and shouted endless insults against the Society and Claver himself, calling him an intriguing villain. Claver heard this in silence, impassively. Taking courteous leave of the judge, he reported to the rector, who sent him back next day with a second petition. This lawyer, a tyrant rather than a judge, treated him as before, calling him hypocrite and plotter, and the members of the Society rebels and traitors, saying that they should be expelled from the country. Claver behaved as before, returning to the college, as the judge went angrily off to his home. God, however, acted on behalf of Claver, for the

judge fell sick in his whole body, so that he could no longer exercise his profession. A short while later he died. The college had another lawsuit, with a woman who kept a wholesale shop, about a sum of money she was unjustly demanding from the Society. Although the matter was brought to court there was no way of getting the truth out of her, or of quieting her indignation. Since a woman's sword is her tongue, this one, like a trodden viper, spat out vituperation against the Jesuits, and told all she met that they were thieves and robbers and highwaymen. Whenever members of the college passed her shop she screamed insults after them, calling on the justice of God. After every remedy had been tried, they sent Claver, arguing that he who silenced demons would silence this their instrument. As Claver appeared before her she attacked him bitterly, calling him thief, deceiver and hypocrite, and all but assaulting him physically. Claver listened to this unmoved, but his companion sought to restrain her by force, thinking that Claver's impassivity irritated her the more. Angered that she had not been able to avenge herself as she wished, she pretended that night to be ill and asked Claver to hear her confession. This he readily agreed to do. She hid in her house two fugitive soldiers, who, as soon as Claver came in, leaped out and locked the door. They abused him, calling him thief and hypocrite like all his Society in that they had robbed this poor woman of her money. Like another St Peter, the companion, fearing that they would be killed, made as if to attack the soldiers, but Claver, like Christ before him, restrained him and begged him to keep quiet and not spoil this opportunity that God had given them to suffer for his love. Those wolves were not mollified by the gentleness of the lamb in their power, and when they seized him the companion shouted for help from the officers of the Inquisition. At this word, the soldiers, terrified, tore open the door and fled. The woman, moved by the gentleness of Claver, repented and knelt before him to ask his forgiveness.

CHAPTER IV

PHYSIQUE AND PERSONALITY

NO authentic portrait of St Peter Claver has survived. In the last days of his life (he would not have allowed it earlier) two painters were sent to him, one by Isabel de Urbina called Alfonso de la Torre, and the other of his own volition—Juan Pérez de Miranda. In 1690 a citizen of Cartagena, Francisco Velásquez, Knight of Calatrava, is recorded as possessing one of these portraits. In the life by Father Juan Fernández, printed at Saragossa in 1666—that is to say, twelve years after the Saint's death—there is an excellent pen sketch signed 'Marcus Orozco'. It is a half-length study of Claver holding a large crucifix, two negroes kneeling at his feet. The head is large, the eyebrows thick, the eyes deep-set, the hands full of power, the brow spacious as he gazes contemplatively into the distance. As if summarizing his life, the painter shows the words, 'Lord, I love thee,' coming from his closed mouth. They are aimed like an arrow at the crucifix. The title beneath reads: 'The venerable Father Claver, Catalan, of the Society of Jesus, professed in the four vows, illustrious in holiness, prophecies and miracles, through which he converted 350,000 pagans and many Moors; he brought back to our Faith many heretics. For years he served the lepers of San Lazáro. A great penitent, of deep humility and ardent love, he died a virgin in the college of Cartagena in the Indies at the age of seventy-one on 8 September 1654. Our Lord keeps almost his whole body incorrupt and sweet scented.' Apart from the error in his age, all this is true.

We find a description of him in words in the first life written three years after his death and before the Process. This life is especially valuable since it reflects the opinions of his contemporaries expressed in the circular letter which the Father Provincial of New Granada sent to the Spanish Jesuits. Here it says: 'Father

Peter Claver was of medium height, thin faced, his beard flecked with grey, eyes large and melancholy in expression, a thin tapering nose, his complexion dark, but sallowed by his many penances and neglect of his body.' Ten years later his second biographer, Father José Fernández, adds further details to the above, taken directly from the Process:

> Father Claver was of medium stature, by nature erect but become a little bent through his habit of always keeping his gaze on the ground. His head was large, his face thin but long in proportion, a dark complexion which penitence had turned sallow, his brow broad and wrinkled but sunk in at the temples, his brows bushy, eyes well marked but sad in expression, lids reddened with much weeping. The space between his eyes was wide and crossed with two deep furrows from which sprang his nose, large but not excessively so. At either side there fell two deep furrows, originating in the inner corner of his eyes and reaching the roots of his nostrils, thence turning in a semi-circle to run between his cheeks and his beard. His cheeks were very sunken, his beard full and streaked with grey. His mouth large, with thick lips, the lower one a little relaxed, his neck short and wrinkled. His voice was neither loud nor weak, rather resonant than flexible.

Many witnesses comment upon his supple hands; they were even noticed after death. Both the above accounts mention changes in him during life. A robust peasant descent gave him the resistance necessary for his heavy labours. A reference suggests that the climate of Bogotá was not good for his chest. This was the motive which led him to leave the capital for Cartagena without waiting for ordination. It may have contributed to the sallow complexion which all the witnesses note. Possibly also he may have suffered from some digestive weakness, since Brother González says that sometimes he was given a little wine to revive him.

A four-year-long illness began in 1650. The plague which attacked the town in that year, and caused the death of nine members of the college, fell on him. He had travelled down the coast as far as the banks of the Sinú to preach the extraordinary Jubilee dispensation of that year. It was the rainy season, he ate very little on his journeys, and took no care to change his clothing when he arrived drenched at his various destinations. When he fell seriously ill, his superior ordered him to return immediately to Cartagena. He obeyed, leaving his mission unfinished. On arrival his wretched state, face yellow with a deadly pallor, may have been due either to malaria or to jaundice. The city was rotten with plague, and many were dying. Claver caught it, and was so ill that he received the viaticum. He recovered from the plague, but the destruction wrought in his body made him ill for the remaining four years of his life. This is how eye-witnesses describe him: 'The sickness so weakened him that he never recovered. His strength was destroyed, his feet and hands almost useless, his jaws trembled making a continuous clacking. This endless quivering was most painful to him. He could scarcely sit up in bed, and had to be assisted by others when he wished to walk. Later he suffered from painful urinary troubles.' It was really a miracle that Claver should have reached the age of seventy-four considering the rough treatment he had always given his body. Cassani describes thus his last months: 'His sickness ended in a violent palsy. His head and mind remained clear and rational . . . his feet, hands and mouth trembled continuously . . . his teeth rattled as in a tertian fever . . . he was unable to say Mass or even to dress himself or eat without help.'

Towards the end of his life 'he was as if asleep or in a lethargy or coma'. These details enable us with modern medical knowledge to say that he was suffering from Parkinson's disease, or general paralysis, perhaps together with chronic malaria which had affected his kidneys.

In the triennial letters nothing is said of his illness, merely one or two references of value in reconstructing his character. This is a more difficult task than the description of his physical being. He left no personal writings except some family letters and a few schematic notes on spiritual questions. It is impossible to examine his intelligence or his emotional character by direct means. They must be reconstructed through an examination of his deeds, or the remarks of others. In some ways Claver may be seen as an expression of the Catalan national character as described in Pt I, Chap. V, but this must be modified by what we know of him. Father

Gaspar de Garrigas, one of his fellow pupils in Barcelona, describes him when a student as 'humble, devout, obedient, friendly
towards all and never belligerent. His modesty was an example
to all of us. It is impossible to enter into greater detail, because he
was very silent and reserved.' Here we have two keys to his character already there in youth: his reserved silence, and his readiness
to help others while denying himself. The reserve might be seen
as a defect in him, arising from an inferiority complex or inherent
timidity. Thence too perhaps arose his reluctance to be a priest,
the concealment of his intellectual attainments to the point of
being reputed ignorant of Latin. In contrast to this humility we
have the remark of the rector of the college, Father Sebastián de
Morillo, who told Doctor Bartolomé de Torres on one occasion
that Claver, like himself, 'was unfortunately for himself a Catalan
and pigheaded and difficult'.

The voluntary concealment of his scholarship is curious. In
philosophy he stood out as the possessor of a clear mind, in a
public disputation he was once the leader. He knew Greek, and
passed a stern examination which qualified him in the Society for
the profession of the four vows. When he discovered that the
examination was for this distinction he said that if he had known
it earlier he would not have performed so well, but he was consoled by the idea 'of being closely associated with the Pope'. His
advice was increasingly sought by prelates, by commanders of the
Spanish fleets and by his own superiors, but in his personality the
intellectual note is not dominant. The very work he chose pre-
cluded this. When he refused to hear the confessions of the great
ladies of Cartagena he used to say: 'I have no head for those problems of theirs. There are other more learned fathers in the college.'

In the triennial reports quoted above the original comments on
his prudence are illuminating. Until his death the valuation is the
same: *Prudence*, nil. In part it is explained by his work: he was
defending the destitute and forlorn against the rich and powerful,
he was swimming against the stream. But on his holiness and his
skill in missions to the negroes there is no dispute.

The progression from *choleric* to *melancholic* to *sanguine and melancholic* is not so surprising as might appear. Both melancholics and

cholerics belong to the affective category as distinct from the apathetic. Within that category they belong to the group called passionate, itself divided into three sub-groups: melancholic, irritable and violent. From the point of view of his sensibility, he would be classified a passionate affective. From the point of view of his spiritual powers, strong-willed and master of himself. In his social relationships a man of action. It was here that melancholic and choleric were harmonized.

Throughout his life there are cases of firm and rapid decisions. In Mallorca nobody could prevent him going aboard the ship that had been pointed out to him as his. More than once he dispersed dancing groups of negroes with the whip. In his last moments he made clear his unwillingness that his beloved crucifix should be handed to the Marqués de Mancera, and his deep displeasure at the imminent destruction of the college. He insisted on his own views in the catechism and baptism of the slaves, and on their frequent communion, and again and again we can feel his irony when he contemplates the confessions of the rich, or the vanity of some pretensions.

He must have suffered much; he rarely smiled. His face lit up only when he was told of the arrival of a slave-ship, or when he greeted the slaves in the barracks, or visited the lepers in San Lázaro. The dreadful human wretchedness which he witnessed, the cruelty of the slave-traders, the desolation of the hospitals, domestic strife—all this, added to his own strained physical powers, his lack of sleep and his penances, brought about the general sadness which was the background to his life. This led not to mis-anthropy or discouragement, but drove him into consuming toil.

It is asked whether Claver was not psychologically abnormal. The clinical definition of melancholy is unmotivated gloom, a spiritual bankruptcy which seeks solitude in a complete withdrawal. It is a loathing for life, remote from all hope, a total pessimism. The most obvious characteristic is despair and the avoidance of all action. These symptoms are totally alien to the generous, resolute, unselfish spirit of Claver. Sadness in him was the fruit of an immense love for a God he saw rejected: he was an optimist in action and in his estimate of the powers of his negroes.

CHAPTER V

CLAVER AS A FRIEND

CLAVER'S life-story may give the impression of a character rather to be admired than loved. This chapter is included to refute a legend of harshness and inhumanity which has grown up round the Saint.

During the voyage from Seville to New Granada he won the affection of the whole crew, and even of the captain of the galleon *San Pedro*. Children, who soon recognize their friends, used to run after him to kiss his hand and call him 'the Saint'. The lepers of San Lázaro and the sick in the general hospital of San Sebastián counted every day when he was away on mission journeys, and welcomed him rejoicing when he came back. (This is according to the testimony of the prior of the convent of San Juan de Dios.)

Claver was the kind of man who does not open his heart boisterously at the first meeting. But once his heart was won, he gave it without reserve, and for ever. Claver's heart was deeply human, simple, perhaps too sensitive. For this reason he had to be circumspect. To four or five great friends in his life he gave delicate expressions of affection. The extraordinary sufferings of his life brought to his friendships disinterest and untainted love. The only autograph manuscript we have of Claver, the letter to his parents from Mallorca, refers to the companions of his youth.

There are four intimate friends: St Alphonsus Rodríguez, S.J., Father Alonso de Sandoval, S.J., Brother Nicolás González, S.J., and Doña Isabel de Urbina. Besides these, and one or two others, such as the Franciscan Miguel de Ugarte and Captain Villalobos, there are three groups for whom he felt a special affection: the brothers coadjutor of the Society amongst whom he had always wanted to count himself—González, Rodríguez, Lomparte, Bobadilla he especially loved. So also the Brothers of St John of God. Secondly, the negro slave interpreters, his faithful friends and assistants, especially Sacabuche and Monzolo. Thirdly, the lepers of San Lázaro. In wretchedness these were the very dregs of humanity, and for that reason they were the supreme objects of his love. The most heroic moments of his life are associated with them. These relationships throw new light on Claver's biography. No longer is he the saint who almost repels by his superhuman austerity, who receives the adulation due to heroism, but nothing more. He becomes a man saddened by the grief of others, showing in his friendships a marvellous sincerity. We have already discussed his association with Rodríguez and Sandoval. We turn now to the others.

Brother Nicolás González was one of his most intimate friends, his companion for twenty-two years, who knew him for five years before he became a Jesuit. González was his best biographer, the principal witness at the Process, whose testimony, in many ways the most valuable, fills 130 folio pages. But we have little information about him. There is one explicit declaration of friendship: shortly before Claver died, Brother Nicolás asked him about his relationship with St Alphonsus, and we are told that he was moved to do this 'because of the great affection Claver felt for him, and relying on their close friendship'. He declared that in the twenty-two years of their association he saw him every single day, and admired him more each one. Brother Nicolás pronounced the noble sentence: 'Each day he did at least one heroic deed.' Some tasks Claver never carried out without the help of this brother—for example in his ministry to condemned persons, or when he had to visit powerful magnates. Nicolás was the intermediary and intercessor for several ladies, and Isabel de Urbina and others knew that only through him could they gain the Saint's attention. He was not always a model of kindliness towards Claver. Sometimes the latter had to go on his knees before him to persuade him to accompany him, and sometimes, as has been related, the brother reproved him. These incidents did not undermine their mutual respect. It was to Nicolás that Claver went with his doubts, with him he went down to the harbour and the slave barracks, to him he gave his most precious memento, the notes of St Alphonsus, his hair shirts and scourges, and he gave him his crucifix as a pledge of friendship. Nicolás was with him when he died. The final conversations between them are most moving. Claver begged Nicolás to have him buried at the door of the church, 'where all may tread upon me'. 'I will not,' he replied, 'I will have you buried in the chapel of the Crucifix.' 'Brother Nicolás,' said Claver as he passed through the sacristy after receiving the viaticum, 'I am about to die. Have you any errands for me in the next life?' 'Pray for me and for the college.' So that he should not forget, Nicolás made a list of people and got the old man to sign it. 'Put your signature, here, Father Claver. No, a little lower, in case there are more names to add.' Nicolás never forgot his teacher and became the most insistent propagandist for the canonization.

The apostle of the negro slaves was not, as has been suggested by some modern tendentious writers, a revolutionary priest, hater of the rich and embittered protector of the poor. He favoured the poor, and he demanded that the rich should carry out their duties, but his work was constructive. As a Christian sociologist he believed that the solution lay in the Christian co-operation of the powerful and the weak. It will surprise some readers to learn that Claver had friends in the upper strata of society in Cartagena, amongst them the Urbinas. Eight days before Claver died Brother Nicolás came into the room where he lay paralysed and reminded him that it was Saturday, the day when he heard Doña Isabel de Urbina's confession. The Saint closed his eyes for a moment, and then asked that he might be carried there in a litter; it was the last time that he would ask this favour of them. Doña Isabel was very downcast. As her spiritual director he had brought her strength and consolation. Claver told her that she ought to select as her confessor Father Fariña, who had just arrived from Spain. He was to be his successor in the mission to the negroes. As he left he blessed Doña Isabel and her family, and contrary to his custom allowed her to kiss his hand. She was a great benefactress of Claver's work. She sent food, clothing and money to San Lázaro and to condemned criminals. In his last days she was most solicitous about Claver. Her servant, Margarita of Cape Verde, was charged with preparing for him then certain special dishes which were sent down to him by another slave, the negro Liseta, who had the most careful instructions to serve them himself to the dying man, for otherwise they would be appropriated by the negro Manuel, Claver's servant and, in effect, jailer. Margarita received her freedom from Doña Isabel on the day of Claver's death.

It was Doña Isabel who sent the painter Alfonso de la Torre to make a portrait of Claver, and on his death she ordered his coffin from Luis Hernández, who lived in the calle de San Agustín. She got the mulatto Pedro Suárez to line it with white fabric and adorn it with golden ribbons and a huge palm leaf decorated by the nuns of St Teresa with flowers and festoons. On the night of his death she went down to the church where he lay at ten o'clock. The whole family enjoyed his intimate friendship. Don Hipólito Salazar, the husband of Doña Isabel, was commandant of the castle at the Punta del Indio, and while there fell sick of the plague. Claver was summoned, and took with him relics of Alphonsus Rodríguez. Don Hipólito offered 500 pesos towards the cost of the canonization. He died a few day later. His wife, who had great faith in her confessor's prayers, meekly complained of this failure.

'Señora, I prayed for him, as also did brother Alonso, but it was proper that he should die, for never would he be better prepared.'

On several occasions Claver asserted that he had joined the blessed. From that moment the widow dedicated herself to God's service. Doña Isabel's sisters were Doña Juana and Doña Jerónima. The former caught a high fever and the doctors despaired of her. As always, they summoned Claver. Already paralysed, he arrived in a litter. He saw the sick woman, and turning to Isabel said: 'You need no longer fear that your sister will die, because death has passed by like a huge tidal wave up a river.' Doña Juana lived, and the family's respect for Claver was intensified. On another occasion Father Francisco de Urbina was on his way to Cartagena from Peru. On arrival at Panama he fell gravely ill. The family begged Claver to pray for him. The Saint smiled and said: 'Do not worry. He will soon arrive here in perfect health and take

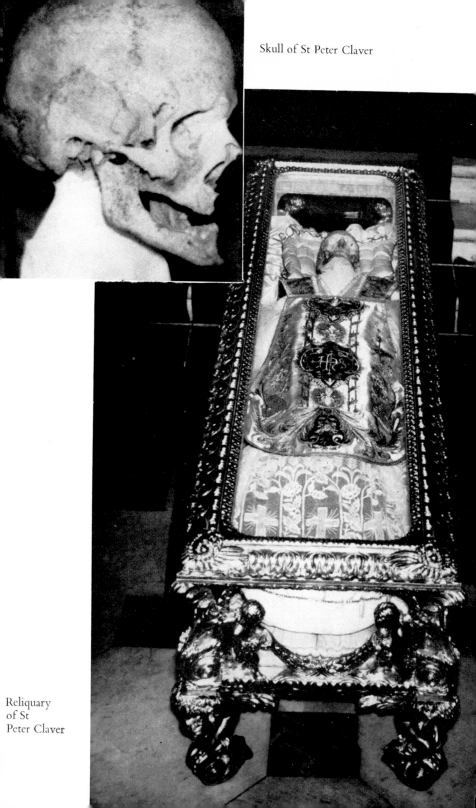

Skull of St Peter Claver

Reliquary
of St
Peter Claver

Reliquary:
Side view

charge of us all in the college.' And so it happened. The most private family problems were presented to the Saint. Doña Jerónima complained to him that she was worn out by her many children, that another was soon to be born, and this addition would make her situation even worse. 'It will not,' said Claver, 'he will only live a short while; just long enough to be baptized and thus acquire rights in heaven.' So it happened: the child lived only a few moments. One day, while hearing the confession of this same lady, he asked her to remember her slaves in her prayers, and gently added, 'And that poor fellow, that poor fellow, who suffers like a martyr.' It was found that at that moment a servant was beating one of the slaves so badly that he died.

In this matter of slaves Claver was very firm with the owners. Doña Jerónima's husband had an old slave, Sebastian, and Claver begged Doña Jerónima to free him. She said that she could not as he was indispensable. He answered sternly, 'Very well, but he will not be much use to you.' A few days later the slave fell ill, and they had to free him. Once Claver went into Doña Jerónima's house, and met her sister. He said to her, 'This Lent you will not wear your farthingale.' Their father, Don Juan de Urbina, was ill from the first day of Lent until Palm Sunday, and the daughters stayed at home to look after him, getting no opportunity to wear the garment so hated by the Saint. He was at the death-bed of Don Juan, and said, 'I wish that I were such a man as he: God has a crown ready for him in heaven, and this will be his holy week.' In that week he died. Now another member of the family plays his part: Don Lope de Estrada, son of Doña Jerónima and Don Pedro de Estrada, another friend of the Saint. One day he was punished by his teacher, and thinking that as a Knight of Santiago he should not put up with such an indignity, he decided to enter the convent of San Diego as a monk. Claver was told of this, and he announced, 'Lope will not become a monk, but his two brothers will.' The situation was difficult. The father, Don Pedro, was in opposition, but heaven arranged events otherwise. Lope joined the navy and went aboard the flagship on its first trip to Santa Catalina. There was a terrible storm, but what was left of the fleet reached land. There was great commotion in

Cartagena, and prayers were said before the famous Christ of the Expiation, and Don Pedro vowed that if Lope were saved he would permit this two other sons to enter a monastery. Good news of Lope came from Portobello, and a solemn *Te Deum* was sung in the cathedral. The prophecy was fulfilled. But there was a sad prophecy too, Claver's last to this family, that Lope, saved from shipwreck, would die in the siege of Barcelona. Claver told Doña Isabel that the news of the death would arrive in November. She pressed for more details, and looking sadly at the two sisters he said: 'In October, in October.' In November letters came from Spain telling of Don Lope's death in the siege on 7 October.

For his work with the negroes Claver needed the assistance of outstanding men of the same race. In this he and Sandoval were revolutionaries, using a method widely adopted in modern times. His friendships with these collaborators were astounding. He demanded for himself and them extraordinary privileges of self-rule. When they were sick he looked after them with great care, allotting them many honours, such as the best places at meetings. One of the major difficulties in his mission was the variety of negro races; there were twenty-five, each with its own language. Many difficulties were encountered in retaining interpreters, until, as we have seen, the Father General himself had to intervene. At the time of the heaviest slave traffic there were eight to ten of these assistants. Their names are in the Process, and are repeated here in Pt II, Chap. II. To the Saint every one of these men was as the apple of his eye. He spoke with difficulty the language of Angola, doing everything possible to get money for his interpreters. By asking for alms from door to door he got together the price of three slaves in Africa. He asked a merchant who was leaving for Guinea to get them for him. In a storm he lost everything except Claver's purse of money, but after considerable difficulties he was able to carry out the task. 'Claver was very happy with these slaves; he could work with them. He spared no pains in their instruction, nor kindness in order to win their trust. It was a difficult task to teach them the elements of the Faith; merely to teach them the sign of the Cross took several days. This is a measure of the problem of teaching them the catechism so that they might instruct others. He taught them each day at the same hour, usually in leisure time after meals.' The superior ordered him to have them taught some trade, suggesting shoemaking or tailoring. This was done, and the money they earned was used to buy more slaves. A witness tells us: 'His natural melancholy turned to affability itself with them. No mother ever cared for her children as Claver watched over his slaves.' His care for their clothing, food and medicines was systematic and methodical. Begging from house to house for their medicines, he would have only the most costly for them. If they were gravely ill he had them taken to his own room and put into his own bed, while he slept on the mat on the floor. He himself administered their medicines. For four months he watched by one interpreter. He was so benevolent with them that on more than one occasion an interpreter became a tyrant towards the Saint, who responded to this by making him his favourite adviser. In the lives of few saints is it possible to find a kind of headquarters staff more efficient and more humble than in the case of Claver and his interpreters.

The following humble souls he used in their various ways, selecting them from among slaves: At ten years old Isabel Folupa was at the point of death. Claver baptized her and cured her miraculously. She later spent her life in his service. She says of him in the Process: 'He was the refuge and help of all negroes.' Her particular task was the preparation of her companions for communion. Antonia was the slave of Don Manuel de Estremoz. Her special care from the beginning was looking after the lepers of San Lázaro. She was, as it were, the provider, keeping all her small savings, made by denying herself, in a money box. On the eve of the Saint's name day she gave them to him to pay towards the annual banquet for the lepers. Margarita of Cape Verde, the slave of Isabel de Urbina, had the duty of preparing special dishes for the poor. The task was not an easy one. There were exceptional meals on great feast days, meals for the wretched beggars at the lodge of the college, and meals for the hospitals. She did her job well, and Doña Isabel was generous in providing the raw materials.

Claver could not possibly attend to all the sick himself. To help him there was a veritable charitable association, whose

members did house-to-house visiting. Angela Rodríguez was one
of these. She was a freed slave, and looked after Ursula for four
years as if she were her mother. Claver spent many hours with her.
When she died he asserted that she would spend only three years
in purgatory. Another negress, Bernardina, made house-to-house
collections for the hospitals for thirty years. Two others, Justina
and Martina, were chosen by the Saint to collect and bury the
bodies of slaves thrown aside to await the passing of the mortuary
cart. Don Pedro Calderón, a familiar of the Inquisition, begged
Claver to extend their activities to the prisons. When a body had
been recovered, Claver was informed, and he always arranged
singers for the funeral and said a Mass for each one. This had a
tremendous effect on the slaves, especially as it modified their
pagan ideas of death.

More important than all his infinite kindness to the slaves was
his confidence in them; he believed in them, in their capacity for
virtue, for faithfulness, for holiness. This made him inexorable
towards those who criticized his work with what they called
hopeless savages. His friendship for the negroes was deep and
sincere. It is not surprising that the great workers' Pope, Leo XIII,
exclaimed: 'No life, except the life of Christ, has so moved me as
that of St Peter Claver.'

Chapter VI

BE YE PERFECT

BY its nature the religious life implies subjection. Hence the fundamental vows of poverty, chastity and obedience. These are the essential virtues of the religious man as he seeks perfection, and the episodes related in this chapter reflect the formation by these means of an instrument useful in the service of God.

Claver was ill and a friend sought to give him a present. Finally he was persuaded to accept a tiny flask of wine and asked whether he wanted white or red.

'The poor do not choose, they take what they are given.' The wine went to a sick monk nearby in fulfilment of Claver's life principle to be a slave. We have seen already the poverty and inconvenience of his cell and he dressed accordingly: 'He never used new cassocks or cloaks, his shoes were secondhand.' Brother Manuel Rodríguez tells us that 'his biretta and clothes were tawny-coloured through long use.'

Andrade has reproduced letters he received soon after the Saint's death. (Care should be taken not to interpret literally the 'nevers' and the 'always'.)

He dressed like a beggar. He never used anything that was not rejected by others. In his cell, itself refused by anyone else, his bed was an old blanket or a heap of flour sacks, his chair a box. His breviary was the one he had had at his ordination, and so old and worn that it was almost impossible to read it. Both backs were missing. His daily service book was even worse; its binding had all gone, and it was held together with string. His hat, so old that its original colour had disappeared, its lining gone and its seams open, his cloak so worn and ragged it scarcely stayed on his shoulders, his cassock full of patches, his stockings old and darned. If ever he was obliged to get new shoes, he would not put them on until someone else had worn them and taken the shine of newness from them. A superior once forced him to wear a new cassock, but he was so upset and so clumsy in it, constantly catching his feet in it, and concerned lest he might be wearing the garb of the world instead of that of Christ, that the superior relented and gave him an old cassock, to the great delight of Claver. His underwear did not deserve the name of clothing. It is exhibited today as a symbol of poverty. He wore a vest without sleeves and quite shapeless. It was like a few old rags of sacking wrapped round his body and tied together with string. Even his amice and other vestments for Mass were of the poorest. Because one of the chasubles had some flowers embroidered on it he could not be persuaded to wear it. He even looked for the 'poorest' Host, choosing the smallest which others had left. He pushed this to lengths which may seem exaggerated, for at the washing of hands he would not use fresh water which poured forth in abundance from the spring, but insisted on using water left behind by his predecessors, judging it to show greater poverty not to use clean water but that already sullied by others, as if he were a servant making use of what was left over by his master. The same at table, and to light his cell he looked for used toothpicks which he put in a wall lamp with a few pieces of tallow collected from other lamps. He never used a new pen but picked out from the college refuse old ones thrown away as useless. For paper he used old letters and wrappings. For himself he never accepted anything that had the slightest value. The nobles and rich men of the city who held him in respect and reverence willingly offered him large quantities of gold and silver; but it was only when they urged him to take some for the poor that he would put forth his hand and take the smallest coin, for he had no knowledge of money or its value, and take it straight away to the hospital.

Some of these actions of Claver may seem to border on eccentricity or madness. But one must remember the atmosphere and environment in which he lived. It is obvious that Claver pushed his personal negligence to excess, but there is logical force in his behaviour. It was impossible for him to feel at ease amid slavery and acute poverty unless his own life approached the same conditions. Much money passed through his hands: for himself he rejected it, but not for the lepers, or the negroes, or the poor. Captain Sanmartí, a fellow Catalan, longed to give him something during his last illness, but Claver refused to accept the smallest gift. But Sanmartí was so persistent that at last he said, 'Bring me some coarse linen to make clothing for a negro.' The benefactor sent him twelve yards. Four were enough, and Claver sent back the remaining eight.

Among the goods which turned his cell into a warehouse were bales of cloth and heaps of garments for the slaves. They arrived naked from Africa and Claver had to deal with this situation. Andrade writes that the perfect purity he preserved among dissolute surroundings was never in question. 'He was especially careful never to touch directly a living body. He would wrap his hand in the edge of his cloak and then place it upon the sick, and then always in the presence of his companion. If the negro before him was naked he always took off his cloak and laid it upon him, even though often they were suffering from contagious diseases.' He never disobeyed the rule of the Society by going about his tasks without a companion. Captain Balanquecer says that whenever Claver came to his house to hear his daughter's confession, the companion always had to be present. He would not allow Doña Isabel de Urbina to kiss his hand until he took leave of her for the last time just before his death. In that brutal age, when the weak were trampled upon, when the overlord was accorded supposed rights over the bodies and souls of his dependants, Claver's purity was something more than a living example, it was the assertion of human dignity before the slavery of the flesh.

Saint Alphonsus Rodríguez had taught his pupil another ideal: 'Obey. Remember to see Christ in your superior. In that way you will be happy.' Brother Nicolás González one day in answer to a question about Claver replied: 'He loved obedience so much that all his life he behaved like a novice. Before his superiors he always appeared with bare head, and carried out their orders with unbelievable punctiliousness, without complaining or offering excuses.' Often this punctiliousness was very painful, especially when the superior of the moment was a difficult man, as were

Arcos and Sarmiento and Morillo. The notebook by his bed offers
evidence of his struggles.

There is nothing in the religious life which more quickly
leads the soul to the highest perfection than obedience to
superiors. This is the straight and undeviating road; it pleases
God and carries out his will; therefore I must treat one word
from my superior with more respect than a thousand revelations. When a superior orders me to do anything I shall lift my
heart up to God and realize that it is God who directs me.
Therefore, since it is a divine command I shall without hesitation carry it out with blind obedience, considering that it is a
great benevolence in God to make use of me.
It is not right that the inferior should behave towards his
superior as if he were his equal, and although the latter behaves
kindly and informally to him, his soul should see God in him.
And if before he became superior he was well known to me or
my friend, afterwards I must look upon him with changed
eyes.

We see early examples of this rigid obedience in his departure
from Mallorca in a ship avoided by all the others, or his prompt
departure from Barcelona when he received orders to leave for
the Indies.

In the work with the negroes he was the expert of the college.
But as Brother Nicolás says: 'Every day before leaving for the
hospitals he sought permission from his superior to do so. At the
same time he would ask for a companion, and if he found him
busy he would help him to wash the dishes or the vegetables or
set the table until the task was completed. At the beginning of
each month he went to the superior and gave him a report on his
penances and fasts, and all his activity during the month, and then
he would read out an account of his sins before the whole community.'

This submission was not directed only towards his superiors
in the Society. For Claver the sacristan and the porter and the
cook were his superiors. So also his slaves, the negro interpreters.
Gómez is explicit on this point: 'On the mission journeys it was
the interpreters who fixed each day's tasks. When the time came

for catechism or preaching he deferred to them with the utmost obedience and humility.' Andrade supports this: 'He always submitted to the negro interpreter with him, saying that he was his superior.' Claver's last apostolic task ended with an act of obedience. Fernández describes it:

In 1650 he arrived at the village of Tolú on a mission journey upon which he was preaching the special Jubilee dispensation. He received a letter from the father rector to return to the college. This was noised about in the village and all tried to dissuade him from going back until the mission was completed. The local priest, a great friend of the Jesuits, offered to write on his own behalf and that of the town council to explain the reasons for the delay. Claver took no notice; the roads were practically impassible but he set out. As he left he said that a good work performed against his will can never be acceptable to God, and as for himself he would consider it a glory to lose his life for the sake of obedience.

The human side of the Saint is revealed in one of his last acts of obedience. As he lay paralysed his fame had spread beyond New Granada to Mexico, Peru and to Sapin. Shortly before he died the Marqués de Mancera came to visit him in Cartagena. Together with the rector he went to Claver's cell. As the Marqués left he begged Claver to give him a memento. The Saint had nothing to give. The rector, without realizing the storm he was about to raise, ordered him to give the marqués the famous crucifix which he wore always about his neck. The Saint's face stiffened, and the two deep furrows in his cheeks grew deeper. Sadly, without a word, he took the crucifix from his neck and handed it to the marqués. As the visitors left he confided to Brother González that he had most unwillingly parted with the cross because 'it had been his physician and his physic throughout his life'. God had asked him heroically to sacrifice his last possession, the visible symbol of his love. Claver had responded to the summons: 'Be ye perfect.'

CHAPTER VII

SON OF ST IGNATIUS

S T PETER CLAVER is one of the greatest glories of the
Society of Jesus. He is not one of the intellectual saints like
St Robert Bellarmine and St Peter Canisius, or a great
administrator like St Ignatius Loyola or St Francis Borgia.
His place is among the missionaries of genius: Francis Regis,
Francis di Girolamo, and especially with St Francis Xavier. The
Council of Tarragona named Claver the 'Apostle of the West
Indies' as Xavier was called 'Apostle of the East Indies'. The parallel
is unavoidable. Both were unwearying in zeal, both baptized more
than 300,000 pagans. Xavier was the wandering apostle opening
new roads to the Church. Claver was the apostle who stayed in
one spot. The former sought out souls along the routes of his journeys: to the latter souls came as to a safe harbour. In their methods
both were revolutionaries, though Claver was more of a tradi-
tionalist than Xavier, and more of a disciple. They were holy
sociologists, who taught without a plan of campaign and carried
through an immense operation. Xavier freed the east and ended
its isolation from Europe, Claver converted to Christ the Africans
who came to the New World.

We can say that Claver became a Jesuit because of the founder's,
St Ignatius', extraordinary popularity in Catalonia at that time.
From the day when, as a student, Claver had stood in ecstasy on
the spot where Ignatius was beaten, until his death in the college
of St Ignatius in Cartagena, he never ceased to admire the founder
and his creation.

Some modern biographers have exaggerated various aspects of
his experiences within the Society. Some of them we have already
examined. There are others. For example, he was never made a
superior. If this is seen as a deliberate insult, then ninety per cent of
Jesuits suffer under the same affront. Claver was held in great

esteem from the moment when he was selected as a missionary to the Indies. In Cartagena he was made master of novices of the brothers coadjutor in the college: a delicate and responsible task. Five letters to Claver from the General, Father Viteleschi, survive. They are written in defence of his work and show the veneration in which he was held. There is another letter from the General to the Father Provincial of New Granada in which he asks for gratitude and assistance 'for the well-deserving Father Claver'. Other members of his own college held him in great affection. The *Annual Letters*, though, as always, mentioning no names, refer often and clearly to his work: 'to that father who with immense zeal devotes himself especially to the care of the natives'. And there could be no greater mark of esteem than the incident, already reported, of the use of his blood as a relic. Much is made of the abandonment in which he lay sick and paralysed for four years. But the following facts silence criticism: the plague which laid him low in 1651 killed six priests and three assistant brothers out of that small community. Melgar points out: 'According to the *Annual Letters* that community was reduced to seven priests with the rector and five brothers. All these were old men upon whom many duties fell: the work of the Inquisition, the work with the slaves, in the hospitals and prisons, and the teaching in the college. Besides this they were expected to preach in the cathedral and on missions. It was impossible for them therefore to look after the paralysed saint as he deserved. It was impossible to devote to him the time of a Jesuit male nurse.' One of the finest descriptions of Claver the Jesuit is that of Andrade, which is taken from the circular letter sent by the Father Provincial on the Saint's death:

> He spent many years in the college at Cartagena, where he was prefect of spiritual matters, and confessor to all. He was the consolation and the angel of peace in all that happened in the college, both towards his inferiors and his superiors. He it was who normally spoke the homilies within the community. For many years he was master of novices there, that is to say of those novices who came from the sea coasts . . . He was an excellent master of novices, severe with himself but gentle and loving with others. Ready to forgive and slow to punish, he

always inclined to gentleness and mercy, and seeking the joy
of everyone, so far as religious observances permitted. His
homilies to the novices struck home like blazing arrows. With
them he discussed especially contempt of worldly standards,
and he used to lead them through the streets of the town, some
carrying loads of sewage, others brooms and baskets to sweep out
the hospitals and carry refreshment to the sick. They often looked
after the inmates, making their beds, with Claver teaching them
to control their loathing of the stench and filth caused by the
seriously ill. No one inside or outside the college ever saw him
transgress the smallest rule of the Society. However busy he
was he found time each third day to sweep out his cell. Sometimes, his attention attracted by another as he left the college,
he would forget to remove his name tag from the board in the
porter's lodge. As soon as he remembered he would retrace his
steps and remove it in order not to break the rule. He always
asked permission to write a letter, and sometimes, although he
might have been asked to write a letter by the Father General,
he sought permission from the Father Provincial, and when
the letter was written always had it censored. When within the
college he never left his room, thus fulfilling the rule that 'the
cell should be as one's heaven'. He left it for three reasons only,
of which he himself has left a record: 'You shall leave your cell
for three reasons only—for obedience you must; for charity
you may; or through urgent necessity. If for any other reason
you leave it, it is certain that unwittingly you are placing yourself in danger of temptation.' Since these were sayings of his
teacher Alphonsus Rodríguez, he kept them as if they were from
the Gospels. So many entered the Society that the college at
Cartagena was looked upon as a source of supply of assistant
brothers for the whole province. Soldiers and travellers who
decided to reject the world and its pomp entered the Society
there. One Basque, of noble birth, Brother Pedro de Solabarrieta,
who had arrived with the general commanding the fleet, came
under Claver's influence and entered the Society. He was taught
by Claver and lived the life of an angel during his novitiate.
He died shortly after taking his vows. With him Brother
Diego Felipe Monfalue entered the Society, became procurator
of the college in his first year and died in holiness. There was
also a well-known soldier, very courageous and the commander

of his company. Claver brought into the religious life many students of good intellect. Among them was one whom God so fired with his vocation that, when his objecting parents removed his outdoor clothing and locked him in his house, he escaped and persevered in his plans.

This quotation expresses exactly the atmosphere surrounding Claver in the college. All who have written about Claver, from the earliest biographers down to Ledos and Astrain, have been puzzled as to why he was not made superior. The answers may well be, first, that he was too busy, and second, that it was seen that it was not the kind of job for him.

Chosen for the mission to the slaves, the task he was allotted filled all his time. So great was the work involved that again and again other assistants were asked for, and this help was agreed to by Rome. He already did the work of four men, we are told. He himself longed to do the work of forty. As catechizer, priest on the parish, visitor of prisons and hospitals, and rural missionary, his tasks made it quite impossible to add to these that of superior in a place where he would have had to be not only that but at the same time rector of a college with more than 400 pupils. And although the Saint was far from being an ignorant man, he had long been unconnected with teaching the young. The second reason is more personal. In order to become superior certain qualities are needed. These are observed in the priest by his colleagues and reported as a first step to the General's office. The reports we have printed in earlier chapters were not the kind expected for elevation to this responsibility. He is shown as lacking precisely those qualities demanded in a superior. But experiments were made. Father Juan Manuel, rector of the college for a period, and a great friend of Claver, gave him, in spite of these reports, an administrative position. He was made minister of the residence, and the result was disastrous. Too good and too helpful to others, he who had been appointed to command used the opportunity the better to mortify himself. All the most troublesome tasks he took upon himself. He used to say: 'How can he amend the faults of others who has never been able to amend his own? How can he whose own observances are so faulty excite in others a proper zeal? How, when I am so at war within myself, can I impose my will upon others?' A writer puts it well when he says that the slave of the blacks then became the slave of the whites. Fernández writes: 'He began by allotting himself all the most servile tasks. His first appearance in office was as he swept out the whole building, even the most squalid places, leaving everywhere clean and spotless. He went down to help in the kitchen and washed all the dishes ... On the third day he entered the refectory dragging a thin mattress and a few pieces of sacking which he used as bedclothes, and kneeling before us he announced his fault, which was loving his bed over-much. How could one who was scarcely ever in it love his bed too much?'

Claver showed a keen knowledge of affairs in insisting that the inmates be scrupulously cared for domestically to prevent any excuse for not carrying out all their observances! But Father Juan Manuel, 'considering that this minister used his office only to increase his own burdens', removed him from the office and made him master of novices. The failure to appoint him superior is sufficiently explained. But there remains another point.

Claver's solemn profession as a Jesuit, with its particular problems for him, gave rise to his correspondence with Rome. In his natural humility, he thought that it was his duty to propose to his superiors that he be given no fixed grade, but remain admixture of brother, student and priest. This was a new and curious notion. His letter has been lost, but we have Viteleschi's reply (referred to in Chap. V):

> I realize the fervour of your reverence especially in all that touches the evangelization of the negroes. This is evident from your reverence's letter of 23 July of last year. I praise and hearten you exceedingly not only for the great profit that will result to those souls to the glory of our Lord who redeemed them, but also for the great reward awaiting him who carries out such a task with the zeal reported of your reverence. I am moved by the modesty of your plea that you should remain without rank in the Society, but I consider it better that you should withdraw this request and accept the decision of the Society, assuring yourself that this is the will of the Lord, whose blessing I pray may fall upon your reverence.

At the same time the Father General wrote to Father Manuel de Arcos, the Father Provincial of New Granada, on 22 February 1621, the following: 'Peter Claver, in his thirty-third year, should make the profession of the four vows, both because of the fervour of his work with the negroes and because of his performance in examination.' There could be no more discussion. His took his vows on 3 April the same year, and these bound him to the Society. As he completed the formula, he signed his motto which was to pass into history: *Petrus Claver, Aethiopum semper servus*, 'Peter Claver, slave of the negroes for all time.'

The other four letters from Viteleschi to Claver have never before been published, so we give here a complete text. They refute the alleged persecution of Claver.

I am delighted that your reverence works with so much zeal and pleasure for the salvation of the negroes, coming to their aid with so much love and fervour. I send you my encouragement and gratitude, and I beg you to carry on with your work in the certainty that you are performing a great service to our Lord, who will know how to reward such labour. I know that many besides your reverence are of the opinion which you express in your letter of 30 July (1625) that Father Alonso de Sandoval's book should be published. I most willingly undertake to do all that I can to this end, and I shall ask Father Fabián López to take the necessary steps.

Here is revealed Claver's eagerness that his teacher's fine work on the method of converting the negroes should appear. The second letter reads:

It has been a great comfort to me to read your reverence's letter of 17 July in which you inform me of the great deal yet to be done in the mission to the negroes which in obedience you have accepted, to the immense edification of your city and the negroes who are brought there. I am edified by the holy zeal with which your reverence toils in this work of great service to our Lord, and I beg you to continue it with the same fervour, and I trust in the due reward from God for you. In another letter I charge the Father Provincial that there should neither be sold, nor changed, nor taken away from you the eight or nine negro interpreters whom you have, since they are so vital to your work. I rely upon him to see that my request is complied with. I shall hasten with the same pleasure to implement any other request to the comforting of your reverence, as is only just towards one who so much merits it.

This letter shows clearly the feelings of his superiors and gives the lie to the thesis of total misunderstanding which has been put forward. The third letter deals with the same subject, and again the Father General comes to the defence of Claver:

Your letter of 31 March 1623 has much consoled and edified me. I have read its report of your labour in catechizing and other work with the negroes who arrive at your port. You are right, my father, to find solace in so doing, because the work is of great service alike to our Lord and to the poor people who need badly someone to show them the path to salvation. I beg you as urgently as I can to continue in your labour. I charge the Father Provincial that *under no circumstances* is he to employ the negroes you have bought as interpreters for any other purpose. You may teach them to read and any other matter which may enable them to understand more clearly the bases of our Faith so that they may teach the better the new arrivals.

The last letter reads: 'I beg your reverence to inform the Fathers Visitor and Provincial of the matter you treat of in your letter of 27 July. I am confident that they will apply the necessary remedies. I am grateful to your reverence for the energy and earnestness with which you teach the negroes; both qualities very proper in the members of the Society of Jesus . . .' We end these documents with a letter sent to the Father Provincial of New Granada, which also shows the respect of Claver's superiors for him, and lights up a little what might be called his human side: 'I ask your reverence to find some father in the Province suitable to aid Father Peter Claver in his work with the negroes, and send him to Cartagena. It is right that we should love and thank Claver for his work in his ministry, but this should not make us fail to notice and correct any fault in him . . .' The letter continues with the recommendations we have already seen. The assistant sent to Claver was Father

Francisco Mayoral, and reports of the period mention others who
helped him.

The vow 'slave of the slaves' which Claver made to God was
not a dead letter. Brother Nicolás says:

> I had in my possession the letter in which Father Peter
> Claver wrote his profession in his own hand (1622) and in it
> he dedicated and consecrated himself perpetually to God in
> order to seek the salvation of his beloved negroes. That letter I
> gave to Captain Antonio de Loayza, knight of Santiago. To
> fulfil this vow he never ceased day or night to occupy himself
> with the needs of the negroes without noticing the heat, the
> lice, the filth, or their ailments. He taught them, he baptized
> them, he confessed them, he helped them to die. Every day he
> read the collect for their conversion—this was the custom in the
> college—and he did this until the end of his days.

CHAPTER VIII

THE SLAVE OF THE SLAVES

CONSIDERATION of Claver's psychology has purposely been left till now. The central theme which links all his actions and synthesizes his religious personality must be the famous phrase which he himself chose as he made his profession: the slave of the slaves. This is one of the most apposite mottoes in the whole of hagiography. As he finished his novitiate in Tarragona and took his first vows, he chose the motto 'Slave of God'. At the end of his training this general idea was particularized into 'slave of slaves'. The first motto filled his personal life as a student, the second was to fertilize his life as a priest in action.

The notion of slavery lies at the roots of his profound humility, the extraordinary humility which makes his life explicable. Andrade reports some phrases revealing what Claver thought of himself. They were collected by his companions:

He thought himself in importance beneath the soil upon which he trod. He saw himself as a dung-heap full of worms and decay, from which arose an insufferable stench. Whenever he came across a decomposing body or stinking quagmire he would say: 'That is me, that is how I should look.' When he was asked to remember anything in his prayers before God, he would reply: 'That is to make certain of failure.' He thought himself unworthy to be heard, and that if he asked it God would deny it. If he saw some old sacking or rags he used to say that it would do for his shroud, for a little rubbish might well be wrapped in an old sack. When he went into a smithy and saw the iron hammered and put into the fire, he would say: 'I am the man who is unwilling to be moulded by my superiors. For my sins I deserve to be thrown into the forge of hell and hammered by the demons.' Some people once, moved by the opinion they held of his saintliness, came up to kiss his hand. He was as angry as most men are under threat of insult, for to

THE SLAVE OF THE SLAVES 281

attempt to do him honour was to insult him. No amount of persuasion moved him to accept their salutation, for he insisted that he was mere refuse, stinking and revolting.

This view of himself was the fruit of meditation upon maxims he had written in his notebook. Here are some of them:

> If you wish to be wise, be hardworking and humble. True humility sees not the defects of others, but one's own defects. The man who is truly humble seeks to be despised. As St Bernard says, he tries to appear not humble but worthless. He submits to all, obeys all, honours all, reproves none. He seeks that those who watch him should think that he suffers all this not through humility but through lack of will to do otherwise. And as he meditates let him say: 'Think how many servants of God give alms that you may eat, and build houses that you may live a cloistered life. They do this because they believe that you are living for God, but if they knew your heart they would flee from you as from the rotting corpse of a dog. Consider how many people think you a saint, and praise your sanctity throughout the town, and seem to delight to see you; ponder on how they would run from you if they really knew you.'

This meekness of Claver's is an echo of St Alphonsus' teaching:

> It will be asked in what consists the humility which Christ our Lord desires we should learn from him? The answer is, that the heart should be mortified and die; though it be dishonoured and insulted and despised and abused and mocked it is not angered and saddened, because being dead, it does not feel. If it is honoured it receives from the honour neither joy nor a good opinion of itself, neither pleasure nor contentment, because it is dead. If it be praised as saintly it is not puffed up, for it is dead. The mystery of this virtue of true humility of heart is in that it feels joy and happiness when it is despised and spat on, trodden on, trampled like the slimy mud of the market place.

In Claver this virtue was present in the highest degree. We have seen it in his unwillingness to accept his ordination to the priesthood until the will of God was made clear to him through

Father Sandoval. He chose his friends among the humble and the slaves, the sick and the lepers. All his life he sought the humblest tasks: he acted as porter in Bogotá, in Cartagena he took the porter's place while the latter rested. Other details of his humility were made public in the Process: Manuel López said that Claver gloried in that 'he was the son of a carpenter'. Two slaves, Ignacio Angola and Manuel de Caboverde gave evidence that 'he used to feed the poor at the porter's lodge then go to a well in the *patio* and draw water to wash their dishes. He ate with them from the same dish. He behaved in the same way with his interpreters.'

When the time came for him to take a viaticum, although many tried to prevent him, he fell on his knees before the Sacrament. When his successor, Father Diego Fariña arrived at the college, Claver thought nothing of the forty years he had spent with the slaves, nor of the 300,000 he had baptized. He dragged himself to the feet of the new apostle, raised his eyes to heaven and cried: 'It is a worthy thing, a very worthy thing, to come here and baptize slaves.' He then kissed his successor's feet.

This attitude of meekness before life and before men arose from a profound sense of being a mere instrument in the hands of God. Sometimes it led him to excess. Andrade reports the following: 'When he was teaching the negroes he placed chairs for the interpreters, while he stood or sat on the ground. Once a visitor came to see Claver, and seeing him squatting on the ground and the slaves sitting comfortably on chairs, he was so angry that he not only reproved them but was about to lay his hands on them, when Claver held him back, saying that the interpreters were of vital importance to his mission, and deserved the best seats.' Andrés Sacabuche, his companion, refers to similar behaviour on his mission journeys to Tolú, Sinú and the nearby towns:

> As he contemplated the heavens and the stars he would say: 'It is a bewildering thing that those noble creations never cease to obey the will of God, while I, an infamous worm, always resist his will.' When he gazed at the plants and flowers of the countryside, he would say: 'O ungrateful man, see with what fidelity the earth responds to the movements of the heavens; yet your heart, refreshed with the rain of God's gifts,

grows only weeds and thorns, and can scarcely produce a thought of any value.' When he met soldiers or merchants he would cover his face for shame and say: 'Can it be true that these men suffer infinitely more for the empty wind of honour or for a handful of dust, than I am prepared to suffer for an eternal kingdom?' If he saw a workman planing a piece of timber or shaping a piece of iron with his hammer he would exclaim: 'O Divine Lord, unless you do as much to me, you will never soften my obdurate heart.' One day he noticed maggots writhing in filth and said: 'Look at these, there you see a pattern of myself, crawling in the slime of my guilt.' If he had to wade through muddy and smelly ditches, he would say: 'I am like this ditch, into which pure water fell from the sky, and having fallen, rotted and stagnated here. This is what happens to God's word as it falls into my heart.' When he visited the sick who were in great pain, he would say as he came into the room: 'Is there any patience or long-suffering to spare here? I see myself in great need of these virtues, and am come to learn them.'

Nothing disturbed him so much as praise. One day he fed a poor Spanish woman out of the bag he carried with him, and gave her advice to profit her soul. The woman knelt in gratitude before him and began to cry: 'Most holy father, they were right when they said in Lima that because of you God spared Cartagena, and did not lay it waste.' Claver interrupted her, and, his face full of shame, made her get up from her knees, saying to her angrily: 'Be quiet, you are a silly woman, you don't understand what you are saying. Ask God for forgiveness. If I hear you are repeating these things, I will have you punished and exiled from the town.'

The whole of that afternoon he went about as if he had been insulted, never raising his eyes from the ground. As if fearing that the praise of himself he had heard might infect him in some way, he hastened to the hospital and there kissed a sick man's sores. If any addressed him as 'father' (a title to which he had every right) he would open his leather pouch and say: 'Let us drop this father in the bag.' He made this same reply to the governor Don Pedro Zapata. *Petrus Claver, Aethiopum semper servus* was for him no mere metaphor; it represented a real and terrible self-sacrifice.

PART IV

FROM PAINFUL ECLIPSE TO SUPREME GLORY

(1650—1654)

CHAPTER I

THE MAN OF ACTION IMMOBILIZED

FREQUENTLY the life of a man of genius ends in a painful twilight. But in the lives of saints human reason often fails to explain such an end. We must fall on our knees before the mysteries of God.

The last years of Claver's life present one of the most perturbing riddles in religious history. Some aspects of those four years touch the level of tragedy. A man after forty years of labour is about to reach the fulfilment of his aims, a man who has made his life a constant slavery in the service of slaves suffers abandonment in a cell, waited upon by a brutal negro who delighted in tormenting an ageing invalid. A freed man who crucifies his liberator.

When Claver fell ill in 1650 he had overworked for thirty-five years. He had good health, though we are told of several sicknesses which endangered his life. These were nearly all stomach ailments, which were treated by the usual bleeding. The year 1650 was a Jubilee year, and the Church under Innocent X prepared to celebrate it by bringing within the fold those most remote from the faith. In the college at Cartagena it was decided to intensify the mission activity. Claver set off for Tolú, and reached the banks of the river Sinú. In a wretched malodorous village he heard confessions for eight hours in the morning and six in the evening. One day he could go on no longer; his body surrendered, he could not force himself to say Mass. In Claver this meant that the uttermost limits had been reached. He prescribed for himself a remedy typical of the man: he sought to punish his body for its weakness, and began a rigid fast. As already mentioned, his superior summoned him to return to Cartagena where he arrived during a raging storm, and at the height of an epidemic of plague. He become so weak that his limbs were totally useless and he had to accept a cell that was better than his usual room, which he had used for thirty-five years. At one end of the building, near the church, was a room used for those who were chronically ill. It was built upon the city walls, and overlooked the sea and the harbour. Down only a few stairs was the sacristy, and a few further steps brought him to the tribune whence he could see the altar. The ever-active Claver was helped to this new cell by Brother Nicolás, and was heard to say as he entered it: 'This sickness is the reward for my sins. Since I am a bad priest, God no longer desires my services.' He was beginning the unhappiest period of his life: four years of inactivity.

From this moment little is heard of the apostle of the negroes. He was alone with his sickness and his God. Outside his cell he appears only three times, but each a symbolic occasion. This man who had made himself a slave was by the will of God made the object of the service of others even in the minutest detail. As already explained, the destruction wrought by the plague had made it impossible for the community to look after him as he deserved. His regular nurse was a man, a negro, described by Father Astrain as 'not of any great value'. Fernández describes his situation during these years:

He spent the last years of his life in complete abandonment, a pattern of the cross of Christ. Except for the two ladies, Doña Isabel and Doña Jerónima de Urbina, who were always most devoted to him, those outside the college forgot him as if there had never been such a man. Any other man than Claver might have had his spirit broken, but his disdain of the world helped him not to feel this ingratitude keenly. Those who could hurt him most were colleagues within the residence. Their numbers were reduced by the plague, and the few left had so many tasks to fulfil, and Claver's illness went on so long, that the only regular service possible for him was from the negroes. His regular nurse was a young savage, recently bought, whose constant neglect Claver suffered with great patience. He always brought him his food, having picked it over first to select the titbits for himself. Frequently the negro put the food into Claver's mouth with his own hand. One day he would leave him without water, another without bread, often without food of any kind. Claver never complained. He only murmured when the slave, in order to avoid having to be with him, refused to dress him so that he might get out of bed. (Claver needed constant support in order to walk.) Once, trying to walk on his own, he fell and injured his head. The injury was cured miraculously. On this occasion the negro had refused to dress him for Mass. Claver struggled out of bed and fell. Brother Nicolás was often warned of what was happening by the noise of the Saint's fall, and would run to the cell to help him to dress. But Claver did not like Nicolás to help him, since he did it with reverence and infinite care. He used to insist that the slave be sought, who dressed him with great brutality, dragging him this way and that, bending back his arms and pushing him round the cell. Never once did Claver complain. He would say: 'My sins merit greater punishment than this.' Another torture was added to his sufferings; months passed without the cell being cleaned or swept. It was full of rubbish, the fodder of swarms of flies.

This picture is not exaggerated. The slave himself confessed these things to Brother González after the Saint's death. This scene of utter abandonment recalls St Francis Xavier's death on Sanchon Island. Claver spent these years in prayer and suffering. In the morning Nicolás and the negro carried him in a chair down to the church and placed him where he could hear the Masses. Sometimes he went down to the altar where he used to say Mass, and according to the doctor, Bartolomé de Torres, on these occasions the trembling of his hands sometimes stopped. His own uselessness worried Claver, and occasionally he would hear confessions or have negroes brought up to his cell for that purpose.

There is evidence of three occasions when he left the college during these three years. They represent three loves of his life, and three examples, as his life ended, of services returned.

News reached his cell that a ship laden with slaves of the Ararae tribe was approaching the harbour. These men were the most intractable of all the slaves, and the most resistant to the Christian faith. Claver had himself taken to the quay in a litter, a mere shadow of himself. There he saw and spoke to the slaves. This was the last act of his apostolic work with the negroes. As he watched their savage faces, full of terror and mistrust, he wept, feeling in his own flesh the tragedy awaiting them. Back in his cell facing the sea, the whole calamity of the slave-trade must have been very present to him.

The first emergence from his cell was on behalf of the black race, his second on behalf of the white race. For Claver Doña Isabel de Urbina was the good angel who balanced in some way the injustices of her race towards the negroes. During the last years of the Saint's life Doña Isabel was confined to her house by illness. There Claver used to go each week to hear her confession, until his paralysis made this impossible. When his end was clearly approaching he received an urgent message from her, saying that her greatest joy would be to receive absolution and a last blessing at his hands. Two of the interpreters took him in a litter to Doña Isabel's house, where he arrived with twitching limbs and almost speechless.

His third emergence was on behalf of the lepers of San Lázaro. Many times he had walked this road, carrying his gifts in a leather sack. This he could no longer do, and he rejected the proposal of a litter, fearing that a slow journey through the public streets, right across the town, might give rise to scenes of popular homage, and revive the long-silent cries of 'the Saint, the Saint!' There was in the hospital a very gentle horse, a horse which never went faster than an amble. Claver borrowed it, and was painfully hoisted on to it at the door of the college. He could move only with great difficulty, he could neither hold the reins nor press in with his knees. Friends sat him on the horse, and released it. They had complete confidence in the animal, and in its well-known gentleness. Many witnesses guarantee what happened—judges, lawyers and slaves. A child was later to yell 'the horse is bewitched'. This would not be surprising; evil spirits had long lain in wait for their bitter enemy. Scarcely had the horse gone through the main gate on to the jetty and started down the *calle de la Media Luna* than it bolted. It galloped out of control along the sea edge and across the main street. Claver, incapable of any movement, was in great danger, a fall would certainly have killed him. But the horse stopped (people said by a miracle) at the door of the house belonging to Captain José de Julio, and then continued its slow amble to San Lázaro as if nothing had happened. There Claver was welcomed as if he had come back from the dead. The lepers thronged round him. We know nothing of this last interview, we only know that the children yelled as he passed on his way back, 'A miracle, a miracle! The mad horse stopped . . . Claver is on his way again through the streets!' A few days later he died.

CHAPTER II

THE SAINT'S DEATH

THE death of a saint always has about it something of the marvellous. Each individual case varies, but the basic situation is always characterized by peace and the delight of a life lived in the chosen way. There is never the terror of looking back on a sterile life. Saints die in the way they have lived, in serenity and hope. As Claver lay dying, rumours grew in Cartagena. The very people who for months had ignored those windows where a light shone through the night, now began to repeat: 'The Saint is dying.'

On Sunday morning, 6 September, the sick man refused the offer of receiving the viaticum in his cell. He wanted to make a supreme effort, and he got two negroes to help him into the church, where he took Communion. Dragging himself along the floor he made his last visit to Our Lady of the Miracle, in front of whom he had said his first Mass, and confessed many thousands of souls. He went back through the sacristy and said to Brother Nicolás, 'I am dying.' He was carried back to his cell, and that afternoon his fever increased alarmingly. There are eye-witnesses of his last moments. Brother Nicolás gives most details, and in the most moving manner:

> On the morning of the 7th he lost the power of speech. I went up to his cell and found him with his eyes fixed on the ceiling and his hands laid on the bed cover. I sent a message to the superior, Juan de Arcos, that it was time to administer extreme unction. This was done by Father Francisco Jimeno, and as soon as the ceremony was over his colleagues in the college, and some of the most important persons in the city, such as the governor, Don Pedro Zapata, and a familiar of the Holy Office, Don Pedro Calderón, snatched away the hangings, the prints and the crucifix that were in the cell. They kept with

great veneration all they could obtain of his clothing or his wretched bedclothes.

The Saint must have expected this pillage, for a few days before he had given to Brother Nicolás a print which had belonged to Alphonsus Rodríguez, and a little book, saying, 'Take them before they are carried off.'

Father Juan de Arcos, in a letter to all the Jesuits of Spain and America (printed by Andrade), writes:

The rumour ran through the city that Father Claver had received extreme unction, and straightway I was begged by many persons for permission to make portraits of him. Some of these persons were of such authority that they could not be denied entrance. His cell was soon crowded, and soon emptied of anything associated with him; only his bedclothes were left. In their devotion people placed many rosaries about his neck, and as the news spread the atmosphere in the cell became stifling as the crowd forced its way in. Priests, monks, people of high rank in the city, officers from the fleet, ladies, negresses and nuns sent vast numbers of rosaries to be touched by the Saint. People went in and out as if it were a church on Holy Thursday, while groups of children and negroes came crying out, 'Let us go to the Saint, the Saint is dying.' This went on the whole day until nine in the evening when we closed the porter's lodge. Some people of the town, who, because of their great devotion to Claver, did not want to leave him, and his colleagues of the residence, stayed by his side. We all joined in praying for his soul, and between one and two in the morning he gave it up to God, without the slightest movement or gesture, dying with the same peace and serenity with which he had lived. This was on 8 September, the day of the Nativity of the Holy Virgin. Members of the residence cut up the shirt in which he died, and cut his hair and his toenails. His face was more beautiful, and his body less rigid than either was in life. We all kissed his feet and hands, from which came a sweet odour, then according to our custom his body was dressed in priestly robes.

Brother Nicolás's description is detailed and vivid:

Here began the great pilgrimage to one who no longer could see or hear it; here was the apotheosis of one who thought himself abandoned. There came Don Pedro de Estrada, Father Francisco Miguel de Ugarte, Don Antonio Betancur, governor of the Province, and Antonio Farfán, the royal treasurer, and when they saw that I was hanging a rosary round the Father's neck all the priests and the persons of quality did the same . . . then there arrived the immense flood of the common people, the narrow staircases echoed with their feet; even before he died they kissed his hands and his feet, and touched him with their rosaries. A sudden silence fell as the Marqués de Montealegre and the captains of the galleons then in the harbour arrived. So passed the 7 September. At night the college gate was locked and we prayed for his soul. I held the crucifix before his face, but he did not recover consciousness. Between one and two o'clock on the morning of 8 September he died as if he were merely falling asleep, so gently that some people present thought he had not died. But silently, without a sign, he gave up his magnificent soul to God. There was no physical change in his face, and I only realized that he had died because suddenly his pale, thin countenance shone with extraordinary brilliance and loveliness, so that I knew that his soul was in the presence of God, away from his body. I knelt down and kissed his dead feet, as white as alabaster, but smooth and soft as silk. All present did the same, among them Father Francisco Jimeno, the priest Juan Onofre, Brother Francisco de la Vera, Brother Manuel Rodríguez, Manuel López de Estremoz, and Diego de Burgos. There were many other Spaniards and negroes whose names I do not remember.

In this way Claver died.

Chapter III

APOTHEOSIS OF THE KING OF THE SLAVES

ON the morning of 8 September Cartagena seemed as if awakening from a four years' dream. The news of the death of a man who had been abandoned for all that time deeply moved every citizen.

For thirty-five years his face and figure had been part of the city. Wherever there had been need for him he had straightway appeared. Now that his bent body, his serene and melancholy face could be seen again, there was the clatter of feet hurrying to the church of St Ignatius where the Saint lay. The wave of hero-worship which swept the city is described as 'an unceasing murmuring of children, negroes and nobles' or 'a chaos of confusion in the church and the neighbouring square'. Some people are said to have 'rushed into the church and out again so rapidly that their feet scarcely touched the ground'. Others were anxious to get hold of anything that had belonged to Claver. Only an eye-witness can properly describe the events which followed. Juan de Arcos writes:

As soon as day dawned I warned the prior of the monastery of San Agustín that Claver had died. Immediately he ordered the bells to be tolled, and although I warned him that the funeral could not take place until the evening the love which he had always shown us could not suffer to wait, and so at eight o'clock the whole community appeared and sang responses in honour of the dead man in the room where we had the body, and afterwards they sang a Mass for the dead. The whole city was in an uproar of voices praising the dead priest. The slaves from the town itself and from all the surrounding districts as far as the news had reached came hastening to kiss his hands and to touch him with their rosaries. So many sought to do this that not even six corpses would have sufficed. Doña Isabel de Urbina ordered the coffin of cedarwood lined in a rich white cloth . . . Don Pedro de Estrada, His Majesty's treasurer, sent all the candles necessary for the proper laying out of the body. When the governor of the city, Don Pedro Zapata, heard of the death, and of the plan to bury Claver that afternoon, he held a meeting of the town councillors and proposed that the city should defray all the expenses of the burial of a man who had served his city so well. This was agreed unanimously, and two councillors were appointed to see everything was done with proper ceremony. These called on me and informed me of the council's decision, and asked me to postpone the funeral until the following day so that all might have an opportunity of seeing Claver and paying respect to him. They asked also that he should not be buried beneath the floor of the church but in a place of honour separate from other graves, and that a preacher should be selected to make a funeral oration. All this I agreed to, thanking them for the honour done both to Claver and to the Society.

Then there came to the room where he lay an endless succession of clergy who undertook the task of touching his body with the rosaries brought by the teeming crowds, and of emptying the room from time to time so that others might enter. The Brotherhood of the priests of St Peter sent their black velvet pall for use when the body was placed in the church, and all the other velvet cloths necessary for the adornment of the catafalque. Other pious persons sent a beautifully prepared palm-leaf to place in his hands, but since this was contrary to our customs we sent it back.

In the evening an enormous crowd gathered together, persons of importance and slaves of both sexes and others of all social degree. There were many who could not get into the church, and they crowded into the streets nearby. The body was taken down to the church on the shoulders of the most illustrious men in the city, their candles shining on the faces of the many nationalities which hemmed in the procession. To get the body into the church it had to be brought through the porter's lodge, the main door being crammed with people. As it passed, so many pressed forward to kiss his hand or touch him with their rosaries that the hangings and other adornments of the coffin were ruined. Don Pedro de Estrada and a few priests forced their way through and placed the palm between his left arm and his side . . . At the same time the superior of the Mercedarians arrived with all the members of his monastery. They too had to force their way through the crowd to get near the body. With great devotion they sang a set of responses, an action which was an especial honour since this was their most important feast day, a day when normally they do not leave the monastery. Then arrived the admiral in command of the fleet, the Marqués de Montealegre, accompanied by the flower of Spanish chivalry. On their knees they kissed Claver's hand and touched him with their rosaries. The press round him was so great that all of us from the residence could not clear a space round him, and priests and monks from San Agustín and La Merced had to come to our aid.

Then came Don Matías Suárez de Melo, a canon of the cathedral and vicar general of the diocese, and he and all the clerics of his suite kissed Claver's hands and touched him with their rosaries. The church was never empty for a second of crowds of people entering and leaving, and towards nightfall so great was the concourse of slaves and people from all the district round about that we feared the body might be torn to pieces in their eagerness to see and touch it. Several devout men had the idea of removing the hands from the chalice and placing them in the form of a cross, so that they might be kissed without the necessity of leaning right across the body and so disturbing it. The hands were so soft and pliant that they moved easily in all directions, and visitors touched their heads or their eyes with them, or moved them to any part of their bodies where they felt pain, in the hope that the touch might cure. Everyone who came touched him with a rosary or a wreath or a silk stocking or ribbon or handkerchief—with anything that could be taken away and kept as a relic. A slight sweat appeared on the face of the corpse and immediately there was a rush to wipe it away with pieces of cloth, which were then highly prized. As night fell the crowd increased at such a rate that the town guard was asked for to protect the body. The governor sent them, and they made their way through the throng with brutal blows to left and right. In their wake followed six Augustinians led by their prior. These relieved us so that we might rest from our endless struggle to control the multitude. An attempt was made to cover the body with a velvet cloth in order to protect it, but there was such a grumbling and muttering from the mob that it had to be abandoned. In spite of the soldiers and the Augustinians members of the crowd squeezed through and snatched Claver's cap and his stockings and pulled out his toe-nails. Although the body was surrounded by blazing torches hands were pushed through the flames in search of anything that might serve as a relic. All present called upon Claver as 'the Saint'.

The following morning the crowd returned, as if many of them had not already seen him. The hale and the sick, children and adults, everyone from the city and from the surrounding countryside came to venerate him. At eight o'clock the community of San Juan de Dios sang a Mass. Then every member of the Augustinian house came, followed at nine o'clock by the city authorities in procession led by the maces. The whole town council was accompanied by the governor and his lieutenant-general. All of them kissed Claver and touched him with their rosaries. The service was sung by the Augustinians, whose prior said Mass. The preacher was Father Miguel Bretón, of the order of the Mercedarians, whose text was: *Qui crediderit etiam si mortuus fuerit vivet.* He did much honour to the Society as he talked of the glorious task of the salvation of souls and compared the Society's work with that of other orders who praise God by singing in the choir. He praised the virginity of the dead man, his rigorous penances, and his zeal for souls, to the great satisfaction of the congregation.

Then we proceeded to the burial, beginning with fierce arguments about who should have the honour of bearing the corpse. Finally it was won by the governor and the aldermen and one or two of the highest officers of the fleet, together with those clerics who could force their way among them. As he was taken off the bier to put him in the coffin the weeping crowd surged forward, seeing their last opportunity of grabbing relics. In spite of the resistance of the guards they cut his cassock and alb and seized him by the feet and arms in an attempt to sever them too. They tore his brocade chasuble to pieces, and we decided that the sacristan should take away the pillow upon which he lay and share it out to the people, thus attracting them to a spot far away from the grave to enable the entombment to go forward at all. But the crowd swarmed around him so eagerly that he was almost suffocated; they snatched away the pillow and tore it to shreds, so that he who ended with a thread counted himself lucky. The sacristan climbed into the pulpit to escape the crowd which pursued him in search of relics, and from there he threw to the crowd vast numbers of confession tokens which Claver had made and signed. While the crowd was engaged in searching for these, the burial took place. The body was placed on the epistle side of the altar of the Holy Christ. This ended the funeral, but not the persistence of the crowd which still today clamours for relics of the man they considered a saint.

On Monday 14 September the city paid civil honours to Claver in the form of a magnificent tomb bearing its coat of arms. The civic authorities were present in procession, a choir came from the cathedral, Mass was sung by the rector of the college, Fray José de la Concepción preached a sermon in honour of the dead man, and many clerics were present in the congregation. Candles in vast quantities were distributed among those present.

Not content with this, the governor, Don Pedro Zapata, to show the love and respect he felt for Claver, held a ceremony of his own the following day in the same form. Mass was sung by the vicar general of the diocese, and Fray José Pacheco, former provincial of the Augustinians, preached. He spoke of the attacks made on the Society at that time, and said that God had taken away Claver so that he would not see the punishments that were being prepared for Cartagena. At this all those present applauded. The negroes too played their part in these ceremonies in honour of Claver. All the various tribes among the slaves joined together to provide candles and music and a sermon preached for them by Father Gregorio Bellín, treasurer of the church of Popayán. He excelled all the others in his praise of Claver, proving by excerpts from the Scriptures that his great influence and the honours he had received from God, all arose from his ministry to the negroes. There were present all the officers from the fleet, and the governor with his officials. Again there was a munificent supply of candles, and the congregation formed in procession, each section in a tribal group, carrying candles. It moved out of the church, giving an impressive proof of gratitude to the man who had done so much for the negroes. Many events, apparently miraculous, have taken place, witnessed by reliable persons. In order not to make this letter too lengthy I will not list them here. I trust that God may be pleased one day to permit a detailed report of Claver's full life to be published.

On that night of 8 September a curious thing happened, which may be dismissed as a dream or imagination. A freed negress named Lucrecia Angola, who had known Claver for many years, had a vision as she slept, while she was about sixty miles away from Cartagena. She saw a long procession of people bathed in brilliant light, at the end of which walked Christ with Claver at his side, both dressed in gorgeous robes. She knew then nothing of his mortal sickness. Next morning she asked her neighbours what news there was from Cartagena, whether in particular there was any news of Claver's death. Nobody had heard anything. No news came until the arrival of the mule-trains, when the whole story of his death and the attendant ceremonies was made known.

These local celebrations of the glory of Claver were to be made world-wide through the decision of the Church.

CHAPTER IV

THE SUPREME HONOUR

HARDLY had Claver died when negro slaves were trying to force the doors of the college so that they might see him. For the same purpose came inquisitors, high officers of the fleet and governors. Many biographers, in order to emphasize Claver's attitude of 'slavery and humility', have suggested the picture of some second-rate provincial missionary, ignored by those of social or political eminence. There is some truth in this picture: as we have seen, he himself cared nothing for social rank or influence. But the picture needs to be corrected. The commanders of the fleets which entered the harbour felt that they could not visit Cartagena without calling on this reputed saint. Among his last visitors were the Marqués de Montealegre and the Marqués de Mancera, the latter ex-viceroy of Peru. Bishops on their way to the principal sees of the Indies looked upon a visit to Claver as a duty. Senior members of the Society of Jesus were in continuous correspondence with him. Many eminent and learned priests, such as Gaspar Sobrino, have written in praise of him. In Lima a pious and holy man was granted a special revelation about the apostle of Cartagena, 'a city so rich and so full of sin'.

According to Andrade, a popular saying runs: 'Because of Claver God has left one stone upon another in Cartagena.' Fernández and others give an expanded version: 'Because of a donkey and Claver God has . . .' The word donkey refers to the childlike brother Bobadilla, who led his saintly life in the city.

Canonization was foreseen from the moment of Peter Claver's death. In 1657, three years after it, Andrade wrote that if in that century public opinion had had the power it had in antiquity Claver would already have been canonized. But the Roman Church moves more calmly. Its solemn pace is a guarantee of certainty. Around the simple tomb in the chapel of the Holy

Christ the faith of a whole people began to crystallize. Many miracles were reported as worked by the relics of Claver, especially by the six stoles which he had worn. By these means so many of the sick were relieved that Brother Nicolás González lost count, and he stated in the Process that 'no man can count the cures performed through Claver'. 'Without any exaggeration,' writes Fernández in 1666, 'I can affirm that if I had to list the miracles reported to me by private individuals I should have to begin another book.' Among many others who sought relief at his tomb were Isabel de Betancur, the negro Juan, Bartolomé Sánchez, Juan de Ribarola, Agustina de Talavera, María de Torres, the blind Teresa and a young paralysed Indian. Hardly a moment passed when there were not people in pain with their heads resting on the stone plaque which said simply: 'Father Peter Claver'. So many came that Father Gaspar de Cujía thought that all these sick persons, 'especially the children, were defiling the tomb when they were placed upon it in the hope that they would recover, and it was decided that in the same chapel a niche should be cut in the wall, covered by a securely-locked door.' This was done and the body was transferred there on 1 March 1657, two and a half years after its first burial. When the coffin was opened the body was found to be incorrupt, without a sign of decay. Although it was covered with quicklime the skin was completely unaffected. According to Fernández, this was certified by the doctor Bartolomé de Torres. The moment had come to initiate the cause of canonization. First to act was the governor, Don Pedro Zapata, who proposed to the town council that they should solicit from the Chapter—the see was vacant—the inauguration of the necessary collecting of information about the life, virtues and miracles of Claver. Father Diego Ramírez Fariña, Claver's successor in the mission to the negroes and rector of the college, allied himself with the council in their request, and became the most energetic supporter of his predecessor's cause.

The Commission was appointed on 7 September 1657. It consisted of Juan Guerrero Freile, judge of the Inquisition, as commissioner, and Juan Téllez as secretary and notary. The enquiries and interrogations lasted until 1660. We have selected a few passages from the original document, sent from Rome by Tridiano Castagnori, Procurator of the College of the Sacred Apostolic Palace of the Vatican. He was the deputy selected by the Congregation of Rites for the causes of canonization. The document (now to be seen in the National Archives at Bogotá) mentions 124 regulations 'for the proper conducting of the enquiry into the virtues and miracles of the venerable servant of God, Peter Claver'. For example: 'The witnesses must be eye-witnesses in so far as they deal with miracles done before or after death. In so far as they deal with the holiness of life of Claver evidence may be admitted from those who have heard reports from eye-witnesses. Before examination each witness must take an oath, swearing both to tell the truth and to keep it secret.'

Here follows the report of the Council of the Indies on the letter which had been written to the King urging Claver's beatification: 'The city of Cartagena of the Indies informed your Majesty in its letter of 12 November 1669 that among other worthy men who served God and your Majesty was the venerable Father Peter Claver, a native of Verdú in Catalonia. [Here follows a recital of Claver's activities.] The city beseeches your Majesty to instruct the ambassador at Rome to intercede with his Holiness to give the necessary instructions so that the enquiry may begin into the life and virtues of that holy man.'

The great official correspondence was on the move. Documents, both secular and ecclesiastical, urging the canonization were arriving in Rome. He who during his life had signed himself 'slave of the slaves' was now moving all Christendom to act on his behalf. The Bishop of Cartagena, Miguel Antonio Apis, wrote three letters to the Pope on Claver's behalf. The first reads:

Holy Father: As soon as I arrived here in Cartagena as bishop in 1681 I gained a clear understanding of the reputation for sanctity among the people of the venerable Father Peter Claver. This was earned by his magnificent toil and his heroic virtues, which he exercised in the spreading of the Catholic faith and the winning of souls, and it was confirmed by the miracles worked through him after his death. He suffered many things for the Faith, he led out of the darkness of paganism many thousands of souls, he loved God fervently, and he loved his neighbours, particularly those who were poor, or sick, or black. He was an apostolic man in all things. To put the matter briefly, I can say that I have no hesitation in comparing him to St Francis Xavier . . . For these reasons I humbly beg your Holiness to grant that the Process begun some time ago in this city may be discussed by the Sacred Congregation of Rites, and that all things necessary may be done in order to set in motion the cause for the beatification and canonization of that wonderful servant of God, a deed which will redound to the profit of the Catholic religion. I kneel at your Holiness's feet. Cartagena, 30 April 1690.

The other letters are in the same vein. Further petitions arrived from Europe and America. On 1 August 1695 the Sacred Congregation voted for the introduction of the cause. Twenty days later his Holiness Pope Innocent XII confirmed this vote. Three years later the reports of the Process, which have been our authority throughout this biography, were published in Rome. They contain the evidence of 154 witnesses of all social classes, the majority of whom had known Claver or seen the results of his labours. Four great popes took part in the glorification of Claver. Innocent XII in 1695 approved the opening of the Process. Benedict XIV on 24 September 1747 declared his virtues heroic. Pius IX on 21 September 1851 beatified him. Leo XIII on 15 January 1888 canonized him, and declared him on 7 July 1896 patron of all the missions to the negroes. In the interval between the opening of the cause and the declaration of his heroic virtues there was presented a petition which is perhaps unique in the ecclesiastical history of the Church. The Council of Tarragona, famous in the Middle Ages, and venerated in modern times, presented a petition to Rome for the beatification of Claver. In it he was given the titles of 'second Xavier' and 'unshakeable pillar of the Western Church'. The Archbishop of Tarragona summoned to the city a council at which were present the bishops of Tortosa, Vich, Barcelona and Gerona, and representatives of the bishops of Lérida, Urgel and Solsona, together with the abbots, priors and other members of the monasteries and religious communities of the Province. The document begins: 'Most Holy Father: The Council of Tarragona, in order to promote the exercise of virtue in its province, prostrates itself at the feet of your Holiness to beg for the beatification of the venerable Father Peter Claver ... The Council begs it with the greater sense of right since this second Xavier of the Society of Jesus was born in this province ...'

The Council met first on 12 October 1727 and had its last meeting in December of the same year. The petition was sent on the day of the feast of St Francis Xavier to Pope Benedict XIV who, with the unanimous agreement of the Sacred Congregation of Rites, pronounced on 24 September 1714 that 'the virtues of the venerable Father Peter Claver were in the highest degree heroic, and the cause of his canonization may safely be continued'.

So that a man may be canonized two things are required: that his virtues be seen to be heroic or excellent, and that miracles be done through him after death. 'Is there evidence of the theological virtues, faith, hope, charity, prudence, justice, fortitude, temperance and the associated virtues? Are they present to an heroic degree?' These questions are asked in the Process under the title *super-dubio*. The word heroic means heroic in the highest degree, that is to say the saint loves God *perfectly*, with the help of Divine Grace, that he has achieved dominion over his passions so that he does not consciously consent to any moral imperfection, to the slightest degree of sin.

Thirteen miracles were recognized as due to Claver during his life. Others followed after death. The report of the Process mentions twenty, and the brief of beatification, 'apart from many remarkable happenings which the judges did not admit, more than forty miracles'. Two especially were selected: the first the sudden and perfect cure of a tumour in the arm of the child María Torres, and the cure in Micaela García de Saavedra of an internal disease. In the medical language of the time we are told that 'an artery in her right arm was cut, and a huge tumour the size of an orange appeared. The doctors pronounced it incurable. She was taken to the tomb of Claver. Her screams of pain as she was carried there moved all who heard them. The sacristan put her on a bench near the tomb so that she could rest her arm upon it, and he placed on her arm one of Claver's stoles. With successive visits the tumour decreased in size to an almond, then disappeared altogether. The doctor Bartolomé de Torres declared this miraculous.'

This miracle was part of the evidence accepted for the beatification, which took place on 21 September 1851 in St Peter's, under Pope Pius IX. At half-past ten in the morning the Cardinals entered in their splendid robes. Then came in the Chapter of St Peter's and the members of the Sacred Congregation of Rites. Next the Provost General of the Society of Jesus, the Very Reverend Father John Roothan, presented himself to the Prefect of the Congregation, Cardinal Luigi Lambruschini, and asked that the brief of beatification might be promulgated. The brief was read, followed by a solemn *Te Deum*, during which a portrait of Claver was unveiled and the bells of St Peter's rang out, mingling with salvoes from the guns of the castle of Sant' Angelo. The Archbishop of Acrida, Monsignor Cardelli, celebrated Pontifical Mass, and said the prayer of the Blessed Peter Claver. In the afternoon, after vespers, the Pope venerated the image of the new Beatus and received the customary offerings. He who had made himself a slave now rose as a king to the altar of the first church in the world.

Now that he was beatified, only one step of the ladder remained. The miracles which had led to his beatification were done in South America; those which were to lead to his canonization were done in North America, and they were so remarkable that ever since the United States has had a special devotion to Claver. There are in that country more than 200 churches dedicated to him.

Barbara Dressen was born in Germany in 1779 but had emigrated with her husband to Milwaukee. She was told one day by her doctor, Bayer, that the wrinkle which was spreading across her face was a cancer, that there was no cure for it and that it would be fatal. She assured him that she would not die of it, and she would consult a priest. Bayer was not impressed. The priest she consulted was Father Francis Xavier Weninger, of the Society of Jesus, a missionary and a great admirer of Claver. He told her to have faith and to pray. For three years the cancer continued to grow and became ulcerous. But the sick woman, in spite of her eighty years, longed to live. She had great faith in Claver and prayed to him. On the return of Weninger the old lady went to the church of St Gall where he was and begged him to apply a relic of Claver to her cancer. He did so while she prayed fervently. The pain ceased. She was cured. In her own words: 'I went out into the open air and I felt not the slightest pain. I noticed that the wind had no effect on me, though before the tiniest breeze caused thunderbolts of bitter agony. I felt tiny scales falling from my cheek. I caught them and blew them away from my hand. I went home, and just as I arrived I felt the last scales fall. Since then I have been well, and no sign remains of my sickness.' Five years later she testified before the apostolic judges and the miracle was admitted.

Ignatius Streckel too was a German emigrant to North America. He lived in St Louis, where he worked in a soap factory. Towards the end of 1861 he struck his chest hard, just on the breast-bone, with an iron bar. 'At the time there was no wound, but soon afterwards I felt a pain and a burning sensation.' Inflammation and cancer followed, attacking the bone and spreading to the ribs. Other symptoms were an exhausting cough, high temperature and painful breathing. Two doctors, Joseph Heitzig and William Schoenemann, declared him to be incurable, the latter giving him fourteen days to live. Again Father Weninger appeared. The sick man went to him to ask for help for his wife and children, threatened with starvation. He found the Jesuit blessing the congregation and holding a relic of Claver. Streckel was much moved and joined the congregation. He felt the touch of the Blessed Peter Claver on his head. His faith increased. He declared that he said to his wife on returning home: 'I believe that I shall be cured. Tomorrow I shall leap about in sheer joy.' The wound began to close. In a few days the rotting in the bone suddenly disappeared. 'In a few days', he declared, 'I felt in myself my old strength. I could work throughout the day at the heaviest tasks.' This miracle happened in 1863.

Both these events were scientifically and minutely scrutinized. When the General Congregation was held on 9 August 1887 in the presence of Pope Leo XIII and the question was put whether these were miracles, all those present replied affirmatively. From his throne in the Vatican the Pope on 1 November in the same year announced as miraculous the two cures, and everything was ready for the canonization. On the same day the miracles of the Blessed Alphonsus Rodríguez were admitted.

The solemn ceremony took place in the vast room over the portico of the Vatican basilica. Leo XIII was celebrating the fiftieth anniversary of his first Mass, and it was fitting that the working-man's Pope should canonize the greatest social worker the Church had seen in the seventeenth century. We take the description of the scene from an eye-witness:

The hall was transformed into a rich and splendid chapel. Two hundred chandeliers and thousands of candles made a blaze of light. Princes and ambassadors, cardinals and bishops, abbots and priests were waiting to receive Leo XIII who appeared wearing the triple crown. As the Pope appeared in the Sedia Gestatoria the choir of the Vatican intoned the motet *Tu es Petrus*, and the Pope took his seat on the throne surrounded by the fourteen senior bishops and archbishops. Then followed the customary homage of the cardinals and other dignitaries. Then amid profound silence Cardinal Bianchi, Procurator of the Canonization, approached the throne, and the consistorial notary Gioazzini read in a loud voice the petition begging his Holiness to inscribe in the catalogue of saints Peter Claver, the Blessed Bomfilio and his seven companions, the Blessed John Berchmans and the Blessed Alphonsus Rodríguez. The Litanies of the Saints were sung, and the second petition was read, *instanter et instantius* (the first was called *instanter*). His Holiness intoned the hymn *Veni Creator Spiritus*, and again took his place on the throne. Then the third petition, *instantius, instantissime* was read, whereupon the successor of St Peter, seated on his throne as infallible doctor of the universal Church, pronounced in the following formula the decree of canonization: 'In honour of the holy and undivided Trinity, for the exaltation of the holy Catholic faith and the spreading of the Christian religion, with the authority of our Lord Jesus Christ, of St Peter and St Paul, and of ourself, after mature deliberation and after imploring again and again divine favour, and in agreement with our venerable brothers the cardinals of the holy Roman Church, the patriarchs,

archbishops and bishops in Rome, we decree and assert that
Peter Claver, John Berchmans, and Alphonsus Rodríguez, etc.,
are saints, and we inscribe them in the catalogue of saints and
we proclaim that in all the universal Church their feasts shall be
devoutly celebrated each year, that of Peter on 9 September . . .
In the name of the Father, the Son, and the Holy Ghost, Amen.'
At this moment was heard the shrill sound of the trumpets
announcing to those without the proclamation of the decree,
and the bells of St Peter's rang the glorious news throughout
Rome, and all the bells of Rome replied.

From Michelangelo's dome above St Peter's the figure of Claver
shone in all the glory of the saints. The slave of the slaves had been
exalted.

CHAPTER V

THE LIBERATOR OF A RACE

THE Catholic Martyrology sums up Claver's personality thus: '9 September. St Peter Claver. In Cartagena in South America. St Peter Claver, confessor, priest of the Society of Jesus, who, with admirable self-sacrifice and most excellent charity, worked for more than forty years in the saving for Christ of nearly 300,000 negro souls. He was canonized by Pope Leo XIII, and later declared patron of the missions to negroes.'

Claver was born in an heroic age, an epic age, an age when the task was to consolidate and absorb a new world, both physically and morally. He was born into a country that was living through its golden age. It was an environment full of the problems of conquest, of a search for *El Dorado*. Sacrifices were readily made in both causes. Deeds which appear to us today heroic even in saints were carried out by soldiers as part of their normal duty. There appeared to be a competition in tenacious courage between sword and cross. The thirst for material glory produced military and political geniuses, and the thirst for souls produced a company of saints. The heroism and courage of Pizarro, Cortés, Magallanes, Quesada and Almagro were mirrored in the heroism of the missionaries. Loyola, St Teresa and Claver sought the conquest of the new world of the spirit, spurred on by the errors of heresy, the growing moral laxity or pagan ignorance.

In Claver there was a powerful reaction against the cruelty of this expanding world. If the slavers and plantation owners could live in Cartagena and Africa, putting up with heat and epidemics, why should not the apostle of Christ do likewise? This reaction against man's cruelty to man was a mainspring of his activity. What Father Las Casas was for the Indian, Sandoval and Claver were for the negro. Sandoval always refused to recognize the lawfulness of the slave-trade. It is idle to seek for moderation and sweet reasonableness in a man who witnessed the abject misery of these human beings treated as brute beasts. In his environment Claver was an extremist in fearless love. He was a man of his times. He lived his life in the greatest slave-port the world had then seen, and he lived there within the Jesuit mission which specialized in the apostolate to the negro. There is not in ecclesiastical history a case of a man who has brought into the Church through baptism so many non-white pagans. A million slaves passed through Cartagena, and before they went on their way to Portobello, Quito, Lima and other places to the south, one-third of them came into contact with Claver. His name was well known in Africa. In Loanda and Cape Verde were missionaries who received frequent letters from him, expressing his anxiety about this commerce in human beings, and his sorrow that they were so ill prepared in spiritual matters before they set sail. Towards the end of his life he had wanted to go to Africa. He was known in Europe. People in Seville were always asking for details of his work. The archbishops of Seville all supported the missionary who was applying in America the mission code drawn up in their city. He was discussed throughout South America, from Lima to Mexico. Wherever there were slaves, in the mines and the plantations, there were some who had heard from his lips a word of love and redemption, who wore a medallion given to them by their friend in Cartagena.

For three reasons Claver deserves the proud title of 'Liberator of a Race'. First, because as these poor wretches landed in Cartagena, their faces reflecting their terror, he was able to offer them in the midst of their abandonment the joy of sensing that they were individuals, and human. Second, because by making himself—a white man—the slave of black men, he showed that there exists a fundamental equality in men behind all appearances. This ideal was to be the seed of the future incorporation of their successors into Christian nations. And third, because not merely with words, but with the sacrifice of his own life, he proved that pity and love still remained in the world, and that they might reduce the load of hatred placed on each slave by so much injustice.

Through his tremendous and heroic sacrifice Peter Claver

P.C.—21

brought into the seventeenth-century world the message of the redemption of the poor through love. After 300 years this message has its tasks to perform today. There are still millions of slaves, with no brand on their arms, but the mark of slavery in their tyrannized souls. Many spiritual liberators are needed, slaves to sacrifice themselves for the modern bondsmen.

Appendix

FATHER ALONSO DE SANDOVAL

NOT enough emphasis has been laid on the vital influence of Sandoval on the work of Claver. As often happens, the pupil is better known than the teacher. Even the man himself, apart from his association with Claver, has remained in the background of history. His book *Naturaleza, policía sagrada y profana, costumbres, ritos y supersticiones de los etíopes (Negros)*,[1] published in Seville in 1627, produces a tremendous impression on the modern reader. Bartolomé de las Casas has become an historical figure, and rightly so, but in fact his defence of the Indians from slavery led to the enslavement of the negroes. He was one of the first to suggest the importation of negro slaves into America. Later he repented bitterly, but the damage was done. Sandoval's book was a textbook for the missionaries who faced the consequences of Las Casas' work. St Peter Claver used it continuously and followed it in every detail. We have seen that he urged the General of the Society to have it published.

All that we have called his 'applied sociology' the Saint owed to Sandoval. Claver's association with Alphonsus Rodríguez had inspired in him a desire to imitate especially the latter's humility, and on arrival in America he sought out only the most humble and menial tasks. His superior in Bogotá and Tunja thought him fitted for different employment. At this moment of indecision the influence of Sandoval must have been decisive. Their first interview took place when Claver arrived in Cartagena in 1610. Claver went with him to the slave barracks and was shown the misery of those poor wretches. This experience began to clarify Claver's notion of what slavery really was. On the day when he was ordained priest he was placed under the tutelage of Sandoval.

We have no private papers of Claver's which might tell us

[1] *The Nature, Religion, Customs, Rites and Superstitions of the Negroes.*

something of his method of working. However, it is clear from the evidence given at the Process that both his intimate life and his public life were modelled in astonishing detail on the ideas of Sandoval as far as method is concerned, and on the ideas of Alonso for what concerns his asceticism. So that by reading Sandoval much can be learned about his work with the negroes, while a study of Alphonsus helps us to understand the inner workings of his spirit. Hence the necessity of a study of the life and works of Sandoval.

He was born in Seville, one of a family of seven children, all of whom entered the Church. His father became a royal treasurer in Lima, and the boy went to school at a seminary in that city. He entered the Society of Jesus, and some proof of his diligence is seen in that the rector allowed him to start upon his theology and philosophy before he had completed his novitiate. Contemporary writers describe him as 'frank, very sincere, without the slightest suggestion of duplicity, and very determined'. A new Jesuit sub-province had been established in New Granada, and Sandoval answered a request for help in its establishment. He arrived in Cartagena at the new college which had just been founded with the purpose of answering the needs of the flood of negro slaves arriving in the town. José Cassani describes what he found and what he did:

> He found a house serving as a college, a house where every-thing was lacking, even a kitchen. Since there was nothing to eat, no one had concerned himself with somewhere to cook 'it'. He looked around, examined the building and its surround-ings, and decided, since he was the youngest there, to begin begging for alms. He went out each morning to get enough to keep the college in food for that day. As soon as he had it, whether in money or kind, he took it off to the house of a woman named Beatriz López, who would thereupon cook the food, and keep a little back for her own needs. This he did for three years, until he was relieved by an assistant brother. This freed him for his priestly duties.

Sandoval was a quiet man but a determined one. He had an excellent mind, lacking all narrowness of vision. 'What a triumphant thing it is', he writes in his book, 'to haul even one of these negroes from their abyss of sin, and hold him in the divine grace, if only for a night.' We are told that he used to go about the city seeking out the slaves. A supernatural event fixed the manner of his life. He had the soul of a missionary, and while on a journey with the rector of the college, Father Juan Perlín, they went to preach in the mining villages of the modern district of Antioquía in Colombia. Sandoval stayed to preach in Saragossa, a most unhealthy spot. He caught a severe fever, which almost killed him, and his biographer says that 'not only was he anointed with holy oil, but they even placed a sheet over him, thinking him to be a corpse'. Father Perlín prayed for him and begged God to take him, a useless old man, and preserve Sandoval in all his youth and energy to serve the Church. He prayed St Ignatius to intercede, and Sandoval was preserved to use his life for the salvation of the slaves. This supernatural intervention plays the same part in Sandoval's life as the vision of St Alphonsus played in Claver's. It was in Saragossa also that Sandoval was given the picture of the Virgin of the Miracle which later hung in the Jesuit chapel in Cartagena. Sandoval had a great devotion to this picture, which Claver inherited from him. As we have seen, before it Claver said his first Mass, and near it he confessed his negroes.

Sandoval's mission was not an easy one. He himself confesses that when he got news of the arrival of a slave-ship his whole body trembled. From 1607 to 1610 twelve to fourteen slave-ships unloaded their cargoes in Cartagena. The poor wretches arrived with the idea that their blood was to be used to paint galleons. The *Annual Letter* for 1611 tells us that very few of them were properly baptized. Most of them had not the slightest idea why they had been anointed with water; many of them thought that it was a hygienic measure. Sandoval took notes, and discovered that out of each 200 negroes about twelve to fourteen had been certainly baptized, and these were usually the artful ones who had been used as guards for the rest. No attempt had been made to baptize from fifty to sixty in each group, while the others had had water slopped over them as they went aboard, an action which was to them absolutely meaningless. Sandoval divided the new arrivals into appropriate groups to facilitate their instruction.

Those who had been correctly baptized he prepared for confession, the others he prepared for baptism, choosing for immediate tuition those who were seriously ill. Once properly prepared he baptized them in groups of thirty to forty, giving to them a tin medal to hang about their necks so that they might be readily distinguished from the unbaptized. The *Annual Letter* for 1611 tells us that the slaves highly prized these medals and that if they lost them they used to seek out Sandoval and beg him for another. They always greeted him with great respect when they saw him about the streets, and were clearly conscious of the great service he had performed for them.

One of Sandoval's major difficulties was the language problem. The slaves spoke many different dialects, and very few knew a single word of Spanish. Sometimes an interpreter was found who understood the negro dialect of another tribe, but knew no Spanish. Then Sandoval had to employ a second interpreter to put the already translated ideas into Spanish. Often he would struggle for hours in this three-way linguistic traffic in his desire to baptize some poor wretch who arrived seriously ill. The same *Annual Letter* explains another grave difficulty: the arrival of slaveships whose occupants were suffering from contagious diseases. These ships were forbidden entrance to the harbour. When the victims *were* allowed ashore, Sandoval was always there to receive them and do everything possible to baptize the most seriously ill before they died. He worked so hard and so endlessly at his task that his superiors were forced to ask him to rest more.

It was clear to him that many negroes said that they were baptized when they were not, and that many who were baptized continued to live as pagans. These facts led him to develop the method of work which Cassani describes: 'He went out from the college and visited the plantations and other places where slaves were to be found. Many of them lived either ignorant of religion, or lax in their observance. For this reason he always carried with him a phial of water and baptized on the spot if necessary, provided that the slave was aware of the significance of the sacrament. He kept a record of the baptisms according to names, tribes and addresses. It was later found from this record that in seven years

he had baptized more than 3,133 formerly alleged to be Christians.'
Claver carried out this part of his task in exactly the same way.

Sandoval's work aroused opposition. The ecclesiastical authorities of the town were apprehensive of the intervention of the Jesuits and they ordered Sandoval to cease his activity. The Jesuits insisted on their right to administer the sacraments. The argument was brought to court, the judge examined witnesses, and ultimately the ecclesiastical authorities were invited to share in the missionary work. But the infinite toil of inspecting the slaves, educating them, looking after them in all their filth and disease moved the new missionaries to announce that it was not their business but that of friars and monks. The bishop was advised of this, and gave permission to Sandoval to carry on with this task. The General of the Society heard of it and congratulated Sandoval by letter. At the same time he recommended the local Jesuit authorities to select assistants who might in time succeed him. This point has not been sufficiently emphasized. The mission to the negro slaves in America was not a sporadic activity brought to great fruition by the genius of Claver. It was one of the tasks which the Jesuits undertook with the greatest determination and persistence. There is a letter from the General Viteleschi which assures Sandoval of his great interest in the mission, and promises him all the help he may require.

The following pages from Sandoval's book summarize the ideals of these two missionaries:

Spanish merchants used the Indies as warehouses from which they might take gold and silver and pearls and precious stones. For these purposes they sent their agents and their servants. Christ, the supreme merchant, exploits these Indies to enrich his own capital with another kind of gold and silver and precious stones, which are the souls of the natives of those lands, and the souls of those transported thither, as were the negroes. And he sends thither his own agents and servants, religious men of all the orders, laden with cargoes of virtue, holiness, and learning. Well, then, suppose that a rich and powerful merchant had agents in the Indies who worked to his great profit, supplying with all kinds of rich and elegant merchandise only, ignoring cheap and everyday goods. And suppose that among them was one who, while not forgetting the rich products of commerce, occupied himself with the cheaper and more ordinary goods, yet so presented them and adorned them that their sale brought in as much, or even greater, profit than the sale of luxuries. I ask, would not this man be as much esteemed, and as much rewarded, by his master as the others? It was the will of God to set up his shops in this New World, and to that intent he sent rich merchandise of wealthy men of good lineage and women of high and delicate birth. But so that his shops might be complete he sent the cheaper sort of stuff, Indians and mulattoes, and savage negroes. As his agents he sent there men of all the orders in his holy Church, but of these the majority concerned themselves with the luxurious merchandise only. Nevertheless they brought a great trade to their master, and much increased his wealth. But our Lord has his cheaper merchandise, which he esteems highly, and he would be better pleased if his agents occupied themselves with the whole range of his wares. What would happen, then, if one of his agents went to him and said: 'Lord, rather than busy myself with the most prized of your goods, the whites, I would prefer to deal in the cheaper commodities, the black savages, held by men to be common rubbish.' And so he buys and sell blacks, which is to say he teaches them, and catechizes them, and baptizes and confesses them, and seeks their salvation, Who can doubt that his master will prize that servant as much as, or more than, the others? Who, in order to receive the prize of *that* master would not make every effort, even such as seem beyond his strength?

BIBLIOGRAPHY

I. The most important document is the Process of Beatification and Canonization. *Sac. Rituus Congregatione . . . Beatificationis Canonizationis Ven. Ser. Petri Claver . . .* Romae, Typis, Rev. Camerae apost. MDCXVI. It is in a number of parts. There is the *informatio super dubio* in Latin, thirty-four pages long, and the *sumarium super dubio* in Italian, 403 pages. It ends with the observations of the promoter of the cause. The text used by us (from the National Library of Colombia in Botogá) has a manuscript copy (102 pp.) of the reports *non cultu*. This work is the major source. In it 154 witnesses, many of them eye-witnesses, give evidence under oath.

II. *The Life of the Venerable and Apostolic Peter Claver*, Maria de Quiñones, Madrid, 1657, octavo, 172 pp. This was published by the Licenciado Gerónimo Suárez de Somaza. There has long been uncertainty about his role in the work. In the prologue he writes that 'it came into' his hands, and he decided to publish it. This is repeated by the censor Father Antonio de Herrera: 'Published by the Licenciado Gerónimo Suárez de Somaza'. However, Father Agustín de Castro, when granting a certificate for the work, writes 'the life . . . put together by the Licenciado Gerónimo Suárez de Somoza . . .' which suggests some closer connection. Father Charles Sommervogel (Bibliothèque de la Société de Jesus, vol. I, Paris, 1890), attributes this life to Father Alfonso de Andrade, native of Bogotá. (This is not the Toledan Jesuit Alfonso de Andrade who appears in the *Varones Ilustres*, vol. VI.) He writes of him that he wrote this life 'on the basis of information received from the Father Provincial in letters from Cartagena'. Father Eugenio Uriarte, in his book *Catálogo razonado de obras anónimas y seudónimas de autores de la Compañía de Jesús* (v. III, Madrid, Ribadeneira, 1906, no. 4564) finally decides the argument in favour of Alfonso de Andrade, of the province of Toledo, who handed it three years after the death of the Saint to the printer Suárez of

Madrid. This work, which we have consulted in a microfilm belonging to the National Library in Madrid, is of great value. Based on contemporary materials, it was written before the beginning of the Process. Its sources are letters from the Father Provincial of New Granada and the personal correspondence and conversation of Andrade with those who knew Claver. It is a little over-burdened with pious reflections, a defect of the period, but it is the first life of the Saint, and has some invaluable passages.

The second biography, one which might be called scientific since it is based on the Process, is José Fernández, S. J., *Apostólica y penitente vida del Venerable Padre Pedro Claver*, Zaragoza, Diego Dormer 1666, quarto, 680 pp., one plate. It completes the life above by adding details from the Process. It is the basis of all succeeding biographies. We have used the first edition (Archivos San Bartolomé, Bogotá). Like the first life above it suffers from the continuous ascetic commentary which will not allow the events to speak for themselves. This dehumanizes the story of Claver's life and appears to dissociate it from the environment in which it was lived. But little new information can be added to what this book gives us.

Father José Cassani's excellent monograph must be mentioned. It appears in *Historia de la Provincia de la Compañía de Jesús del Nuevo Reyno de Granada en la América*, Manuel Fernández, Madrid, 1741, 618 pp. The second part consists of the lives of 'famous men' and it begins with Claver. It is a tiny masterpiece, written in perfect taste, and flavoured with irony and a delicate maliciousness. As well as being useful for Claver, it is a rich source of information about Sandoval.

III. *Vita del venerabile servo di Dio Pietro Claver*, Rome, Salomoni, 1748, quarto, adds nothing new to Fernández. It was re-published by Father Andreassi in 1888. Father Bertrand Gabriel Fleuriau, S. J., wrote the first French biography in 1751: *La vie du vénérable P. Pierre Claver*, Paris, Bordelet, duodecimo. He reduces a little the pious commentary, but his ignorance of the environment leads him into exaggerations about the climate of Cartagena, among other matters. This work was republished by J. M. Daurignac in 1854: *Histoire de Bienheureux Pierre Claver*, Lyon, Paris, and many editions have followed. The most complete of the older biographies is Fernández—Sola—Fiter, S. J., *Vida de San Pedro Claver*, Barcelona, 1888. It is based on Fernández. Father Sola himself tells us that it is a rewriting of the 1666 edition of Fernández's work. It suffers from pious digressions and a lack of historical background but the appendix on documents is excellent. The canonization in 1888 inspired several biographies, most of them copies of the older works. Monsignor Brioschi, for many years Bishop of Cartagena, published the following year *Vida de San Pedro Claver*, Garnier, Paris, an octavo volume of 542 pp. The book is concerned above all with the promotion of piety. The foundation is factual enough, but it is obscured by too many pious observations. In Germany Fernando Hover published a life which was later edited in 1905 by Father Martin Hagen, S.J. In the year of the canonization Van Aken published *Vie de Saint Pierre Claver*, Ghent. This is an adaptation and abridgement of Fernández, Ongaro and Fleuriau. Nearer to our own time, interest in the Saint has notably increased, but apart from a few useful books, most of the publications are historical novels. Two studies are worth especial notice. A chapter by Father Antonio Astrain, S.J., in Vol. V of *Historia de la Compañia de Jesús en España*, Razón y Fe, Madrid, 1916, is a masterpiece in its compression. He published for the first time documents from the Roman archives which threw new light on the Saint. He is especially interesting in his discussion of life in the residence and on the missionary journeys. The other worthwhile modern work is published by Gabriel Ledos in the *Collection Les Saints* in 1923 : *Saint Pierre Claver*. The author is an archivist of the Bibliothèque Nationale in Paris, who specializes in paleography. He knows the original documents and the early lives, and, more important, he uses for the first time Sandoval's work and the *Annual Letters* of Father Sebastián Hazañero. This is an historical life, without pietistic embellishments. Apart from the natural absence of the latest discoveries, it is a sound and well written popular book.

IV. *Other books*

Arnold Lunn, *A Saint in the Slave Trade*, *Peter Claver*, Sheed & Ward, London.

Mabel Farnum, *Street of the Half Moon*, Bruce Publishing Co., Milwaukee, 1940.

Luis Mejía, *Historia de San Pedro Claver*.

Mariano Picón Salas, *Pedro Claver, el santo de los esclavos*, F.C.E., Mexico, 1949.

The above are more or less *biographies romancées*, the last-named vitiated by an unhistorical viewpoint and a marxist social philosophy. Among the popular short lives written with the object of pious edification, Father Martindale's essay on St Peter Claver in *What are Saints*, Sheed & Ward, London, deserves special mention for its acute observations on the Saint's psychology.

INDEX

326   INDEX